COLLAGE OF MYSELF

Collage
of Myself

Walt Whitman and the
Making of *Leaves of Grass*

MATT MILLER

University of Nebraska Press
Lincoln and London

An abbreviated version of chapter 1, "How
Whitman Used His Early Notebooks," appeared as
"Composing the First *Leaves of Grass*: How Whitman
Used His Early Notebooks" in *Book History* 11
(2007). Brief excerpts from chapter 2, "Packing
and Unpacking the First *Leaves of Grass*," and
from chapter 3, "Kosmos Poets and Spinal Ideas,"
appeared in *Walt Whitman Quarterly Review* 24 (Fall
2006–Winter 2007): 85–97. Various typographic
transcriptions herein originally appeared in
"Selections from the Talbot Wilson Notebook of
Walt Whitman," *Double Room* 3 (Fall–Winter 2003).

∞

Library of Congress Cataloging-in-Publication Data
Miller, Matt (Matthew Ward)
Collage of myself: Walt Whitman and the
making of Leaves of grass / Matt Miller.
p.   cm.
Includes bibliographical references and index.
ISBN 978-0-8032-2534-3 (cloth: alk. paper)
1. Whitman, Walt, 1819–1892 — Technique.
2. Whitman, Walt, 1819–1892. Leaves of grass.
3. Whitman, Walt, 1819–1892 — Notebooks, sketchbooks, etc.
4. Whitman, Walt, 1819–1892 — Manuscripts. 5. Collage. I. Title.
PS3241.M55   2010
811'.3 — dc22   2010020826

Set in Minion by Bob Reitz.
Designed by Nathan Putens.

For Mona Jorgensen
and Lana Miller

Contents

Illustrations

Acknowledgments

This book would not exist without the generosity of Professor Ed Folsom. How he manages to give so much to so many is his secret. The book would also not exist were it not for the online Walt Whitman Archive (www.whitmanarchive.org), coedited by Ed Folsom and Kenneth Price, which provided the digital images of Whitman's manuscripts essential to this study.

Many thanks also to the editors of *Book History*, *Double Room*, and *Walt Whitman Quarterly Review*, in which portions of this book have previously appeared.

Introduction

This book is a case study of the creative process, a demonstration of how Walt Whitman composed his early poems, and a reevaluation of the origins of collage as a practice in Western art. Here, I explore an enduring mystery in American literary studies: the question of how Walter Whitman, a rather undistinguished newspaperman and author of potboiler temperance fiction, transformed himself with astonishing speed into the author of America's most celebrated collection of poems. This book documents a new and surprising achievement by America's most famous poet: over a half-century before the word *collage* was applied to Picasso's pioneering use of the technique in the visual arts, Whitman was conceptualizing and practicing a similar artistic method with language in the groundbreaking poems of *Leaves of Grass*.

Many theories have been proposed to explain Whitman's creative breakthrough, but prior research has faced significant obstacles due to scant and inaccessible manuscript evidence and misunderstandings about the period in Whitman's life leading up to the first edition of *Leaves of Grass*. After more than a century of Whitman scholarship, we still know surprisingly little about how he came to write his first mature poems, and almost all investigations thus far have explored his breakthrough by way of speculative accounts of his biography, with most recent scholarship stressing incidents related to his politics and sexuality. Rather than use an outside event to explain his creative maturation, I look at his writing process itself, using the Walt

Whitman Archive's online collection of digital images to reveal his discovery of an enabling new process of composition. My findings force a revision of our understanding not only of *Leaves of Grass*, but of the origins of collage, a technique increasingly seen as the most important and enduring contribution of modernism, as well as a signature creative method of subsequent postmodern artists.

Given the intense critical interest his work has received, it might seem remarkable that this is the first book-length study of Whitman's notebooks and manuscripts. This lacuna in Whitman scholarship is largely due to the fact that collections of Whitman's manuscripts are scattered around the world in more than thirty archival repositories, making systematic access to them extraordinarily difficult. The Whitman scholar Edward Grier published transcripts of most of Whitman's prose manuscripts in 1984, yet no effort was made to edit and collect the poetry manuscripts until the Walt Whitman Archive undertook this massive, ongoing task. These scholarly obstacles are compounded by the fact that many of the most precious and important collections are sealed from public view because of their fragility and limited availability in facsimile editions and reproductions. Editorial scholarship hasn't yet adequately addressed these issues, and the material that Whitman left behind has never been systematically collected and transcribed. My involvement with the Walt Whitman Archive's comprehensive online collection of digital manuscript images has allowed me to move beyond these problems and address some important misunderstandings.

Until recently it has been assumed that Whitman was drafting lines for *Leaves of Grass* long before its 1855 debut, but I use the notebooks to demonstrate that until around 1854 he was unaware that his literary ambitions would assume the form of poetry at all. I show that there is no extant evidence that Whitman, who once speculated that

Leaves would be a "spiritual novel" or a play, drafted any poetic lines whatsoever between 1848 and 1853. Shortly thereafter he discovered a remarkable new creative process, allowing him to transform a diverse array of text, including diary-like observations, reading notes, clippings from newspapers and scholarly articles, and language stolen or paraphrased from books, into the breakthrough poems of *Leaves of Grass*. Long before a term for the method was coined, Whitman pioneered the creative technique now most commonly known as collage, anticipating subsequent work by the modernists, including Ezra Pound, T. S. Eliot, and Marianne Moore, as well as the visual and literary collage work of the Dadaists and Surrealists. Equally prescient was the attitude toward language that allowed for Whitman's innovations, and this study also details the critical resonance between Whitman's approach and more recent theoretical discourse describing how the use of found materials — creative methods known variously as collage, montage, and bricolage — have been critical in the development of literary and visual art.

In the first chapter, "How Whitman Used His Early Notebooks," I examine the most important of Whitman's earliest literary notebooks and show how editorial misunderstandings have led to misconceptions of the poet's life in the years just prior to the publication of the first *Leaves of Grass*. Even the best-informed Whitman scholars have assumed that he was drafting poetic lines for years prior to his literary debut, but my corrected dating of his notebooks demonstrates that until about a year before his book's publication Whitman had no idea that his literary life's work would be undertaken as a poet. In his manuscripts composed just prior to the publication of the first *Leaves of Grass* Whitman seems to be seeking some altogether new genre in which to express himself, which underscores just how malleable his concept of genre had become and suggests that *Leaves of Grass* might well have taken a radically different form. His diverse experiments in fiction, oratory, and poetic theory bore little fruit until he discovered his signature poetic line, a capacious vehicle that allowed him to transform aborted forays in other types of writing into major poems such as "Song of Myself." From scraps of language both original and stolen Whitman pieced together his poetic body; thus his role in the conception of *Leaves of Grass* is less its midwife than its Dr. Frankenstein.

The second chapter, "Packing and Unpacking the First *Leaves of Grass*," demonstrates the ferocity of Whitman's textual manipulations. Influenced by his nomadic lifestyle, his words too were constantly on the move, not only from house to house, reflecting his migratory ways, but within his notebooks themselves, as he simulated a kind of primitive word processor, "cutting and pasting" his lines into multitudinous arrangements and forms. This chapter emphasizes the fragmentary nature of Whitman's compositional method, stressing how the poet's pervasive and ferocious approach to revision broke language down into increasingly smaller and more portable units. This approach to writing, at once compositional and deconstructive, allowed Whitman ready access to various and multiple formulations for his poetic ideas, drafts that were continually shifting and adjusting to new artistic priorities and conceptualizations of his audience. I use a sexually charged passage later published in "The Sleepers" as a case study of this process and juxtapose its manuscript stages to expose Whitman's evolving motivations. What was once an explicitly homosexual depiction evolves into an ambiguous scene that encourages readers of various sexual orientations to project their own desires and come away with satisfying readings.

Where the second chapter emphasizes the mobile, fragmentary nature of Whitman's approach to language, the third, "Kosmos Poets and Spinal Ideas," examines the conceptual frameworks that hold his poems together. Whitman called these organizing principals "spinal ideas," structural paradigms that allowed him to organize his scattered drafts without sacrificing the fragmentation, multiplicity, and fluidity essential to his project. In practice these concepts became mobile centers of gravity that could attract and structure his words without subordinating them to predictable metrical, narrative, or rhetorical ideas of order — ideas that Whitman believed reflected a rigid, unitary outlook too closely bound to outmoded European conventions. The phrase *spinal ideas* suggests both the spine of a book and that of a human body, but his bodily metaphor exists in tense relation to the decentered and asymmetrical results. Anticipating the formulations of Gilles Deleuze and Félix Guattari, Whitman's rhizomatic formal constructs eschewed the unitary architectural model of his poetic contemporaries and embraced a fluid, adaptive approach whereby text and meaning accrete around key nodal concepts. This chapter explores one of the most important of these spinal ideas, the poet's concept of *dilation*, and traces its development in a manuscript passage in which Whitman "enters into" a slave and a slaveholder in the same breath.

In the fourth chapter, "Poems of Materials," I relate Whitman's collage-like creative method to his underlying attitude toward language and text. The idea of a "poem of materials" holds dual meaning, suggesting work that offers the materials for readers to construct their own lives and poems, as well as a poem stressing the material nature of the printed word. The idea is especially apparent in Whitman's catalogs and lists, where language is presented as something fundamentally exterior to one's identity and selfhood, while at the same time it is something that, through his particular poetic alchemy, can be assumed into a new and poetically enlarged self-formulation.

In such passages Whitman attempts to conflate word and object, promising readers a more direct and physical engagement with language than previous poets had indicated was possible. Focusing on an underappreciated poem, the 1856 "Broad-Axe Poem" (later titled "Song of the Broad-Axe"), I map the concept of a poem of materials onto a specific published work. As subsequent artists did with found-art objects, Whitman deployed "ready-made" examples of language to critique the nature of his medium, the role of the artist, and the locus of reception for art in its audience.

In the final chapter, "Whitman after Collage / Collage after Whitman," I explore the significance of Whitman's discoveries in relation to subsequent artists and writers. So revolutionary were some of these ideas that, in order to come to grips with them, we must read *back* to Whitman through the lens of what we now know. Although the poet himself may not have accurately anticipated the scope and application of the concepts he pioneered, history has begun to catch up with him, allowing us to more fully assess his accomplishment. This chapter suggests that many of the most important concepts of recent, forward-thinking art movements were anticipated directly by Whitman's poems and critical statements. Using concepts from the visual arts, focusing especially on Marcel Duchamp and subsequent conceptual art practices, I interpret the significance of Whitman's achievement in this coda to my exploration of his creative process, revealing how the conventional, transatlantic conception of the roots of modernism is complicated and enriched by our recognition of Whitman's originality.[1]

Abbreviations

COLLAGE OF MYSELF

I

How Whitman Used His
Early Notebooks

As we look back on *Leaves of Grass* today, over a century and a half after the publication of the first edition, we are still at a loss to explain how Walt Whitman came to create such a groundbreaking book. As a result of scant and often misunderstood documentary evidence from the period leading up to the publication of the first *Leaves*, many scholars have regarded the book's genesis as an unsolvable mystery, and those who have tried to explore the puzzle have often been hindered by misconceptions about Whitman's life and his creative process. Readers exploring Whitman's writing process have usually tried to understand what inspired him, and inspiration, I would contend, is something easily misconstrued. We tend to look at the idea from the outside, explaining creativity in terms of the kind of events that transform us as people, as important incidents in the stories of our lives. But artistic inspiration is often something more closely related to the experience of art itself. Rather than try to use an outside event to explain Whitman's creative maturation, I look at his writing process, using his notebooks and manuscripts to approach the question from the inside.

Another misconception is related to a problem that has troubled his readers from the beginning: the question of what creative category we should use to assess him. For most readers, and probably even for most writers, the issue of genre is something rather more fixed and stable than it was for Whitman. He was foremost a poet, so most readers interested in the genesis of *Leaves* have emphasized the *verse* in his manuscript notebooks, but in Whitman's case the focus has been too narrow. This is not to say that Whitman's development of his poetic line wasn't crucial. In fact his notebooks suggest that it was probably the single most important factor accelerating his development. But Whitman's prose was fundamental to his line, and it remained critical throughout his compositional process.

Another important misconception relates to the chronology of events in his writing leading up to the first edition. Misunderstandings about the dating of his notebooks have led to some substantial misrepresentations in accounts of Whitman's life in the years just prior to 1855. We need to address this issue first to lay the groundwork for exploring the others.

A particularly problematic notebook is one that is usually now called the "Talbot Wilson" notebook, a title derived from a note Whitman wrote to himself on the front cover verso.[1] Filed in the Library of Congress under the title "Notebook LC #80," it often used to be called "Whitman's earliest notebook," in part because it was long ago labeled that way by the twentieth-century biographer and critic Emory Holloway in a note glued to its cover. The notebook is among the most important, but it is certainly not the earliest documenting Whitman's writing toward the first edition. It was acquired by the Library of Congress as a part of the Harned Collection in 1918, and scholars had access to it from 1925 until 1942, when the Library began to disperse its collection for safekeeping during World War II. When the containers for the Harned Collection were returned in 1944 the Library discovered that this and nine other notebooks were missing; they remained missing until 1995, when the "Talbot Wilson" notebook and three others turned up for auction at Sotheby's and were eventually returned.[2] Since then only a few scholars have had direct access to them, although scans have been provided online.[3] From 1942 to 1995, however, scholars had access only to Holloway's transcription from 1921 and a poor quality microfilm copy made by Floyd Stovall in 1934 that itself was believed lost until it resurfaced in 1967.

In the first printing of the "Talbot Wilson" notebook in 1921 Holloway dates it to 1847–50 based on an 1847 date found in the notebook and some addresses in Brooklyn that Whitman jotted down on the inside front cover. One of these addresses was for the Brooklyn *Weekly Freeman*, which Whitman edited between 1848 and 1849, and Holloway extrapolates from this that Whitman began drafting the lines of poetry in the notebook at about that time.[4] From 1921 until 1942 Holloway's printed transcription of the notebook was the only source available outside the Library of Congress, and from the time the notebook was lost in 1942 until Stovall's microfilm appeared it was the only way to read the notebook at all. The late 1840s dating was eventually challenged in 1953 by Esther Shephard, the first scholar to accurately date it.[5] Shephard based her argument on the fact that the only other early notebook lines that found their way into the 1855 edition and had been conclusively dated were from 1854 — a five- or six-year gap — and those lines seemed less advanced than the ones in "Talbot Wilson," sometimes, for example, being written in the third person (whereas in the "Talbot Wilson" notebook Whitman writes with his mature, full-scale "I"). Shephard also cited two of Whitman's own statements claiming that he began writing *Leaves of Grass* in 1854; however, because Whitman is a notoriously unreliable source (and also made statements contradicting those cited by Shephard), and because the possibility remained that there could have been notebooks written in the early 1850s that had simply been lost, few scholars went along with the 1854 dating.[6] A subsequent study by Edward Grier in 1968 reaffirmed Holloway's 1847 dating, and because Grier later went on to edit Whitman's *Notebooks and Unpublished Prose Manuscripts*, the most frequently cited source for Whitman manuscripts to this day, his views on the "Talbot Wilson" notebook have had a powerful and, at least in respect to the dating of this important document, deleterious effect on Whitman scholarship.[7]

When the notebook resurfaced in 1995 scholars finally had access to the actual artifact (or at least relatively high-quality, though grayscale instead of full-color, digital scans), and a crucial fact finally became clear. In addition to literary writings the notebook also contained stubs of cut-out pages that had not been visible in the 1934 microfilm. Many of these stubs reveal fragments of numbers that appear to be the remnants of fiscal ledgers that Whitman kept for business purposes (see figure 1). These stubs showed that Whitman, who was an omnivorous recycler of old notebooks and paper scraps, had cut out

FIG 1. A cut-away leaf showing Whitman's fiscal ledgers. Charles Feinberg Collection of Walt Whitman, Manuscript Division, Library of Congress, Washington DC (loc.00141.006).

FIG 2. Leftover material from 1847, previously used to erroneously date the notebook. Charles Feinberg Collection of Walt Whitman, Manuscript Division, Library of Congress, Washington DC (loc.00141.053).

the mundane ephemera in a notebook so that he could use the blank pages that remained for his poetry and prose. Because two of the pages were mostly blank and could still be used, he left them intact, even though they contained some notes related to the notebook's former purpose. One of those pages contained the 1847 date previously discussed (see figure 2). Once it became apparent that this was a recycled notebook, the primary evidence for dating used by Holloway and Grier no longer applied, and Shephard's argument from 1953 suddenly became a lot more convincing. Recently this new manuscript evidence has been used by Andrew C. Higgins in an essay that convincingly demonstrates an 1854 dating for the notebook's literary content.[8] Far from being the "earliest notebook" Whitman used for *Leaves of Grass*, "Talbot Wilson" is actually antedated by several notebooks and manuscript fragments.

Because of this mistaken dating, almost all Whitman scholarship is misleading in regard to the question of when he began to actually draft poetic lines for the first edition of *Leaves*, and many important arguments and portrayals are, at least in this respect, based on a shaky foundation. For example, Higgins shows that David S. Reynolds, Betsy Erkkila, and Martin Klammer use the "Talbot Wilson" notebook's status as Whitman's earliest notebook to emphasize, as

Erkkila writes, that when Whitman "breaks for the first time into lines approximating the free verse of *Leaves of Grass*, the lines bear the impress of the slavery issue."[9] The notebook does not, however, show us the first time Whitman "breaks into" his signature lines. Because his writing in prose at this time is just as fervent and was often used later in his poems, why should the poet's discovery of his line be used to estimate his interests? The notebooks and manuscripts that antedate "Talbot Wilson" suggest that Whitman was more concerned with several other emphases than slavery, especially poetic theory, spiritual expansiveness, and sympathy for suffering anywhere (including but hardly limited to slavery).

Until recently Whitman's biographers have also been misled about the notebook and the probable beginnings of his mature writing. Gay Wilson Allen, for example, mistakenly refers to the "Talbot Wilson" notebook as "the earliest" of Whitman's manuscript notebooks for *Leaves of Grass* and states that Whitman "could have used this book any time between 1847 and 1852" (though he does add "or even later").[10] The habit of using the notebook for chronological arguments dies hard, even for later scholars aware of the notebook's revised status in the poet's development. Jerome Loving states that "one of Whitman's notebooks ('[T]albot Wilson') suggests that 'Song of Myself' may have been in the poet's imagination" as early as 1850, when Whitman published his "Letters from a Travelling Bachelor" in the *New York Sunday Dispatch*. Shortly thereafter, however, in a footnote, Loving gives an abbreviated history of "Talbot Wilson," stating much of what I've just presented and adding that the notebook's poetic lines "were probably written long after 1847."[11] Many time lines and chronologies of Whitman's life also continue to erroneously date facts about the origins of his mature writing, including Joann P. Krieg's useful and otherwise diligently researched *A Walt Whitman Chronology*.[12]

"Talbot Wilson" is by far the most frequently cited of Whitman's early manuscript notebooks, and the threads of misunderstanding related to its mistaken dating spread far and deep.

An 1854 dating for "Talbot Wilson" forces a revision of any number of arguments about Whitman's early development, one of the most important being how to understand his writing process for the first edition. To do this we need to come to grips with the fact that without the erroneous early dating of this notebook, there is no extant evidence to suggest that Whitman discovered his mature, long-lined style until late 1853 to 1854. Importantly, Whitman did publish three free-verse poems in 1850 — "The House of Friends," "Resurgemus," and "Blood Money" — but these poems are a far cry from the mature work of the 1855 *Leaves*, and even the inchoate writing of the 1854 notebooks. As many have noted, these poems do show Whitman breaking from the rarified and traditional exercises of his early, rhymed verse toward more specific and engaged political concerns. "Resurgemus" in particular is important because Whitman later relineated it and included it with only minor changes as the eighth poem of the 1855 edition that eventually came to be titled "Europe, the 72d and 73d Years of These States." However, refitting "Resurgemus" to the line and syntax of his mature style does little to hide its difference from the work he composed later. With its narrow focus, stilted rhythms, and lack of personhood and voice, the untitled eighth poem of 1855 still feels like a throwback. These early free-verse experiments offer only a glimpse of Whitman's mature style, and given the four-year gap between them and evidence of any other writing with line breaks they seem more like dead ends before a long gestation period than the first steps of a steady evolution. In 1850 Whitman recognized that none of the poetry he had written at that point could serve as an adequate model for his ambitions; his new style seems to have demanded that he stop experimenting with "poetry," at least for a while, so that he could gain the perspective necessary to make a decisive break.

So, to briefly describe Whitman's early career in writing poetry as far as we can tell: His earliest known poem, "Our Future Lot," appeared in the *Long Island Democrat* in 1838. Over the next twelve years he published at least nineteen individual poems in various newspapers, many of which were reprinted in slightly altered form and under different titles. All of these poems except three of the very last were written in a cramped and conventional formal style that bears almost no resemblance to his mature work. In 1850 he published three poems in free verse that anticipate the poems of *Leaves of Grass* but also show that he had much to learn before he began drafting the lines that were later included in his best poems from the first edition. After writing these three poems he left behind the conventional formalism of his early verse, and with a few exceptions, such as "O Captain! My Captain!" and "Ethiopia Saluting the Colors," he never looked back. He seems to have abandoned fiction by this point, having published his last original story, "The Shadow and the Light of a Young Man's Soul," in 1848. Little has been conclusively determined about Whitman's writing habits between 1850 and 1853; he published little journalism, took odd jobs, indulged his passion for opera, and presumably, at some unknown point, began thinking his way toward *Leaves*. Notebooks and various fragments from this period show him pursuing a number of intellectual interests, including a career as an orator in the tradition of Emerson and a substantial, focused study of language and linguistics. There is no evidence that he wrote anything with poetic line breaks during this period. Then suddenly, sometime around 1854, the long lines appear, in various syntactic and grammatical manifestations, moving with incredible speed through less successful efforts such as the unpublished "Pictures" and the poem that came to be called "A Boston Ballad" to the scope and accomplishment of the untitled work later known as "Song of Myself."

Obviously this narrative is highly abbreviated and elides many crucial factors in Whitman's development, but it highlights something that should be of interest to anyone concerned with Whitman's poetry: the poems of the 1855 *Leaves* appeared in a boiling rush, the size and suddenness of which continue to beg for explanation. Many accounts so far have either stressed the idea that he experienced some kind of religious illumination or had some spectacularly eye-opening sex (or that sex opened his eyes to some kind of religious illumination). His earliest admirers, such as Richard Maurice Bucke, often emphasized a mystical experience the poet is said to have had in 1853 or 1854; this line of thinking has been continued by Malcolm Cowley, who championed Whitman as mystic in his introduction to the widely distributed centennial reprinting of the 1855 edition, and V. K. Chari, whose book-length study explores Whitman's specific mystical relation to Vedanta.[13] Others have explained Whitman's breakthrough in terms of sexual experience, which was at first presumed to be with a "Lady of the South" during his 1848 trip to New Orleans. Beginning with Henry Brian Binns in 1905 and continuing with Emory Holloway, the "New Orleans theory" of Whitman's transformation endures in its updated, same-sex variation, despite the fact that there is no real evidence to support the notion of either a gay or a straight romantic tryst.[14] More recently scholarship has tended to emphasize Whitman's politics, and though these accounts help explain an important factor informing the content of the first *Leaves* it's hard to relate them to the actual breakthrough Whitman experienced with his writing. His evolving political sympathies and frustration with the Democratic Party were things he clearly felt compelled to write *about*, but it is difficult to imagine them as the primary cause of his artistic quantum leap in *how* he wrote.

As I shall explore in more detail later, Whitman's notebooks of 1854 reveal writing that is mystical, sexual, and political (though his more sexually inflected descriptions seem to date long after his New Orleans journey). None of these aspects of his creative process should be discounted, though they all rely on a relatively narrow selection of the overall notebooks, and with their biographical emphases there is much in the manuscripts and notebooks that these explanations would seem to exclude. What is clear is that *something* important to Whitman happened in late 1853 or early 1854, something that crystallized his ambitions and allowed him to write profusely and in an entirely new way. It is the suddenness of his poetic maturity that fascinates, and perhaps it is this very suddenness that has encouraged biographers, critics, and disciples to devise spectacular and at times fabulous explanations. Looking more closely at these narratives we find that they have at least two things in common. First, they assume that some important biographical event in Whitman's life must be responsible for his creative catalyst; second, they privilege a relatively narrow selection of his notebooks and manuscripts, ignoring otherwise compelling passages that don't seem to fit the focus. But why is it necessary to regard Whitman's breakthrough as the result of something *outside* his writing instead of something he discovered within the writing itself? That is, what if we look at Whitman's creative transformation as something grounded first and foremost in his artistic medium and his life as a practicing writer? And what if, rather than cherry-picking the notebooks for an outside focus, we instead regard these writings as articles of intrinsic interest and explore the poet's breakthrough with an approach involving as broad a span of his notebook writings as possible?

There are certainly some early notebooks and manuscripts that have been overlooked or inadequately investigated. One of the most important is a little-known document from the Feinberg Collection at the Library of Congress: two pages left from a larger notebook that either was lost or has not been associated with these leaves.[15] I refer to these two tall, salmon-colored leaves filled with small, relatively neat handwriting on both recto and verso as the "Med Cophōsis" notebook fragment (based on the first legible phrase on the recto of the first leaf). The writing on these two leaves continues from page to page; they are attached delicately at the center; and the parallel tear-marks on the inside of each leaf suggest that they have been torn from a tall notebook, the remainder of which either has been lost or has never been associated with this fragment by scholars. These pages have not been dated, and to the extent that they have been examined at all they have been viewed in the context of *Daybooks and Notebooks*, where they were assimilated by the editor William White into a rather arbitrary sequence White calls "Other Notebooks, &c. on Words" (*DBN* 3:773–77). Buried in this framework, the "Med Cophōsis" notebook fragment seems to have been overlooked or regarded only from the perspective of Whitman's language studies. But this fragment only minimally relates to Whitman's linguistic interests, and there are clues here that provide a reasonably good idea of when it was written.

The first lines of two of the poems Whitman eventually included in the 1855 *Leaves* are drafted here in prose in what appear to be their first incarnations. At the bottom of the recto of the first leaf we find this passage:

My Lesson
Have you learned the ᵐʸ lesson complete:

It is well — it is ‸^{but} the gate to a larger lesson — and ~~And~~
    that to another ~~still~~ —
And ~~every one of us~~ ‸^{each successive one} to another still

On the verso Whitman writes in prose, "There was a child went forth every day — and the first things that he ~~saw~~ looked at with fixed love, that thing he became for the day." These passages, which contain lines from untitled 1855 poems eventually called "There Was a Child Went Forth" and "Who Learns My Lesson Complete?" date these pages prior to 1855. There are other clues that suggest these leaves may contain some of Whitman's earliest extant writing toward the first edition of *Leaves of Grass* — perhaps the earliest (except for the reprinted "Resurgemus"). For example, the same page where he drafted the first line of "There Was a Child Went Forth" contains notes that clearly articulate the formational idea of the poem eventually titled "Song of the Answerer":

<u>The answerer</u>

Plot for a Poem or other work — A manly unpretensive philosopher — without any of the old insignia, such as age, book ~~oth~~ etc. — a fine-formed person, of beautiful countenance, &c. — Sits every day at the door of his house — to him for advice come all sorts of people. — Some come to puzzle him — some come from curiosity — some from ironical contempt — his answers — his opinions
  2 A man appears in public every day

This passage alone would do little to more clearly date this manuscript fragment; however, in notebooks that can be definitively dated to 1854 or later we find Whitman drafting lines — sometimes in prose and sometimes in his mature, long-lined style — that came to make up significant parts of this poem.[16] Though not conclusive evidence, the preliminary nature of Whitman's notes about these 1855 poems suggests that the "Med Cophösis" leaves probably antedate the major known notebooks in which he began to conceive and draft his first major works.

Other clues support this early dating. At the top of the recto of the second leaf Whitman jotted down, "*Man's Muscular capability*. Phren. Jour. Vol 7, page 96," a reference to a miscellaneous note about a Norwegian runner and adventurer at the end of volume 7 of the *American Phrenological Journal*, originally published in 1845. Whitman's reference to "spiritualism" toward the top of the first leaf verso suggests, however, that he must have been looking through an old issue. Spiritualism, a kind of pseudo-scientific religious movement, enjoyed considerable popularity in New England in the fifteen years leading up to the Civil War and seems to have interested Whitman prior to his publication of the first *Leaves*. In its preface he refers to the "spiritualist" as one of the "lawgivers of poets," and in his anonymous self-review of the same year in the *United States Review* he refers to himself as "the true spiritualist."[17] The reference to spiritualism in the "Med Cophösis" fragment definitely dates the fragment as after 1847, the year he could have first been initially exposed to the movement by way of Andrew Jackson Davis, the movement's early popularizer, whose first book was published in 1847 and went through eleven editions by 1852.[18] As an editor and book reviewer Whitman probably heard of spiritualism during that year since Davis's book received a good deal of popular press; however, it seems likely that the poet's interest developed somewhat later, as the movement was absorbed into public consciousness and its mystical vocabulary developed into culturally recognizable images and tropes. Spiritualism really caught on in the early 1850s, when a fad for séances, "trance writing," and "trance lecturing" spread throughout New York, and Davis and others began to produce book after book dealing with spiritualism, including several volumes of "trance poetry."[19] Though dismissive of spiritualism in its pop-cultural manifestations, Whitman appears to have been interested in Davis, who was the most famous and prolific "philosophical spiritualist," a term he used to distinguish himself from the movement's more sensational figures.[20] Davis published a slew of books throughout the early 1850s, including two issued by Whitman's friends at Fowler and Wells, *The Philosophy of Spiritual Intercourse* (1851) and *The Seer* (1852), either of which seems a likely candidate to have been on Whitman's mind at the time he was writing these notes.

We can say with certainty, then, that these pages date from after 1847 (after the publication of the journal article and Davis's first book) and almost certainly before 1854 (before the "Talbot Wilson" notebook). The crude nature of the proto-poems described therein support the pre-1854 dating, and the likely time of Whitman's serious involvement with spiritualism suggests that the notes were written after 1850 and probably after 1851 or 1852, when Fowler and Wells published Davis's books. Based on this evidence I contend that the "Med Cophōsis" notebook fragment was composed between 1852 and early 1854. If this notebook fragment dates from the earlier part of this span, this would have to be the sole extant example of Whitman writing in poetic lines from that period, and we would have to believe that he conceived of at least three of the poems later included in the 1855 *Leaves* years before there is any evidence that he continued to work on them, implying that he thought of these poems (and in the case of "Who Learns My Lesson Complete?" began drafting lines), then abandoned them for years, which seems less likely than the notion that the notebook fragment dates from closer to 1854, the year of the other datable pre-*Leaves* notebooks. Also, as the top of the recto of the first leaf suggests, Whitman was

FIG 3. Whitman contemplates genres for a major early work. Charles Feinberg
Collection of Walt Whitman, Manuscript Division, Library of Congress, Washington DC
(loc.00005.002).

at least somewhat involved in his language studies at this point, but
there is no other evidence of his having engaged in this project so
early in the decade.[21] For these reasons the most likely date for "Med
Cophōsis" would seem to be either late 1853 or early 1854.

I linger on the question of dating this notebook fragment because
of some comments Whitman made on the verso of the first leaf (see
figure 3):[22]

> Novel? – Work of some sort ˄ Play? – instead of sporadic characters – intro-
> duce them in large masses, on a far grander scale, – armies – twenty-
> three full-formed perfect athletes – orbs – take characters through the
> orbs – "spiritualism" Nobody appears upon the stage simply – but all
> in huge aggregates nobody speaks alone, whatever is said, is said by an
> immense number

Just to the upper left of this passage is an asterisk with a note indicating
that Whitman continued this thinking with another, asterisk-marked
section further down the leaf (see figure 4):

> Bring in whole races, or castes, or generations, to express themselves – per-
> sonify the general objects of the creative and give them voice – every thing
> on the most august scale – a leaf of grass, with its equal voice. –

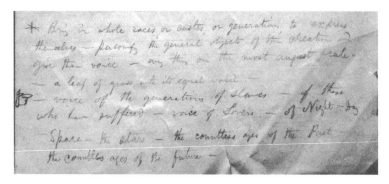

FIG 4. Probable source manuscript for title phrase "leaf of grass." Charles Feinberg Collection of Walt Whitman, Manuscript Division, Library of Congress, Washington DC (loc.00005.002).

☞ — voice of the generations of slaves — of those who have suffered — voices of Lovers — of Night — Day — Space — the stars — the countless ages of the Past — the countless ages of the future

What was Whitman thinking of in this passage? Clearly he seems to be considering some kind of major work, and he has no clear idea what genre such a work might assume. What this passage sounds like, though, is "Song of Myself." It is in "Song of Myself," with its catalogs, that he introduces "large masses" of "characters" on a grand scale, in "huge aggregates," and where he attempts to speak for "generations of slaves — of those who have suffered." Through his trope of universal identification Whitman works to "personify the general objects of the creative and give them voice" and to speak for "Lovers . . . Night — Day — Space — the stars." In "Song of Myself" he also gives voice to "the countless ages of the Past" and exhorts "the countless ages of the future." No other work Whitman published in his subsequent career really comes close to fitting this description.

The most suggestive part of this passage, however, may be his reference to a "leaf of grass." Previously scholars have dated Whitman's earliest mention of the phrase "leaves of grass" to the important, though misunderstood, "Talbot Wilson" notebook, but this fragment, as I have shown, almost certainly antedates that writing. According to the information we have available to us, then, this seems to be the earliest extant manuscript in which Whitman uses the phrase (here in the singular) that would become the central image of his greatest poem and the title of his life's work. The implications are compelling. For one, Whitman seems at this stage in his thinking to have no clear idea that his masterpiece *would even constitute a poem.* "Novel? — Work of some sort ₍Play?₎" Whitman asks himself, searching for the right word to describe the grand conception hatching in his mind. Perhaps not comfortable with the prosaic implications of the word *novel* (he had already published his hackneyed temperance novel *Franklin Evans*), in the top margin of the recto of the next leaf he amends his description, writing in brackets "A <u>spiritual novel</u>?" Perhaps he was toying with ideas from his readings in spiritualism, though this seems rather unlikely. Even in the passage in these notes he puts "spiritualism" in quotes, suggesting his distance from the movement and its thought. Whitman never seems to have taken spiritualism seriously enough to base such a major work on it, and the semantic difference between "spiritual novel" and "spiritual*ist* novel" is significant. Aside from the descriptions found in the passages just quoted, it's hard to guess what he means to indicate by this phrase, but his notes on these leaves do hold some provocative implications.

Most crucially, Whitman's uncertainty in this passage suggests that well into the early 1850s he wasn't sure what genre his creative ambitions might assume. In fact judging from some of the writing here none of the conventional generic parameters of his era seems to fit with what he had in mind. Because of the misunderstanding about when he first started writing in his mature line, the assumption has been that he knew his ambitions would assume the form of poetry when he jotted down these remarks. But in fact he hadn't written any lined verse in a long time. He seems to be seeking some new genre altogether in which to express himself, which underscores just how malleable his concept of genre had become and suggests that *Leaves of Grass* might well have taken a radically different form. In a passage just below where he contemplates his "novel? — Work of some sort" he seems to be considering something between a novel and a verse play:

> Shade — An ^twenty-five old men old man with rapid gestures — eyes black and flashing like lightning — long white beard — attended by an immense train — no warriors or warlike weapons or helmets — all emblematic of peace — shadowy — rapidly ~~approaches and pauses~~ — sweeping by

This passage, in which Whitman changes his mind from one "old man" to "twenty-five old men," sounds like a potential scene from the play considered just above in which "Nobody appears upon the stage simply — but all in huge aggregates." Apparently, however, as indicated by a bracketed qualification Whitman added just to the right, he isn't sure: "if in a play — let the descriptions ~~not~~ that are usually put in brief, in brackets, in italics, be also in poetry, carefully finished as the dialogue." So the image preoccupying him here doesn't seem to fit well with any of these categories: it might be a novel or a "spiritual novel"; it might be a play, but if a play it must straddle the line with poetry, with even the stage directions in some kind of poetic line. On the recto of the second leaf he also seems to have considered rendering this concept as a poem proper (whatever that might have meant to him): "A poem in which all things and qualities and processes express themselves—the nebula—the fixed stars—the earth—the grass, water, vegetable, sauroid, and all processes—man—animals." We can see here how Whitman's concept of this work floats between genres, never settling. These passages, which seem like proto-formulations of "Song of Myself," suggest that early on his masterwork was conceived in *sui generic* terms.

In this same notebook fragment Whitman also considered another work included in the 1855 *Leaves* that might have taken another form besides poetry. In the notes quoted earlier anticipating "Song of the Answerer" he begins by describing his idea as a "Plot for a Poem or other work," not sure what form that work might assume. There is plenty of evidence elsewhere that his attitude toward genre remained quite malleable until late in the development of his pre-*Leaves* writing. The "Talbot Wilson" notebook contains as much prose as poetry, and in fact the most finished piece of writing in the notebook is a work titled "Dilation" that today we would probably call a prose poem. Readers have described this notebook as the place where Whitman "breaks into" the line of *Leaves of Grass*, implying that a definite separation developed in his mind between the poems he began drafting and the prose style that antedates his line. We've tended to overlook or minimize the fact that he continued to write lyrical prose equal to the lyricism of his newly found line in all of his 1854 notebooks—that his experiments with the long line that he eventually settled into seem to have been conducted concurrently with a sustained interest in poetic *prose*. The other manuscript notebooks dated from 1854 in fact contain considerably more prose than poetry, and he culled more lines from the prose in these experiments than he did from the work in lines. Some of the lines in these notebooks later reverted back to prose in the form of the 1855 preface, only to reemerge as poetry in the piece eventually called "By Blue Ontario's

Shore." Rather than breaking into his line, Whitman seems to have been unclear about what formal body he wanted to inhabit until quite late in his development of the first *Leaves*, vacillating between different formal conceptions as he gradually moved toward his signature line. Though he used the label "poem," it is not at all clear that he regarded the words he used as "poetry" in any essential form, and it seems to have been crucial to his creative process that the boundaries between genres remain unstable. Given this flexible attitude toward generic distinctions, it's hard to say when Whitman saw himself as beginning to write the thing that would fulfill his artistic ambitions. All we can really say is that at some point between late 1853 and early 1855 he decided that the work he was going to publish would be set in lines and that he would refer to these writings in lines, if only by default, as "poems."

It is difficult to pinpoint with certainty the moment Whitman first started writing in his line, let alone when he decided it would be his formal vehicle for the thing that became *Leaves of Grass*. If there was a specific early notebook in which he discovered his line, it's entirely possible, probably even likely that it no longer exists. We can only estimate the dates of the extant notebooks, and, as we've seen, even that is problematic. A few, such as the early "Med Cophösis" notebook fragment, provide evidence of their position in his development, but it's impossible to give an exact chronology. There are, however, some clues worth considering. The "Talbot Wilson" notebook and another notebook, filed in the Library of Congress as Notebook 85 and sometimes called the "Poem incarnating the mind" notebook, seem to document similar stages in Whitman's development: in both he writes with poetic concentration in both verse and prose; in both he writes with his signature poetic device of anaphora; in both he concentrates on identifying with those who are suffering, including

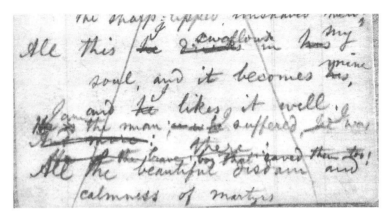

FIG 5. Whitman revises from third- to first-person address. Thomas Biggs Harned Collection of Walt Whitman, Manuscript Division, Library of Congress, Washington, DC (loc.00346.020).

slaves; and in both he has developed an early version of his inclusive, declarative, broadly figured first-person voice. As Floyd Stovall first noted, however, this last point suggests an order.[23] In the "Talbot Wilson" notebook, Whitman seems more comfortable and aggressively expansive writing in the first person, and the most significant poetic passage in the "Poem incarnating the mind" notebook was originally drafted in the third person (see figure 5):

> All this ~~he drinks~~ I swallowed in ~~his~~ my
> soul, and it becomes ~~his~~ mine,
> and ~~he~~ I likes it well,
> ~~He is~~ I am the man; ~~[illeg.] he~~ I suffered, ~~he~~ I was
> there:

Putting aside for now the fascinating implications this passage holds regarding the development of Whitman's "I," this suggests that the "Poem incarnating the mind" notebook antedates the "Talbot Wilson" notebook, if only slightly. Further evidence supporting this is the fact that the punctuation in the lines in the "Poem incarnating the mind" notebook is in the more conventional mode in which he first experiments with his line, whereas in the "Talbot Wilson" notebook, perhaps for the first time, we find him toying with the ubiquitous ellipses he used to punctuate the first edition. The passage where he changes from third- to first-person address describes the wreck of the ship *San Francisco*, which happened in January 1854, so we know that he had found his line by then, though he was still developing it, as "Talbot Wilson" shows.

There is at least one other place where Whitman writes in his long line that antedates the "Talbot Wilson" notebook, which is in "Med Cophōsis." The lines described earlier, included in the poem eventually called "Who Learns My Lesson Complete?" appear at the bottom of the recto of the first leaf (see figure 6). There are only three lines, and no others on either leaf, so this is a very modest flirtation with his signature form. What is intriguing about these lines, though, is that, as with those in the "Poem incarnating the mind" notebook, they were not originally written in the first person but were later, at an unknown point, changed: "Have you learned ~~the~~ my lesson complete." In another early notebook that seems to antedate "Talbot Wilson" Whitman also writes in a free-verse line (though one not as long) that never speaks in the first-person address (*NUPM* 1:131). What all this seems to indicate is that Whitman found his line before he found his voice, and that many of the lines now in the first person in the 1855 edition were originally drafted from a more detached, third-person point of view. At some later point he probably went through many of his earlier drafts and rewrote them in his assertive new first-person address. We see him doing this with his prose as well. Passages that were originally written as discourse on the role of

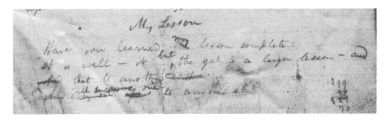

FIG 6. Whitman revises from third- to first-person address. Charles Feinberg Collection of Walt Whitman, Manuscript Division, Library of Congress, Washington DC (loc.00005.001).

"the poet" Whitman later assumed for himself personally, refitting them as verse and changing the point of view. What was once poetic theory became instead poetry, often with no more manipulation than putting line breaks at the end of sentences and changing a few pronouns from "he" to "I." The notebook passage describing the wreck of the *San Francisco* was drafted under the title "The Poet," a role Whitman later assumed in the poem merely by changing it to the first person. This passage, like others scattered throughout the pre-1855 notebooks, shows how Whitman's concept of what a poet should be was worked out before he became that poet. These early notebooks reveal a passionate (yet also methodical) idealist who was able to negotiate the gap between abstraction and reality with what he portrayed as a casual, even cavalier confidence in his own imagination. Later poetic revisions of himself—with the "Calamus" and "Children of Adam" clusters, his Civil War poems, and his old age poems—could rely on qualities that he had already defined and, increasingly, a life he had already lived as a poet. But in the early notebooks he is already revising (even as he invents) his own identity, piecing his poetic selfhood together out of disparate discourses.

It could be, of course, that much of the time Whitman wrote of "the poet" he was already thinking of himself but was hesitant to make such bold claims. In many cases, that is, the move to first person may have simply been restoring the point of view to the way it was originally conceived. This is far from certain, however, and we really don't know when he developed his artistic self-confidence. There is also the possibility that much of his self-confidence resulted from the poetic quality of his prose writing in the third person — that he became a poet by writing in prose about "the poet." Judging from the sheer amount of poetic theory Whitman was writing around the time he discovered his line, this would appear to be a strong possibility. Of course some of his writing in the third person stayed that way in the form of the 1855 preface, which was, so he later said, "simply another poem."[24] Readers often take the third person in the preface as a rather transparent stand-in for the "I" of "Song of Myself," so the line between forms of address has always been somewhat foggy. There are implications, though, to the fact that some of Whitman's most famous first-person lines were originally cast as something more neutral. It means that such famous passages as line 832 from "Song of Myself" — "I am the man, I suffer'd, I was there" — began in a manner far different from how they are now received, and the intimacy we attribute to Whitman's voice, at least in some places, is an afterthought. The possibility that at almost any point in a poem like "Song of Myself" Whitman may have originally been writing impersonally and only later appropriated the first-person pronoun sends some cracks down the foundations of a number of biographical readings. Just as the young woman in "Song of Myself" fantasizing about the twenty-eight bathers can be read as a surrogate for Whitman, so the "I" we have assumed was Whitman in other places may have once been someone else.

The line Whitman found or invented in the third person may

have had even more impersonal origins than I've suggested. Since *Leaves of Grass* was first published readers have often assumed that Whitman developed his line from the Bible. This explanation has been explored by critics ever since, perhaps most definitively by Sculley Bradley and Gay Wilson Allen. Bradley discusses Whitman's biblical affinities in terms of what he calls "periodic rhythm," emphasizing Whitman's use of "more ancient and native meter based on the rhythmic 'period' between stresses." This "periodic rhythm" creates a wave-like "pyramidal" structure, an "envelope" of rising and falling lines, the rhythm of which resembles the rising and falling of waves.[25] Allen is more hesitant to assert a direct biblical relationship, exploring the relation in terms of analogy rather than influence.[26] That Whitman was aware that his line seemed biblical is undeniable, and he was surely influenced, even if only unconsciously, by English translations of the Bible's Hebraic rhythms. But the Bible of course must have always been present as a potential influence in Whitman's mind, so *something* had to have turned him toward the idea (he certainly took his time discovering it).

Another explanation is that Whitman's line was influenced by Martin Farquhar Tupper, an enormously popular figure in the early 1850s who wrote in an unrhymed, long line somewhat similar to Whitman's and who made a fortune with his now forgotten *Proverbial Philosophy*. Tupper, who like Whitman also frequently used catalogs in his verses, may indeed have been a kind of influence. Tupper's sold-out public readings in Manhattan in 1851 were hosted by Whitman's friend William Cullen Bryant, and Whitman surely noticed the acclaim. As with the Bible, Whitman's readers almost immediately noted the parallels with Tupper, and some readers disinclined toward Whitman (including Henry James Jr.) have used the comparison to dismiss the notion of Whitman's originality.[27] More thoughtful responses have been scarce. C. Carroll Hollis's 1983 description of the possible Whitman-Tupper relation points out that "no other writer [besides Tupper] has lists and catalogues so near Whitman's in 'Song of Myself,' not in substance, in thought, but in external form." In retrospect the correct dating of the "Talbot Wilson" notebook strengthens Hollis's case, since he erroneously concluded, based on the late 1840s dating, that "manuscript evidence in the early notebooks indicates that Whitman was already working [with his line]" before Tupper published his blockbuster.[28] As we've seen, Whitman didn't find his line until after Tupper came to New York in 1851, so the possibility that Tupper provided some kind of an initial impetus now seems more probable. Joseph L. Coulombe traces Whitman's awareness of Tupper by way of an analysis of contemporaneous periodicals, showing that Whitman's active involvement with newspaper journalism would have affected how Whitman regarded him, and Matt Cohen's study reveals that if Whitman was influenced by Tupper's line the influence is still biblical, since "Solomon's proverbs were the model for *Proverbial Philosophy*."[29]

The notebooks don't offer much evidence either way about the Bible or Martin Tupper, but one intriguing early passage does suggest another possibility: Whitman's use of his long line may have been influenced by a form of prose notation he used for items in a list. In what appears to be the remnant of a very early notebook, Whitman jotted down the following, copying it from entries in J. P. Giraud Jr.'s comprehensive 1844 tome, *The Birds of Long Island* (see figure 7):

"wood drake"

"Summer Duck" or "Wood Duck", very gay, including in its colors white, red, yellow, green, blue, &c crowns violet — length 20 inches — common in the United States — often by ~~creeks~~ streams and

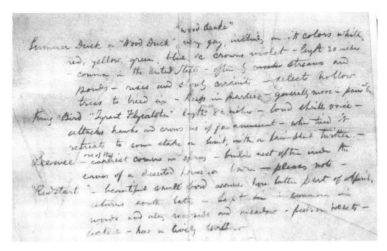

FIG 7. Prose notations in verse-like form. Charles Feinberg Collection of Walt Whitman, Manuscript Division, Library of Congress, Washington DC (loc.00158.001).

>   ponds — rises and slowly circuits — selects hollow
>   trees to breed in — keeps in parties — generally move in pairs at least
>   King Bird "Tyrant Flycatcher" length 8½ inches — loud shrill voice —
>   — attacks hawks and crows as if for amusement — when tired it
>   retreats to some stake or limit, with a triumphant twitter. —
>   Peewee — one of the earliest comers in spring — builds nests often under the
>   eaves of a deserted house or barn — pleasing note —
>   "Redstart" — beautiful small bird arrives here latter part of April,
>   Returns south late in September — common in
>   woods and along roadside and meadow — feeds on insects —
>   active — has a lively twitter.[30]

Few would contend that this constitutes poetry, but it is a very early passage from Whitman's notebooks that at least looks like his signature line and has some of the impetus of his poetic catalogs.

It's certain that he looked back on this prosaic notation after he was actively engaged in writing *Leaves of Grass,* because he extracted some phrases from its first line that were later used in lines 237–43 of the poem eventually titled "Song of Myself":

> My tread scares the wood-drake and wood-duck on my distant and
> day-long ramble,
> They rise together, they rise together, they slowly circle around.

> I believe in those wing'd purposes,
> And acknowledge red, yellow, white, playing with me,
> And consider green violet and the tufted crown intentional
>   (*LG* 40)

The leaf on which the "wood drake" passage appears has so far been dated as simply "pre-1855," and there are indeed few clues in the text that help pinpoint it any more accurately. However, the leaf, which was torn from a larger notebook, looks exactly like the leaves of the "Med <u>Cophōsis</u>" notebook fragment (see figure 8). The meticulous, clerkly handwriting characteristic of Whitman's very early notebooks appears the same on these leaves, and both contain notes related to his study of the Greeks. The rather unremarkable writing in the "wood drake" "lines" probably wasn't the first time Whitman wrote in his signature form, but the passage may have suggested to him some of the elastic possibilities that his mature line later developed; no other lines from around this period are as long as the pseudo-lines in "wood drake," and this very well may be the first extant example, however prosaic, of Whitman's use of the catalog form.

At whatever point Whitman finally settled into his line he seems to have realized something else that became crucial to him: that his newly found verse form was capacious and flexible enough to accommodate

much of what he had already written. Without the musical prerogatives of meter, working with a highly variable line length that was
determined only by the sentence (or speech unit of the sentence) that
he was writing, there was nothing to stop him from plundering his
old notebooks for sentences and phrases that fit with his new poetic
conception. From an early, pre-1855 notebook that contains nothing
but brief prose jottings, Whitman extracted language that later came
to be the famous passage at the end of section 26 of "Song of Myself"
describing "A tenor large and fresh as the creation" (601-10).[31] In
another early, all-prose notebook he repeatedly works over much of
the infamous "boss-tooth" passage from the poem eventually titled
"The Sleepers," only here the boss isn't a phallic tooth but a poet.[32]
The "prose poem" "Dilation" later became lines 1220-22 in "Song of
Myself," and many other prose passages in the "Talbot Wilson" notebook were also resurrected as poetry.[33] These are only a few of many
examples where Whitman mined his notebooks' prose for lines, and
a similar kind of rehabilitation occurred with "Resurgemus" and, as
we have seen, with the "wood drake" notes, which themselves recycle
writing from *The Birds of Long Island*. It would seem that sometime
after he found his poetic line Whitman went hunting and gathering
through his old notebooks for lines, images, and phrases that he
could use anew for his evolving poems. Many of his prose jottings,
he came to realize, already constituted poetry; all they were waiting
for was a vehicle that was finally supplied by a sufficiently expansive
concept of poetry and its formal possibilities.

In addition to the recuperative properties of his line, a generative
facility shortly became apparent. Put another way, sometimes what
Whitman recuperated were merely lists of words that became the
skeletal basis for poems or sections thereof. In this fascinating manuscript he reveals his awareness of this compositional process:

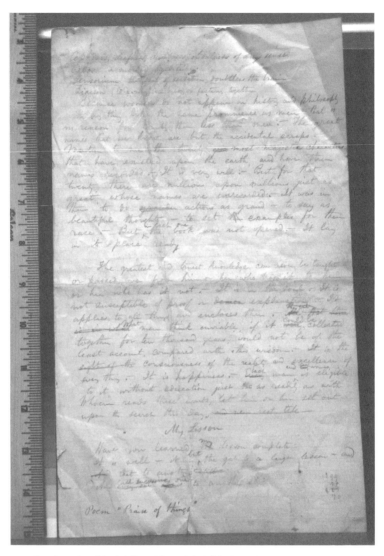

FIG 8. "Med <u>Cophōsis</u>" leaf (*left*) and "wood drake" leaf. Charles Feinberg Collection of Walt Whitman, Manuscript Division, Library of Congress, Washington DC (loc.00158.001).

summer Duck or "Wood Duck" very gay indeed in its colors, white, red, yellow, green, blue &c brown violet - light is colour - common in the United States - often & amid streams and ponds - rivers and slowly currents - select hollow trees to breed in - keeping particularly fewnels, more - ...

King bird "Tyrant Flycatcher" ... regular ... loud shrill voice ... upper hawks or crows &c if permanent ... when tired it ... flies to low state of bush ... a kind of broad tail twitter ... nests of course ... builds nest often under the eaves of a deserted house ...

... beautiful smell and manner eggs late part of which ... storm aid &c - dispirion ... woods and alone ... in meadow - four ... lustre when in bud ...

... Young Sapsucker

... Ophonote Salignan

... though he will ... for beyond ... And all other ... some upon the heart of the whole ... are utterly perfect of anything ... against ... it -

... when the world is finished at ... like a perfect ... how a street down to you suppose ... bottom ... the human ground has been found, and ... ... we have still more ... ... & noble ... and ...

... of the term ...

... at all ... by ...

The ... these probable ... terrible agency of nature - the ... ... of the suggestiveness of ... the end of a ...

Whole poem

Poem of Insects ?

_____

Get from Mr. Arkhurst the names of all insects —

_____

interweave a train of thought suitable — also trains of words[34]

_____

According to Grier this note is written on what appears to be wrapper stock for the 1855 edition, and "Mr. Arkhurst" is John Arkhurst, a taxidermist who lived in Brooklyn from 1854 to 1857. Whitman seems to have let his idea for an insect poem alone for a while, then returned to it later, reiterating and expanding on the same skeletal concept in the "Scope of Government" notebook (Feinberg #926), which dates from sometime between late 1855 and early 1856 (*NUPM* 1:283):

The insects

get from Mr. Arkhurst a list of just *American insects* —

_____

? Just simply enumerate them
with their sizes, colors, habits,
lives — shortness or length of life
what they feed upon
(A little poem of a leaf, or two
leaves only)

~~end the insects~~ —
First enumerate the insects —
then end by saying

I do not know what these are but I believe that all these

are more than they

seem

I do not know what they are

I dare not be too assuming over them

I have advised with myself

. . . I dare not consider

myself, in anymore for my place than

they are for their places[35]

Whitman's insect poem was never to be, but the process he describes is richly suggestive. This, it would seem, is a prime formula for generating his soon-to-be-infamous catalogs, and who knows how many others were composed using this method. Whitman starts with a list, in this case acquired from an acquaintance but in other places culled from a sourcebook, such as the book on birds from which he derived the "wood drake" passage. Reviewing the notebooks and manuscripts, we find these lists everywhere: of birds, parts of ships, body parts, items crafted from wood, of people at work, of specific men and boys who preoccupied him. Sometimes the words came straight from dictionaries, including the one he himself was compiling around the time the insects passage was written; sometimes the lists came from his old notebooks; and sometimes he probably just brainstormed them himself. In addition to the skeletal list he generates a set of qualities he can use to flesh it out, in the case above "their sizes, colors, habits, / lives — shortness or length of life, / what they feed upon." With this list and the criteria to fill it Whitman improvised his lines and then framed them with lyrical bookends that transform the list into something more: in the case above, examples of mystery and awe in the experience of nature.

When successful he turns what for a less imaginative writer would be a dull exercise into major art. Thus the list, for Whitman, becomes a generative structural framework that in a sense played the same role that rhyme and meter did for other writers.

At first blush this process might seem crude and mechanical, a kind of formulaic stand-in for more sophisticated structural thinking. There are aspects of Whitman's writing process that are undeniably and self-consciously *procedural*. As I explore in greater detail later, the procedural qualities of his work habits reflect an attitude toward language and writing that was ahead of its time. In a genre-blurring book in which the "two rivulets" of poetry and prose commingle on each page, Whitman declared that "the truest and greatest POETRY . . . can never again, in the English language, be express'd in arbitrary and rhyming meter."[36] But it wasn't just meter that was arbitrary; Whitman seemed to see *all* literary conventions as equivocal and ultimately capricious. As such, a poet can pick and choose structural devices, or invent his own, based on a consciously theorized set of poetic values. One of Whitman's values was his Emersonian faith that "every word was once a poem." Emerson anticipated Whitman quite directly in "The Poet" when he wrote, "Bare lists of words are found suggestive to an imaginative and excited mind," a statement that Whitman certainly read and, it would seem, came to embody.[37] Whitman in turn anticipates the procedural strategies of the Surrealists, the Oulipo, and numerous occasional practitioners such as John Ashbery, whose catalog poem of the world's rivers, "Into the Dusk-Charged Air," mimics Whitman's method in a gesture that reads as at once a parody and an homage. The procedural method that Whitman applied to his lists turns away from the idea of generic conventions toward a kind of serial productivity linked to his line and its rearrangeable and duplicative properties.

The discovery of his line and its compositional flexibility must have been an extraordinary moment for Whitman. Suddenly the many years he spent with his journals writing about astronomy, religion, and linguistics, about the sights of New York, the natural world, and his ecstatic response to opera — suddenly all of this was no longer idle jotting or mere diary fodder. His old notes were now the basis for his visionary book, and the "long foreground" Emerson would later describe wasn't just abstract preparation, but a part of his process of composition, even if he hadn't known it at the time. This kind of poetic recuperation by way of his notebook pilferings and procedural generation by way of lists and serial form help explain the extraordinary speed with which Whitman moved from his earliest trial lines for "Song of Myself" to the full-fledged achievement that emerged only a year or two later. Surely it would have taken him considerably longer to write the poems for the first edition if he hadn't resuscitated old material and generated lines in serial form from lists. Because most of the manuscript evidence has been lost or destroyed it's hard to know what portion of poems like "Song of Myself" was appropriated from earlier sources, but the manuscript evidence that survives suggests it was significant. Whitman was never one to waste either his paper or the words he wrote on it; the move to reappropriate must have seemed a natural one once he realized what his new form could do. Readers examine why he chose the words he did for his lines, but it may be equally true that he chose the line he did because of the work it could do for his words. Contrary to most assumptions, his attraction to this line may not have been primarily musical or because it made his lines look and feel something like the "new Bible" he wanted to write for his country, but rather because the line was capacious and plastic enough to involve and absorb the full range of language he had already been composing. It made the transition to writing primarily in poetic form more comfortable, as well as allowing him to rearrange, reuse, and generate from his old material.

Other accounts of Whitman's creative breakthrough are not necessarily excluded by one emphasizing his methods of composition. They can all potentially fit as pieces brought together in the process. We know that his reflections on opera from the early 1850s, for example, were reused in verse form in several places in "Song of Myself." The idea that his concern with slavery helped motivate his early ambitions is borne out in many prose passages from the journals, some of which were transformed into lines also. The same could be said, and with somewhat more manuscript evidence, with regard to the emphasis on social class and economic equality as points of poetic origination. The early notebook writings aligned with Whitman's mysticism cited by V. K. Chari and others were mostly in prose, and some of these also eventually became lines.[38] Interestingly the most sexually inflected passages in his notebooks and manuscript fragments almost all seem to have been initially drafted in lines, suggesting that he may not have had earlier prose descriptions from which to draw and that his discovery of his line may have facilitated his ability to write more candidly about sex. His long catalogs of men and their personal characteristics in the ironically named "Dick Hunt" notebook seem echoed by his catalogs of people in "Song of Myself" and other poems. All of the external sources of inspiration that helped Whitman to fill his notebooks were surely important to varying degrees, but if one event can be described as his strictly *creative* catalyst, judging from the notebooks it would seem to be his realization of new ways of composing derived from his discovery of his line.

Explaining Whitman's breakthrough in terms of line and realization of method helps to reconcile some of the statements he made about writing *Leaves of Grass*.[39] Whitman was reticent about describing his creative process, and the only sources we have to draw on—a few comments he made to his friends and two brief statements he made in his published prose—are contradictory in regard to when he got started. In a book Whitman authorized and partially wrote, John Burroughs provides a short account:

> It is at this period (1853 and the season immediately following,) that I come on the first inkling of *Leaves of Grass*. Walt Whitman is now thirty-four years old, and in the full fruition of health and physique.... In 1855, then, after many manuscript doings and undoings, and much matter destroyed, and two or three complete re-writings, the essential foundation of *Leaves of Grass* was laid and the superstructure raised.[40]

If Whitman didn't come upon "the first inkling of *Leaves of Grass*" until "1853 and the season immediately following," then the poems would seem to have been generated from scratch very quickly, and this passage would support the 1853–54 dating of his notebooks that contain work leading up to the 1855 *Leaves*. The late dating of Whitman's writing process was echoed by his acquaintance John Townsend Trowbridge, who in 1902 wrote, "It was in that summer of 1854, while he was still at work upon houses, that he began the *Leaves of Grass*, which he wrote, re-wrote, and re-rewrote (to quote again his own words), and afterward set in type with his own hand."[41]

This dating is contradicted by other statements, though, especially in a preface Whitman wrote in 1872 to *As a Strong Bird on Pinions Free* and reprinted in *Specimen Days*: "I commenced, years ago, elaborating the plan of my poems, and continued turning over that plan, and shifting it in my mind through many years, (from the age of twenty-eight to thirty-five,) experimenting much, and writing and abandoning much" (*PW* 2:461). On the one hand Whitman claimed to have found "the first inkling" of his poems in 1853–54, but on the other hand he says that be began "elaborating the plan of [his] poems" in 1847, when he was twenty-eight. We might take "elaborating the plan" to mean something other than actual writing, but he also adds that he was "experimenting much, and writing and abandoning much," implying that there were definite drafts being made during those years. This is the view taken by one his friends, Richard Bucke, who backed up the early dating in 1883, writing that Whitman "had more or less consciously the plan of the poems in his mind for eight years before, and that during those eight years they took many shapes; that in the course of those years he wrote and destroyed a great deal."[42] So we have two quite different accounts of Whitman's creative gestation, with the "long foreground" version standing in contrast to the idea that he was brought to a boil suddenly in 1853–54.

Partially because of the mistaken dating of the "Talbot Wilson" notebook, most readers have ignored the claim that Whitman didn't begin actually writing his poems for the first edition until a year or two before it was published. Those who were aware of it likely thought it was one of Whitman's infamous unreliable and boastful testimonies about his own life. From a scholarly standpoint it's a more fertile and attractive prospect to take the view that the first edition was composed over a longer stretch of time, because that allows for more connections to be drawn between his life and work. But looked at in light of his notebooks the accounts don't really contradict each other. Whitman's comments in his 1872 preface help call out this perspective: "One deep purpose underlay the others, and has underlain it and its execution ever since — and that has been the religious purpose. Amid many changes, and a formulation taking far different shape from what I at first supposed, this basic purpose has never been departed from in the composition of my verses" (PW 2:461–62). Discounting for a moment his point about the religious purpose of *Leaves of Grass,* the phrase that stands out is "Amid many changes, and a formulation taking far different shape from what I at first supposed." A different shape indeed – in fact a different form of writing altogether. Whitman didn't even know that he was writing the thing that would become *Leaves of Grass* at the time he composed many of its early lines. The process may have begun as early as 1847 (or even earlier), but *Leaves of Grass,* even in Whitman's mind, didn't become poetry until around 1854. He probably spent some time toying with his line before he realized what it could do for him, and when he decided on it as his formal vehicle his writing picked up steam. So the early date maintained by Whitman in 1872 and Bucke in 1883 probably refers to when he first began to produce writing that was later pieced together into his book, and the late date Burroughs and Trowbridge claim Whitman provided them was when he discovered his "formulation" – that is, his line and the poetic process that allowed him to write in a new style and recover what he had already written.

The descriptions Whitman made (or is said to have made) about his early creative practice actually make quite a bit of sense when looked at in the context of his notebooks and his compositional breakthrough. Just as his 1854 notebooks show a writer vacillating between poetry and prose, seemingly still undecided on what form his writing will assume, Bucke's description suggests a very late date for when he finally settled on a style: "By the spring of 1855, Walt Whitman had found or made a style in which he could express himself, and in that style he had (after, as he has told me, elaborately building up the structure, and then utterly demolishing it, five different times) written twelve poems, and a long prose preface which was simply another poem."[43] Given that he was still writing mostly in prose in 1854, the spring of 1855 seems an accurate date for when he may have fully realized his process and line. The suggestion that Whitman self-consciously regarded his "long prose preface" as "simply another poem" also reinforces just how permeable his concept was of what constituted a poem even after he published the first *Leaves*. Although, as Ed Folsom has noted, the idea that Whitman fully rewrote *Leaves of Grass* "five different times" seems doubtful given what we know about his writing habits, the actual phrasing in this passage — "elaborately building up the structure" — leaves plenty of room for interpretation regarding what this "structure" might have amounted to.[44] Most likely Whitman's various claims about how many times he reworked the first edition simply refer to different processes; "building up the structure" could simply mean experimenting with select passages in different formal arrangements, while Burroughs's description of "two or three complete re-writings" seems to indicate a more wholesale reshaping, probably involving radical rearrangement of the order of various lines.

Throughout his descriptions of his early writing process Whitman repeatedly employs a rhetoric of visual form that frames his statements and hints at the change his writing underwent. He describes a "formulation taking far different shape" not only in his 1872 preface, but also in Bucke's biography, where Whitman tells us (according to Bucke)that he had "the poems in his mind for eight years before [1855], and during those eight years, they took many shapes." Continuing to describe the change in visual terms, he says "the work assumed a form very different from any at first expected," and he also describes Whitman at work on the poems as "writing *Leaves of Grass* from time to time, getting it in shape."[45] John Addington

Symonds, in his 1893 study, also visually framed Whitman's change in writing, describing how Whitman "determined upon the form which this book should assume" and how "at last he shaped that peculiar style."[46] Late in his life Whitman continued to describe his poems in the first edition as having undergone visual change, saying that he "had them in half a dozen forms — larger, smaller, recast, outcast, taken apart, put together."[47] Clearly he wasn't just editing lines in the poems but fundamentally altering their presentation. Although he never actually says that his writing underwent changes in genre or was cobbled together from disparate sources, he does seem to allude to these processes.

One frequently quoted statement that Whitman made about his writing makes particular sense in light of his notebooks. In *Specimen Days* he offers this description of when he printed *Leaves of Grass* in 1855: "Commenced putting *Leaves of Grass* to press for good, at the job printing office of my friends, the brothers Rome, in Brooklyn, after many MS. doings and undoings — (I had great trouble in leaving out the stock 'poetical' touches, but succeeded at last)" (*PW* 1:22). This description was repeated in Traubel's *Camden's Compliment to Walt Whitman* and later by an anonymous interviewer in 1880 who wrote that Whitman claimed he "gave [the 1855 *Leaves*] a great deal of revision, experiencing a difficulty in eliminating the stock poetical touches, if the idea may be conveyed in that way."[48] Although he phrases it differently, the notebooks repeatedly show that leaving out "stock poetical touches" was indeed one of Whitman's overriding concerns during his process of composition. In the "Med Cophösis" notebook, for example, he writes that he would try "never to strain or exhibit the least apparent desire to make *stick out* the pride, grandeur, and boundless riches — but to *be* those" and that he would "give no second hand articles — no quotations."[49] In another manuscript fragment he elaborates on what he means by leaving out "poetical touches":

Rules for Composition

A perfectly transparent plate-glassy style, artless, with no ornaments, or attempts at ornaments, for their own sake — ~they~ only ~coming in where answering~ looking well when like the beauties of the person or character, by nature and intuition, ~and~ never lugged ~in~ in ~in by the colla[r]~ to show off

. . .

Take no illustrations whatever from the ancients or classics, nor from the mythology nor Egypt, Greece, or Rome — nor from the royal and aristocratic institutions and forms of Europe. — Make no mention or allusion to them whatever, except as they relate to the New, present things — to our country — to American character or interests. —

. . .

Too much attempt at ornament is the blur upon nearly all literary styles.

Clearness, simplicity, no twistified or foggy sentences, at all — the most translucid clearness without variation. —

Common idioms and phrases — Yankeeisms and vulgarisms — cant expressions, when very pat only.[50]

Whitman might "lug in" his prose and other early writings into his new style, but his new style wasn't to lug in "ornaments, or attempts at ornaments." It was to be "artless," which meant "no mention or allusion" from the classics or mythology "except as they relate . . . to American character or interests." The process of leaving out "stock poetical touches" was definitely a part of Whitman's American nationalist aesthetics. It meant exchanging European ornaments for "common idioms and phrases — Yankeeisms and vulgarisms" in a new "plate-glassy" American style.

Although he claimed in *Specimen Days* that he "succeeded at last" in leaving out European "poetical touches" with his publication of the first *Leaves*, Whitman continued to declaim his artistic priorities. In a notebook from 1856 in which he composes long sections of the poems that became "Crossing Brooklyn Ferry" and "Song of the Broad-Axe" he is still exhorting himself about the evils of antiquated conventions:

> ☞Avoid all the "intellectual subtleties," and "withering doubts" and "blasted hopes" and "unrequited loves," and "ennui," and "wretchedness" and the whole of the <u>lurid</u> and <u>artistical</u> and <u>melo-dramatic</u> effects. – Preserve perfect calmness and sanity[51]

The image of the manuscript shows that Whitman seems to be particularly incensed in this comment (the leaf contains three of his emphatic "pointing hands," also known as manicules, and numerous underlined passages and oversized words), but the lines drafted in the notebooks show little trace of the qualities he denounces (see figure 9). It is as if he has already left behind the qualities he finds so repugnant but still derives energy from condemning them. Whitman seems to have had a visceral emotional reaction to outmoded Victorianisms, associating them with mental illness. Artifice was akin to a form of insanity, and poetic beauty only "look[ed] well" when presented "like the beauties of the person or character, by nature and intuition."

Whitman's vehemence about the need to purge his poems of the aesthetic priorities of other countries didn't stop him from importing from foreign languages. His "doceurs," "eleves," "koboos," and "quahuags" became linguistic "amies," -creatively spelled "cameradoes" in his ongoing experiment with language. In light of his "Rules of Composition" these foreign-language words might seem anomalous in his conception of American poetics. But words for Whitman could

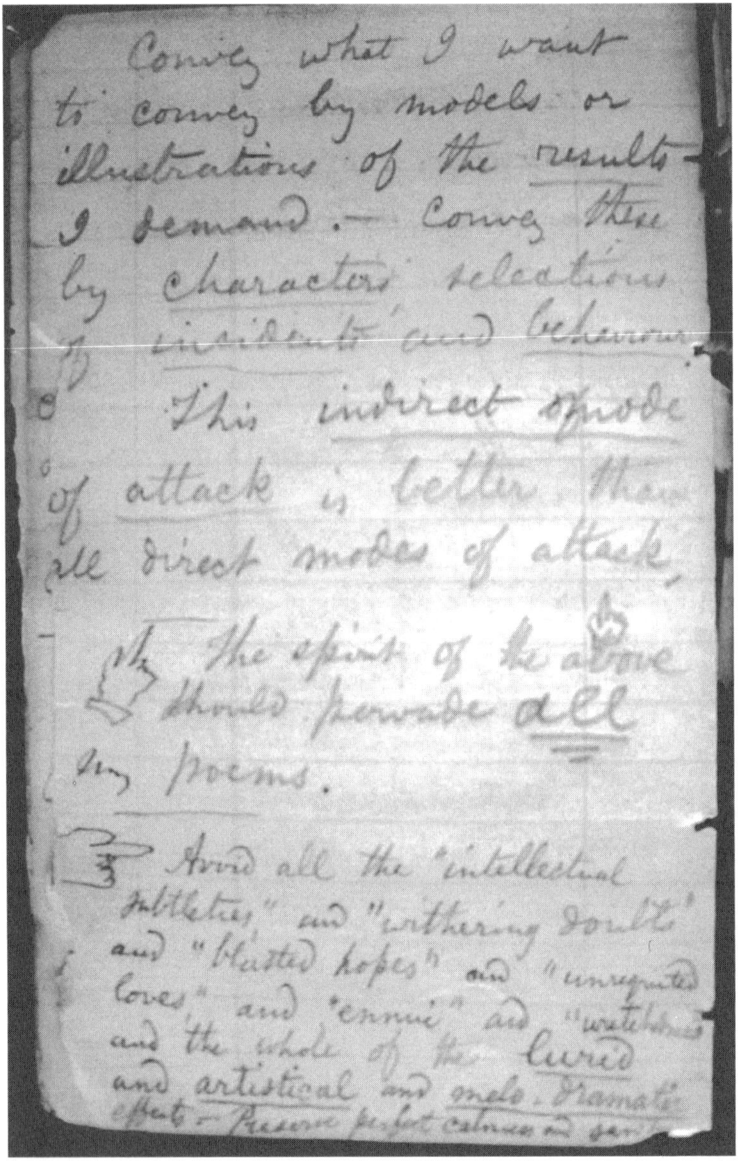

FIG 9. Emphatic comments on Whitman's aesthetic theory. Charles Feinberg Collection of Walt Whitman, Manuscript Division, Library of Congress, Washington DC (loc.00143.073).

always be absorbed by "true noble American character." With the exception of profanity, which he almost never used, it would appear that any form of diction could be lugged in to his vocabulary. But not just any poetic device. Device for Whitman exposed the stamp of its historical origins, whereas language in the raw could always be absorbed. Those poetic devices he retained and made the most use of, especially anaphora, motif, and refrain, are among the most basic generic conventions. They are all forms of repetition, and because most are associated as much with music as with poetry, poetry had no unique claim upon them. Whitman avoided devices that were elaborately entangled with historical definitions of his genre, most obviously rhyme and meter, but also stock mythological allusions, ornate vocabulary, and the kind of inverted melodrama he alludes to when he scorned "lurid and artistical and melo-dramatic effects." Fair or not, Whitman disavowed those techniques as belonging to the sick, aged body of European poetics. When language was put to these devices, it ceased to be something he could mold to his own effects. To the extent that the conventions of poetry were regarded as intrinsic and fixed, its language became encoded with a sense of cultural ownership. To Whitman genre helped copyright language: it kept it from being the "generic" product he needed it to be. His free verse signifies not only metrical liberty, but verse — and language — free for the taking.

In this light Whitman's infamous appropriation of Emerson's letter reflects not so much a breach of literary polity as it does Whitman's attitude toward language as a liberated estate. After all, what he was doing with the words in that letter was no different from what he did with language anywhere. As his notebooks reveal, Whitman's view on language was intrinsic to his process of composition, and surely his experience appropriating words in his notebooks helped encourage him to make free use of Emerson's commendation. Intimate with the mechanics of printing Whitman saw all language as "moveable type," and as a free-soil Democrat he saw no contradiction between assuming his authoritative role as a poet of democracy and disavowing authority over how language is used. That included, of course, disavowing authority over his own poems, or as Gay Wilson Allen observed some time ago, "Whitman attempts less to create a 'poem,' as the term is usually understood, than to present the materials of a poem for the reader to use in creating his own work of art."[52] Whitman is an author who would establish literary authority by giving it away. He wanted to be the steward, not the proprietor, of language. So despite the fact that a terrific selfhood infuses his work, in a sense he anticipates Barthes's "death of the author" by using and presenting language as unmoored from an owner. His attitude toward the poem's authority likewise foresees reader-response criticism by regarding literature as requiring a reader for its completion. These positions help explain why Whitman's work still seems relevant, and why so many of his contemporaries couldn't understand his work at all.

Whitman's attitudes toward language and artistic purpose are thus rooted in his discovery of a process of composition. When he looked back over his notebooks for pieces of language to make into lines he developed a facility to decontextualize words from their original authority. Something freely borrowed from disparate sources surely seemed less his own and encouraged him, in a way, to give it back by offering it to the reader. By the standards of his day these practices were ruthlessly anti-aesthetic. It wasn't just "stock poetical touches" that he derided, but the basic idea of artistry as it was defined for him, which for Whitman reeked of European decadence, "blasted hopes," "ennui," and "wretchedness." He rejected a strictly expressive poetry as "ornamentation" and worked toward a more utilitarian ideal. Ever one to humanize, to furnish his parts toward the soul, Whitman saw his work as an organic, living body. Paradoxically this body was highly constructed; it was theorized into existence; it borrowed from many sources and was "recast, outcast, taken apart, put together." From skeletal lists and pieced-together scraps Whitman built his poetic body from many diverse parts, and his role in the conception of *Leaves* is less its midwife than its Dr. Frankenstein. Strange, variegated, and powerful, it lumbered onto the stage in 1855.

2

Packing and Unpacking the
First *Leaves of Grass*

Between 1853 and 1855, as Whitman was creating his poetic selfhood in writing, piecing together an identity from notes and scraps of written and found language, Whitman moved no less than four times, taking with him not only his family, but also his notebooks, manuscript fragments, and the various texts that he drew upon in the making of the first *Leaves of Grass*. He began 1853 in a three-story house on Cumberland Street in Brooklyn, where he and his family had lived for eight months, having moved there in September 1852 from their residence at 106 Myrtle Avenue, where Whitman's family had lived in the upper floors while he operated a small printing office and bookstore on the ground floor. The men in Whitman's family were experienced carpenters and had built these two houses. They were set to benefit from the housing boom that had begun recently in south Brooklyn as a result of the successful draining of some formerly uninhabitable marshland. But with Whitman's father, Walt Whitman Sr., quite ill and

Walt Jr. distracted by other interests, including his artistic ambitions, the Whitman family profited only a little from the growing Brooklyn economy, despite their carpentry skills and the real estate speculation that led to their many moves. They sold the house on Cumberland and relocated to a smaller one on the same street, where they lived until May 1854, when they moved to a home on Skillman Street.[1] They lived on Skillman for a year until Whitman's mother, with the help of her sons, purchased a new home on Ryerson (Whitman Sr. was by then paralyzed and bedridden), which was where Walt lived when the first *Leaves of Grass* was published. This last home — a plain, blocky house three windows wide — is the only one that has survived. Its address is 99 Ryerson Street, an unremarkable building still standing in the Brooklyn neighborhood now known as Clinton Hill.[2]

Having grown up with a father who was a kind of traveling carpenter, Whitman had moved many times as a boy, so he was probably used to a life on the go. Still the intensely nomadic lifestyle he lived while composing his first major poems must have left its mark. Today, of course, we can move thousands of files and entire libraries in a laptop computer. Whitman seems to have used wooden trunks.[3] Using these, and probably some twine and crates, he would have gathered, bundled, packed, and unpacked every bound and unbound page he had accumulated as a writer almost continually while composing his poems. In one sense Whitman's notebooks were the primary textual structures that he used to order and revise the language that was evolving toward the first *Leaves*. In a larger sense, though, it was the four houses he inhabited during this two-year span — and the packed bundles he moved with — that must have been the overriding containers for his early poetic thought. Although we don't know much about what Whitman's rooms looked like at this time, it seems likely that all the packing and unpacking he did would have resulted

FIG 10. Whitman among his manuscripts. Whitman Archive, Library of Congress, Washington DC (121).

in something like the chaotic jumble of notes and drafts that we know he lived amid later. The pictures we have of him in his room in Camden, New Jersey, show the poet ankle-deep in paper, which he liked to think of as a sea, telling distressed friends that whatever he needed "surfaced eventually" (see figure 10).[4] In fact the papers he needed did seem to eventually turn up; he once became furious when his well-intentioned housekeeper tidied up his mess, telling her that "he had left everything exactly as he wished it to remain."[5] Whitman claimed that his room was "not so much a mess as it look[ed]" and that "the disorder [was] more suspected than real."[6] So finding order in what appeared to be chaos was a skill Whitman seems to have possessed, and it was one he put to use not only with his rooms, but with his notebooks and manuscripts as well. Sometime during the period of all those moves between 1853 and 1855 Whitman came to trust his ability to find what he needed in a jumble of disparate material, and if to the friends who visited him on Mickle Street—and to his readers then and today—the poet's attitude toward discrimination and order has at times seemed a bit cavalier, the end result has usually been effective enough to convince us of his methods.

In this chapter I myself hope to find some order in Whitman's notebooks and manuscripts, only I am lucky enough to enjoy the convenience of one of those laptops I just mentioned, and thanks to the online Walt Whitman Archive, his manuscripts are here as I type this now, stored as digital images, so that I only occasionally have to sift through the rooms in libraries where the poet's various papers are now housed. These manuscripts are no longer on the move, but their mobility and fluid sense of order were once quite important to Whitman. In fact, as this chapter explores in detail, the manuscript evidence suggests that the process of packing and unpacking text was crucial to his writing process, and the idea of mobile units of language powerfully informs most of the first edition, especially the long first poem of the book. This poem, of course, is usually referred to as "Song of Myself," or in more recent scholarship that seeks to respect the autonomy of each edition as a textual artifact, "the first poem of *Leaves of Grass*" or "the poem that would become 'Song of Myself.'"[7] Although up until now I have been employing similar conventions, as I delve further into the specific context of the first edition and the notebooks and manuscript fragments that precipitated it, I attempt to more faithfully approach the historical situation of these texts by discussing the works of the 1855 *Leaves* in the same manner Whitman seems to have done when he needed to distinguish between them. Manuscript evidence suggests that he did so by phrases derived from their first lines, a way of naming poems that he often employed throughout the remainder of his life.[8] In that spirit I refer to the two main poems I discuss here as "I celebrate myself" (for the poem eventually titled "Song of Myself") and "I wander all night" (for the poem eventually called "The Sleepers"). Aside from the fact that Whitman himself referred to the poems of the first edition in this way, using these titles offers some practical advantages: they are brief, recognizable placeholders; derived from first lines, the titles reflect the conventional method by which poets and readers refer to untitled poems; and most important, these titles don't distract from the immediate historical context by summoning a subsequent nomenclature. Like a recent reprint of the first edition in which the works' final titles are inserted in brackets on what is supposed to be a facsimile page,[9] discussing the first poem of the 1855 *Leaves* as "the poem that would become 'Song of Myself'" acknowledges the first edition's autonomy as a unique work. But it also interrupts efforts to consider the work in context and continues to confer authority on a version of the poem that did not exist when the one at hand was conceived.[10]

The manuscript leaf on which Whitman refers to the first poem of *Leaves of Grass* as "I celebrate myself" is one of the most important of all that survived. Aside from its interest in revealing what Whitman called his poems at the time, the verso of the leaf reveals a number of other fascinating clues about the making of *Leaves*. Here we find an alternative order he was considering at the time for the poems, a note about an illustration that he once planned to include that helps to single out an image he seems to have considered especially important, his inaccurate estimate of the first edition's page count, and calculations in which he compares the number of letters on one of his "closely written MS pages" to "letters in [a] page of Shakespeare's poems." This side of the leaf, which Ed Folsom first described in detail, was neglected for years by scholars who were more interested in the equally fascinating recto that I will be examining shortly.[11] However, it is the verso that shows that Whitman originally used shorthand titles derived from first lines for all of the poems of the 1855 *Leaves* except the one he had already published (which he continued to call "Resurgemus"). We find him describing the figure of "A large ship under her full power of steady forward motion," which, though it failed to appear as an illustration, would seem to justify the importance scholars have attributed to his famous line "And that a kelson of the creation is love" (*LG* 33).[12] Because "I celebrate myself" is here divided into five numbered parts, another focus that Whitman scholars have pursued is also verified: the fact that at one time he conceived of "Song of Myself" in terms of distinctive sections. We also learn that although "I celebrate myself" seems to have always been thought of as the "front-page lead" in *Leaves*, all of the other poems were once in a radically different order. Just as he arranged the articles in the newspapers he edited, he arranged and rearranged his poems, mindful of thematic, spatial, and economic prerogatives. He even seems to have considered coupling two pairs of his poems in what we might regard as his earliest conception of poetic "clusters."[13] He bracketed "A young man came to me" together with "A child went forth," and he both bracketed and united with an ampersand "Who learns my lesson complete" and "Clear the way there Jonathan." As with the other shorter works, these poems were later divided and rearranged, perhaps more than once.

Because of the calculations on this manuscript verso with which Whitman attempts to estimate his book's published page count, we know that the notes were made quite close to the time when he and Andrew Rome, a small-job Brooklyn printer, set the type for the first edition. This is further confirmed by a note to Rome at the top left corner of the page stating that Whitman had "left with Andrew 5 pages of MS." Yet even at the late stage when they were apparently made, Whitman's notes here reveal that he was making major changes in the structure and presentation of his entire book. Because the preface is not mentioned it is clear that it was indeed, as Whitman later claimed, "written hastily while the first edition was being printed"—that the bold, radical framing that the preface evoked really was a last-minute addition (*Corr* 2:100). While printing—and even afterward—Whitman continued to amend the first *Leaves*. He stopped the printing process to correct a typo and to revise at least one of his lines.[14] He physically reframed his book with different (and cheaper) bindings in the first edition's subsequent issues, and as Ted Genoways's recent work has revealed, he even had the lithographic plate of his famous 1855 daguerreotype altered to enlarge the phallic bulge in his trousers.[15] At the eleventh hour and later of the conception of the first *Leaves of Grass* Whitman was still packing, unpacking, framing, and reframing his writing. A consistent textual experimentalist, he applied this process not only to his poems, but also to the drawings, photographs, divisional markers, and prefatory text that accompanied them. Having at last arrived at a manuscript that he felt ready to publish, he continued to make changes to nearly every aspect of the book itself. Yet suggestive and fascinating as it is, this kind of last-minute repackaging of the poems seems mild in comparison to what the recto of this same manuscript leaf suggests about Whitman's writing process leading up to that point.

Just as Whitman once described how his poems had been in a variety of forms, "larger, smaller, recast, outcast, taken apart, put together," this leaf shows the process in action and suggests that the comment was not one of his infamous exaggerations.[16] The passage is important enough to quote in full:

25

tr

*And to me each minute of the night and day is ~~chock with~~
~~something as~~ vital and visible ~~vital live as flesh is~~
ins in here page 34 — And I say the stars are not echoes
And I perceive that the ~~salt marsh~~ sedgy weed has ~~delicious~~ refreshing
odors;
And potatoes and milk afford a ~~fit breakfast~~ dinner of state,
And I ~~dare not say~~ guess the ~~the bay mare is less than I~~ chipping bird
~~mocking bird~~ sings as well as I, ~~because~~ although she ~~reads no~~
~~newspaper;~~ never learned the gamut;
And to shake my friendly right hand governors and millionaires
shall stand all day, waiting their turns.

And ~~on~~ to me each acre of the ~~earth~~ land and sea, ~~I behold~~ exhibits to
me ~~perpetual~~ unending marvellous pictures;
They ~~fill~~ the worm-fence, and lie on the heaped stones, and are
hooked to the elder and poke-weed;
~~And to me each~~ every minute of the night and day is filled with a
~~[illegible] joy.~~
And to me the cow crunching with depressed head ~~surpasses~~ is ~~an~~ a
~~every~~ statue perfect and plumb; ~~grouped.~~
[illegible line]

55

Taken as a whole, nothing like this passage ever appeared in *Leaves of Grass*, but if it still seems strangely familiar there is a good reason. The second line, which the manuscript image reveals to have been inserted later, was revised and used in "To think of time" (there as "The earth is not an echo"). The "sedgy weed" of line 3 with its "~~delicious~~ refreshing odors" is revised into "smells of sedgy grass" in "I celebrate myself."[17] Just a couple of lines down, the "chipping bird ~~mocking bird~~" that "sings as well as I [. . .] although she [. . .] never learned the gamut" appears in "I celebrate myself" as "the mockingbird in the swamp never studied the gamut, yet trills pretty well to me."[18] The "bay mare" that Whitman crossed out in that same line was brought back in the line just following the one with the mocking bird, and the first line of the second stanza on this leaf becomes the penultimate line of the unpublished early poem "Pictures." The line after that becomes the final line in one of the most renowned passages of "I celebrate myself": the stanza containing the famous "kelson of the creation" reference.[19] The last legible line of this manuscript also appears in "I celebrate myself" (but in the form Whitman here has crossed out).[20] As Folsom has explored in detail, the image this last line describes of a "cow crunching with depressed head" was one that particularly preoccupied Whitman, appearing in *Memoranda During the War*, *Specimen Days*, and finally, near the very end of his life, in a conversation recorded by Horace Traubel.[21]

We can see how nearly every line in this already heavily edited passage was extracted and used in a slightly revised form elsewhere in *Leaves*. Yet this same manuscript seems to have been part of an extensive and organized draft of "I celebrate myself." This is indicated by the number at the top of the leaf, which labels this passage as section, or perhaps page, 25 in this early version. So Whitman obviously worked through the passage considerably before it assumed its published form. In fact there is evidence that the lines from this manuscript were themselves extracted from earlier notebook sources and in entirely different poetic contexts. We find the "cow crunching" line, for example, developed in another coherent passage in the "Talbot Wilson" notebook, the dating for which I discussed in the previous chapter:

I am the poet of little
       things and of babes

~~I am~~

~~The~~ ¹ Of ᵗʰᵉ each [deletion, illegible] ᵍⁿᵃᵗˢ in the air,
       and ~~the~~ ᵉᵛᵉʳʸ of beetles rolling ˌʰⁱˢ balls ˌᵒᶠ ᵈᵘⁿᵍ,

~~I built a nest in the~~ ᴬᶠᵃʳ ⁱⁿ ᵗʰᵉ ˢᵏʸ ~~here~~
       was a ~~sky~~ nest,

And my soul ~~st~~[deletion, illegible]~~d there~~ ᶠˡᵉʷ ᵗʰⁱᵗʰᵉʳ
       to ᵃᵗ reconnoitre
       and squat, and looked
       ~~long upon the universe,~~ ᵒᵘᵗ

And saw ~~millions~~ ˌᵗʰᵉ ʲᵒᵘʳⁿᵉʸʷᵒʳᵏ of of
       suns and systems of
       suns,

~~And has known since that~~

And ~~now I know~~ that
       ~~each~~ a leaf of grass
       is not less than ₜₕₑᵧ

[page break]

And that the pismire
       is ˌᵉqᵘᵃˡˡʸ perfect and ~~the~~ ᵉᵛᵉʳʸ all
       grains of sand, and
       every egg of the wren,

~~And that~~

And the ~~[runty?]~~ ^{tree} toad is a chef'

 douvre for the highest,

And the running blackberry

 ~~mocks the ornaments of~~

 would adorn the ~~house~~ ^{parlors}

 of Heaven

And the cow crunching with

 depressed neck surpasses

 ~~all statues~~ ^{every statue}

And _^ ~~a thousand~~ pictures [deletion, illegible] of [deletion, illegible]

 and small crowd the [hay on?]

 ~~the~~ railfence, ~~with~~ its

 ~~loose~~ ^{heaped} stones and ~~some~~

 elder and pokeweed,

~~Is picture enough~~

At the time Whitman composed these lines in the "Talbot Wilson" notebook he was nowhere near ready to begin assembling them into a coherent whole. Yet a comparison with the published version of these lines reveals that this draft is actually much closer to the published version than the draft described earlier, which is a fragment left from a relatively complete (if radically different) version of "I celebrate myself." Here is the published version from the first edition:

 I believe a leaf of grass is no less than the journeywork of the stars,
 And the pismire is equally perfect, and a grain of sand, and the egg of
  the wren,
 And the tree-toad is a chef-d'ouvre for the highest,
 And the running blackberry would adorn the parlors of heaven,
 And the narrowest hinge in my hand puts to scorn all machinery,

And the cow crunching with depress'd head surpasses any statue,

And a mouse is miracle enough to stagger sextillions of infidels,

And I could come every afternoon of my life to look at the farmer girl
boiling her iron tea-kettle and baking shortcake.

With the exception of the line "the narrowest hinge in my hand" the published version is almost a line-for-line version of the draft from the "Talbot Wilson" notebook, suggesting a curious evolution in the passage's process of composition. Although we know now that the "Talbot Wilson" notebook is not the poet's earliest manuscript notebook, the evidence I presented in the previous chapter strongly suggests that it must have been composed considerably earlier than the one-page draft of what was once section 25 of a manuscript version of "I celebrate myself." "Talbot Wilson" reveals a poet in the excitement of discovery of his mature and inclusive first-person voice and still tinkering with prose versions of lines that would make their way into his poems. So we can trace an involved development in the relation between these manuscripts. Whitman, pillaging his old notebooks for lines, assembled a version of his long first poem that would seem utterly alien to us if we had it in its complete form; in a period that seems to be quite close to the publication of his first *Leaves* he then disassembled this version (or at least significant parts of it), sometimes reverting to much older presentations of his lines. He unpacked the draft on this leaf with great ferocity, breaking each line apart and using it elsewhere in what became his finished whole. If the manuscript of section 25 of this proto-version of "I celebrate myself" is a reasonably reliable snapshot of Whitman's early creative process, then his revisionary practice of packing and unpacking his lines was astonishing in its intensity and scope.

In fact the manuscript background of these lines can be traced

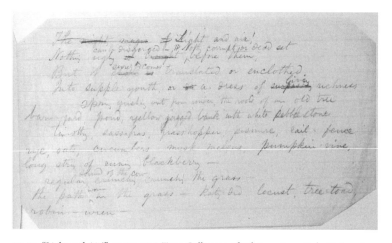

FIG 11. "Light and Air!" manuscript. Trent Collection of Whitmaniana, Duke University Rare Book, Manuscript, and Special Collections Library.

back to yet another, apparently earlier version. A misunderstood manuscript from the Trent Collection at Duke University reveals Whitman's further efforts to use some of this same material. This manuscript has been most commonly known by a transcription of it that was presented by the Whitman editors Harold W. Blodgett and Sculley Bradley as "Uncollected Poem" in their 1965 *Comprehensive Reader's Edition* of *Leaves of Grass*. Their contention that this manuscript represents an autonomous poem is, however, based solely on the idea that this fragment was "given its own title by the poet" (*LG* 652). The argument seems rather specious in light of an actual look at the manuscript, where the manuscript's "title," "Light and Air!" is in no way distinct from the lines that immediately follow (see figure 11). Blodgett and Bradley also associate the manuscript with the poem "This Compost," by which they presumably mean the 1856 version of the poem that was originally titled "Poem of Wonder at The Resurrection of the Wheat." They make this connection in part because of their mysterious inclusion of a line that thematically resembles the 1856 poem, yet the line, which is in turn based on Richard Maurice Bucke's 1899 transcription in *Notes and Fragments*, isn't even present in the actual manuscript — a fact that Blodgett and Bradley themselves admit! Here is an accurate transcription:

~~The nightly magic of~~ Light and air!
Nothing ugly ~~is~~ ˄can be disgorged — ~~brought~~ ˄¶Nothing corrupt or dead set
before them,
But it ~~shall~~ [deletion, illegible] ˢᵘʳᵉˡʸ ᵇᵉᶜᵒᵐᵉˢ translated or enclothed
Into supple youth or ~~dr~~ a dress of ~~surpassing~~ ˡⁱᵛⁱⁿᵍ richness
spring gushing out from under the roots of an old tree
barn-yard, pond, yellow-jagged bank with white pebblestones
        timothy, sassafras, grasshopper, pismire, rail-fence
rye, oats, cucumbers, musk-melons, pumpkin-vine,
long string of running blackberry —
        regular ˄ˢᵒᵘⁿᵈ ᵒᶠ ᵗʰᵉ ᶜᵒʷ crunching, crunching the grass —
the path ˄ʷᵒʳⁿ in the grass — katy-did, locust, tree-toad,
robin — wren

Although Whitman's reference to the "corrupt and dead" might seem to anticipate "Poem of Wonder at The Resurrection of the Wheat," his gesture here is much more impersonal, and the theme of nature's perpetual rejuvenation of life is central to "I celebrate myself" as well. Here again we find our "cow crunching," and also the "running blackberry," "tree-toad," "pismire," and "wren" that appear in both the "Talbot Wilson" passage and the 1855 *Leaves*. Rather than being an independent poem with a thematic relation to "This Compost," this manuscript is a pre-1855 draft of "I celebrate myself," which represents yet another step in the development of the lines I have been tracing through these leaves.

FIG 12. "Light and Air!" manuscript (*detail*). Trent Collection of Whitmaniana, Duke University Rare Book, Manuscript, and Special Collections Library.

We cannot be completely certain when this manuscript was composed in relation to the passage from the "Talbot Wilson" notebook, but there is a clue here that suggests it antedates the notebook passage. By the time Whitman composed the lines in that early notebook he had picked up the phrasing for the "cow crunching" image that preoccupied him throughout his life. Here, however, the phrase begins not as an image at all, but as a disembodied sound, a mere "crunching, crunching" in the grass. As the manuscript makes clear, only later did Whitman insert the cow into the picture, suggesting that the "cow crunching" phrase had not yet formulated itself in his mind when he initially wrote these lines (see figure 12). From then on, every time he used this phrase it was always in the revised form that he seems to have discovered on this manuscript: a "cow crunching." Does this leaf, then, disclose the origin of the phrase, showing us a further step back from the "Talbot Wilson" notebook in the genesis of his line? If so, then we have a revisionary process with at least five steps. He starts with only a sound and locates the sound by giving it a body; then Whitman, probably pleased by the onomatopoetic consonance of "cow crunching," remembers the phrase and renders it more vividly imagistic with the specificity of the cow's "depressed neck." Considerably later, probably just before printing his first edition, he extracts the line whole from his notebook, revising it slightly, and positioning it in a sequence where it makes just as much sense as it did previously. Later still he discards that draft, scattering its lines into sequences new and old, and the cow winds up back in a series of lines similar to where it started in his notebook, though it is now accompanied by other images the poet picked up in its intermediary form. There may have been yet more renditions of Whitman's crunching cow that have now been lost, and who knows how many other key images were shuffled with equal fervor.

For Whitman lines and signature phrases like this one had a striking, even radical portability. He saw the language of his drafts not as a series of interlocking units in an implacable architecture, but as blocks of text to be toyed with, cut and pasted (sometimes literally so) into ever new shapes and forms. We see evidence of this approach to composition everywhere in his manuscripts. Images and phrases are lifted from the manuscript in which they were first drafted—where they were just as likely to have been prose as poetry—and in this process the line is stripped of its original meaning or, as recent theory has described it, deterritorialized from its initial context. This unpacking of a line from its first form had a liberating effect for Whitman, who was deft in seeing new possibilities of meaning. But the stripping away of previous associations was seldom final and complete; Whitman often built upon aspects of his writing's initial significance as it evolved into new and different gestures. Let's explore this process in another of Whitman's mobile fragments of text, one that shows how significantly the meaning he attributed to key images and lines could accrete and change from draft to draft. The image also reveals some subtle relations to Whitman's crunching cow and suggests a surprising unity between two very different poetic sequences. For although this image doesn't involve bovine mastication of the signature trope of "I celebrate myself" (that is to say, grass), it does involve a "tooth." And the resonances of meaning revealed by the manuscripts leading up to the image's final placement show us how Whitman worked through some of his most revealing and sexually charged material in the poem he variously called "I wander all night" (up to 1855), "Night Poem" (1856), "Sleep-Chasings" (1860), and "The Sleepers" (1871 and after).

Because of this poem's eroticism and its dreamlike setting Whitman's critics have often focused on it as one of his most subconsciously suggestive and revealing pieces of writing. The assumption has usually been that because the poem describes what many critics have referred to as a "dream vision," the work is particularly evocative of Whitman's inner psychology. That is to say, because the poem describes a dreamworld, it is often analyzed as one would a dream, with the attendant assumptions about what its imagery reveals of Whitman's unconscious inner life. Whitman's psychologist friend, Richard Maurice Bucke, in his early critical biography, was the first to invite this kind of reading; Bucke described the poem as "a representation of the mind during sleep — of connected, half-connected, and disconnected thoughts and feelings as they occur in dreams, some commonplace, some weird, some voluptuous, and all given with the true and strange emotional accompaniments that belongs to them . . . vague emotions, without thought, that occasionally arise in sleep, are given as they actually occur, apart from any idea."[22] This description, which renders the poem a kind of proto-surrealist or stream-of-consciousness writing, has been echoed by many subsequent readers, such as Malcolm Cowley, who called the poem a "fantasia of the unconscious," and Robert K. Martin, who describes it as among those of Whitman's poems "written in a state of mind somewhere beneath full consciousness, which invoke the experience of the mind in that state."[23] Of the poem's major critics, Edwin Haviland Miller has perhaps taken this line of thinking the furthest,

reading the poem in the specifically Freudian context of an unre-
solved Oedipal conflict in which "the conclusion is sublimation."[24]
An examination of the extant manuscript drafts of the 1855 version
of the poem, which I refer to as "I wander all night," shows that the
poet's writing process was highly self-conscious. Far from being a
stream-of-consciousness poem, written, as Martin contended, in a
state of mind beneath full consciousness, whatever biographical or
psychological significance the poem may express seems to have been
consciously sanctioned by an artist working intensely with various
drafts from his notebooks and manuscript leaves. Although not much
manuscript material is left from "I wander all night," what remains
suggests it was drafted in scattershot fashion concurrently with "I
celebrate myself." Whitman seems to have collaged together both
poems from similar material, extracting text from its original sources
and arranging and rearranging it in ways that gave it new meaning
depending on how it was juxtaposed with other fragments.

In an early, twenty-four-page notebook Whitman drafted two different prose versions of material that eventually became lines 35–41
of the 1855 version of the poem. This small green notebook, which I
refer to as the "efflux of the soul" notebook based on a phrase from
its opening sentence, is impossible to date precisely, though the material later used in "I wander all night" shows that it was written prior
to 1855, and other clues suggest it was probably one of the earlier of
Whitman's notebooks that show him writing in his long, free-verse
lines.[25] Whatever the date, a sentence on the first leaf recto shows the
speaker pondering his love for a man he saw in a railcar and then
editing the passage to change his love object's gender: "Why as I just
~~catch a~~ look in the railroad car at some ~~workman's~~ half turned face, do I
love that ~~being~~ woman?"[26] Apart from what the passage might imply
about Whitman's own sexual or amorous feelings at the time, this

editing demonstrates that his writing, though personal in tone, was composed in anticipation of future public regard, something also implied by the overall intensity of his revisions in the notebook. Why, after all, would Whitman want to disguise the gender of his affection or struggle to improve the artistic quality of his writing if it was being written strictly for himself? Previous Whitman scholars have argued that he intentionally disguised the gender of those he loved to obscure his sexual yearnings from someone who might read his notebooks. The argument seems plausible in such cases as the infamous manuscript in which he refers to his lover, Peter Doyle, by way of a numerical code for his initials, but this is clearly not the case here. Whitman leaves the evidence of his amorous attractions easy to discern, and all of his editorial changes seem to be made for aesthetic, not personal reasons.[27] So this is not a passage from a diary or autobiographical daybook, which begs the question of what mode of writing was intended here.

The first two leaves and the recto of the third leaf read something like what we would today call a personal essay. Though more intensely self-probing — and certainly more sexual — the writing seems close to the manner of such essays as Emerson's "Experience." It shows Whitman pondering the source and nature of his love for the men he encounters on the streets:

> Some fisherman that ~~always stops to pass the time o day with~~ give good morning to and pass ten or twenty minutes as he draws his seine by the shore — some carpenter working his ripsaw through a plank some driver, as I ride on top of the stage, — men rough, ~~rough,~~ not handsome, not accomplished — why do I know that the subtle chlo [page break] roform of our spirits is affecting each other, and though we may ~~never meet~~ encounter not again, we ~~know~~ feel that ~~we two~~ have ~~pass~~ exchanged the right ~~mysterious~~ unspoken password

~~of the night,~~ and ~~have~~ ^{are} thence free ~~entrance~~ ^{comers} to ~~each~~ the guarded tents of each others' ~~love~~ most interior love?

We cannot be sure of course that this particular passage refers to physical love, though crossed-out passages such as "^{exchanged} the right ~~mysterious~~ ^{unspoken} password _∧^{of the night}" do seem fraught with sexual intimation, and Whitman's heavily worked-over writing shows him struggling for a way of expressing what seem to be vital intimate feelings.

Whitman continues with some similarly personal and sexually inflected questions, including one in which he asks why, when these workingmen leave him, do "the pennants of [his] joy sink flat ~~from the~~ and lank in the deadliest calm?" He later extracted the phrase "pennants of joy" in this sentence to revise and use in a different context in line 41 of "I wander all night"; here, as there, the phallic implications of the imagery seem clear. As if Whitman's inquiry had led him to a place too revealing for him to proceed further, he abruptly stops his questioning to begin a different kind of passage, one found frequently in other notebooks composed around the same time: a prose declaration of his view of what it means to be a poet. Though far less personal in address, this passage echoes some of the concerns of the first part of the notebook. It describes a poet who sees through his environment's surfaces to an underlying love that animates the people and things around him. Shifting into a third-person viewpoint, Whitman's tone shifts just as decisively as his form of address, moving from an intimate self-examination to an assertiveness that seems more confident and celebratory but at the same time more brusque, even affected, in contrast with what preceded it. He titles this section of his notebook "The Poet" and after a brief false start launches into this passage, sections of which he later revises and shifts back to the more personal first-person address to use in "I wander all night":

<u>The Poet</u>

I think ten million supple ‸-fingered gods are perpetually employed hiding beauty in the world — ~~hiding~~ burying it everywhere in every thing — ~~but~~ and most of all ~~where~~ in spots that men and women do not think of ~~it~~, and never look — as ~~in~~ death, and [~~illegible~~] poverty and wickedness. — cache [~~illegible~~] ‸after [and?] cache again — ~~they is~~ all over the earth and in the heavens ~~above~~ ‸that swathe the earth, and in the ~~depth~~ waters of the sea. — ~~Their~~ They do their ~~task~~ jobs well; those ~~supple-fingered gods.~~ journeymen divine. [page break] ~~But~~ Only to from the poet ~~do can~~ they ‸can hide nothing; ‸and would not if they could. — ~~Hide.~~ — Him they ~~attend~~ wait on night and day and ~~show where they take~~, uncover all, that he shall see the naked breast and the most private   of Delight.

A variation on some of Emerson's descriptions in his own essay of the same title, Whitman's view of the role of the poet is familiar. The poet is the visionary who sees through the world's drab exteriors to the hidden wellsprings of sensual delight that are always present. His description of this process — the trope he uses to figure it forth — is much more sexual than Emerson's and hints at the more physical imagery that would come to characterize his mature writing. The poet's insight into hidden beauty is described as an erotic disrobing, and in a metaphoric striptease his "journeymen divine" (earlier, "supple-fingered gods") undress worldly delight for his gaze.

At the end of this passage, however, the manuscript becomes less clear and more tantalizing. At just the moment when the "naked breast" is revealed and we are to see the "most private" part of delight, Whitman leaves a gap in the text and frustrates his own unveiling.

What, precisely, is this omitted "Delight" that has been stripped down? The only critic to have described this passage, James Perrin Warren, presents his transcriptions of the notebook in a selectively edited form that doesn't acknowledge Whitman's cross-outs and other manuscript clues about the gender of his objects of affection. He thus unambiguously asserts that what Whitman's "gods" uncover is the "figure of the naked female."[28] Another manuscript leaf separate from this notebook reveals that the poet's writing process is more complicated than Warren's reading would suggest and leaves little room for doubt that Whitman's blank space in the phrase "most private   of Delight" was not, in his mind, occupied by female anatomy (see figure 13). Perhaps because the leaf is a part of the Trent Collection at Duke University, whereas the "efflux of the soul" notebook is part of the Harned Collection in Washington DC, previous scholars haven't associated it with the passage I've been exploring here. One side of the Trent manuscript shows Whitman drafting lines later adapted for "I celebrate myself," and the other is divided into columns on the top half. In the left-hand column Whitman lists a series of suggestive phrases: "Sweet flag / Sweet fern / illuminated face / clarified / unpolluted / flour-corn / aromatic / Calamus / sweet-green / bulb / and melons with / bulbs ~~swee~~ grateful / to the hand." The phrase "sweet flag" faintly echoes "pennants of joy" from the "efflux of the soul" notebook, though "sweet flag" is also a colloquial expression for the same hardy grass known as calamus, and this is likely Whitman's primary meaning for the phrase in this list. Although in hindsight we know that Whitman later used "Calamus" as a title for his cluster of poems about masculine love, here this might be a list of words associated with plant parts, and we have to squint to see any sexual implications so far. The phrase "illuminated face," however, sticks out from the others, and some writing below this list suggests the "bulbs" aren't those of plants: "bulbous ~~bulbous~~ / Living bulbs, melons with polished rinds the ~~[illegible]~~ that ~~soothing the hand to touch~~ smooth to the ~~[illegible]~~ reached hand / Bulbs of life-lilies, polished melons [illegible] flashed for the ~~gentlest~~ mildest hand that shall reach." These "bulbs" seem more like metaphors for testicles, and there is little doubt about what Whitman means by "life-lilies." The phallic connotation is clinched by some writing above and to the right of this passage:

The ~~sweet trickling~~ trickling sSap that ~~trickles~~ ~~drops~~ flows
    from the end of the ~~pole~~ little
manly maple
    tooth of delight
tooth — prong
— tine

_____

spen~~d~~t spend

This leaf is suggestive in its own right, demonstrating, among other things, that Whitman associated "calamus" with male sexuality long before he published his group of poems under that title in the 1860 edition of *Leaves*. But it also shows that here, where he is experimenting with imagery to represent the ejaculating penis, he is also completing the blank left in the passage "most private   of Delight." The associations between the phrases "pennants of joy" and "sweet flag" and more obviously between his manuscript blank "of delight" and his "tooth of delight" are strengthened in juxtaposition with these lines from the published poem:

The cloth laps a first sweet eating and drinking,
Laps life-swelling yolks . . . . laps ear of rose-corn, milky and just
    ripened:

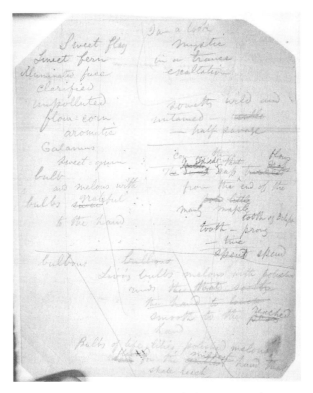

FIG 13. "Sweet flag" manuscript. Trent Collection of Whitmaniana, Duke University Rare Book, Manuscript, and Special Collections Library.

> The white teeth stay, and the boss-tooth advances in darkness,
> And liquor is spilled on lips and bosoms by touching glasses, and the
> best liquor afterward.

Robert K. Martin was Whitman's first reader to (at least publicly) acknowledge that this passage is a description of oral sex, and the manuscripts confirm this critically belated honesty. Lingering for a moment on the critical and biographical significance of these drafts, I would suggest that there are a number of connotations to Whitman's revisions of his erotic poetry. For one, it is a misguided effort to read these poems as if Whitman was subconsciously revealing his personal psychology. The drafts are too self-consciously worked over to endorse such a reading; also, as early as 1854, and perhaps earlier, Whitman was keenly aware of and struggling to express homosexual eroticism in his poems. In addition, it is clear that he was sensitive to how readers would receive this eroticism, and he succeeded in encoding his sexual metaphors with sufficient ambiguity to render them acceptable to readers with more conventional ideas of sexuality than his own. The fact that this frequently scrutinized passage persisted through more than a century of readings before its homosexual content was acknowledged testifies to the poet's command of polysemic imagery and diction. In his struggle to come to terms with how to best express his imagined gesture, his "boss-tooth," his "tooth of delight," evolved, under the poet's control and scrutiny, over multiple drafts; it is one of the more revealing of the fragments of text that he collaged together, with a skillful combination of candor and metaphoric ambiguity, to form the poetic self of his early poems.

We can better understand Whitman's sensitivity to how different readers would receive his writing by looking at the double meanings encoded in his language in this passage. One such intentional doubling is in his use of the word *lap*. The dictionary that Whitman owned and used while composing these poems, *The Original Webster's Unabridged Dictionary*, shows two competing meanings for the word.[29] On the one hand, for a cloth to lap is for it to swathe or enfold, so the line "the cloth laps a first sweet eating and drinking" could simply mean that clothing covers up the physical source of sexual pleasure. But with his repetitions of the word in the next line, the word *lap* begins to suggest its common meaning, to "lap up" or lick "life-swelling yolks . . . . ear of rose-corn, milky and just ripened." It's hard for contemporary readers to avoid hearing a description of what Martin describes as "the act known politely as fellatio."[30] Yet in the other sense of the word *lap* "yolks" could be construed as a metonym for the womb, so that the line could be taken to mean that cloth covers both the male and female genitals. Whitman's double meaning here permits readers who are compelled to maintain a heterosexual reading of the line to do so; for readers ready to hear the other, more biographically significant meaning the image is quite clear.

In Whitman's "tooth of delight" and the lines that follow the ones just described an even more nuanced double reading unfolds from his careful choice of words. In Whitman's edition of Webster's dictionary the primary definitions of *boss* read as follows:

1. A stud or knob; a protuberant ornament, of silver, ivory, or other material, used on bridles, harnesses, &c.
2. A protuberant part; a prominence; as, the *boss*, of a buckler.
3. A projecting ornament at the intersections of the ribs of ceilings and in other circumstances.
   Oxf. Glos.
4. A water conduit, in the form of a *tun-bellied* figure.
   Ash. Bailey.[31]

Though the word didn't signify the same broadly conceived social role that it does today, a similar nascent definition for the contemporary meaning of *boss* had recently arisen in the United States. It is listed as the secondary definition for the word in the dictionary Whitman consulted: "Among mechanics, the master-workman or superintendent. [This word originated among the Dutch settlers of New York, but is now used extensively in the other States.]"[32]

Boss, then, in the sense we think of it, was a new coinage that had only recently spread from where it originated in Whitman's native ground to the rest of the country. Coming from his very home and the Dutch settlers among whom his mother could count herself a member, this slangy definition of *boss* surely would have appealed to Whitman. He uses it in this colloquial context the first time it comes up in "I wander all night," when he says, "Only from me can they hide nothing and would not if they could; / I reckon I am their boss, and they make me a pet besides." The second time he uses the word, however, in its more explicitly phallic presentation, he surely had in mind the primary definition. He must have known that most Americans would have understood the word in terms of its older and more common usage as "a protuberant part; a prominence." I believe that when most readers today hear the line "The white teeth stay, and the boss-tooth advances in darkness" they interpret the "boss-tooth" as one among the other "white teeth" — that is to say, their leader — and the line probably has an absurd and even humorous effect, especially if read in a sexual context. From this point of view the line can be taken to present an orgiastic scene in which the boss penis advances from the other penises, and it is this reading that has allowed critics for over a century to interpret the passage — if they mentioned its blatant sexuality at all — from a heterosexual point of view. The "boss-tooth" advances from the gay gang of blackguards to have sex with the passive woman. The phrase connotes an eminently heterosexual and even adolescent perspective; crudely put, the "boss-tooth" is the "big dick" in this reading, in terms of both size and masculine dominance. Yet the colloquial ring of "boss" and the odd metaphor of the phallus as "tooth" temper the image's potentially aggressive implications and present the scene in an ambiguously comic light.

74

Whitman, who had the representation of his own lapped penis enlarged in successive versions of the frontispiece to the first edition of *Leaves*, was surely aware of this possible reading. The care with which he worked over the passages leading up to these lines in his manuscripts suggests an intense self-awareness of the connotations his sexual imagery could evoke. As what we would today call a gay man writing in an age when the underlying meaning would have been utterly unacceptable—and even, as over a century of chaste reactions to the poem suggest, unthinkable—if he were to attract the audience he craved it would be necessary for him to allow readers to see these lines only in a heterosexual light. However, when we consider "boss-tooth" in terms of the primary definition of the word *boss* as a "protuberance," the more biographically salient of the two readings is clear. The "boss-tooth" is not being presented as one *among* the other "white teeth"; it is being presented *in contrast* to those teeth. The "white teeth" are the teeth in one's mouth, and the "boss-tooth" (the "protuberance," the "tooth—prong—tine," the "tooth of delight") is the only penis in the image. In other words, the "white teeth stay" back as the "boss-tooth advances" into the "darkness" of the mouth. Although Martin seems not to have been aware of these manuscripts or of the definition of *boss* in the dictionary Whitman used, they confirm his groundbreaking reading of the poem.

In the "boss-tooth" image Whitman thus skillfully walks the line between extraordinary, culturally transgressive homosexual candor and an equally extraordinary but not quite so transgressive heterosexual allowance. Furthermore it's entirely possible that many readers in Whitman's time weren't even aware of any sexual connotations here and were simply baffled by these lines. Just as it wasn't until Martin's 1979 reading that anyone acknowledged these lines' homosexual content, it wasn't until the twentieth century that readers acknowledged any kind of sexual content in these passages at all. It's possible that Whitman may have come to see them as too suggestive, since he eventually edited out the "boss-tooth" stanza and two other suggestive stanzas that preceded it. He didn't do this, however, until 1881, suggesting that he remained publicly comfortable with these lines for the greater part of his life.

As with the "cow crunching" passage, the "boss-tooth" lines allow us to trace a suggestive pattern of development in Whitman's manuscripts. In a very old notebook Whitman begins by writing some contemplative self-reflections about his love for other men. He quickly realizes the gender-related implications of this writing for his immediate potential audience and changes his love object to a woman. He continues in this revealing, almost confessional mode; protected by his heterosexual persona, his descriptions grow increasingly erotic and troubled until he stops. He then draws a line to indicate a new draft, titles this section "The Poet," and rejoins his discourse on the hidden love and eroticism in everyday life, this time from the third-person point of view and in an explicitly declarative mode that contrasts with the inquisitive tone of the previous first-person passage. Although written in prose and in the third person, this is the confident, assertive mode of his major early poems. Whitman recycles some of the material from the previous passage in the notebook for this new third-person writing and develops some explicitly sexual descriptions, but now the gender of his love object is ambiguous. It's as if he has learned from his previous attempts at sexual disclosure that neither overtly homosexual nor deceptively heterosexual modes of address approach his audience with the versatility he craves. Instead he presents a sexually charged but indeterminately gendered subjectivity that allows different audiences — male and female, queer, straight, or otherwise — to project their own desires onto the imagery and come away with a satisfying reading. Drafting a metaphoric striptease of his beloved, however, he runs into a problem with how to reveal the body while maintaining his intentional ambivalence, so he leaves a blank space in the manuscript that he is unable to fill at the time. Considerably later, as his poems are coming together toward their completed form, Whitman decides to return to his old "efflux of the soul" notebook for some useful material. With an apparently renewed interest in the problematic striptease passage, he turns over the leaf of a relatively finished draft and attempts to find a new solution for how to depict the erotic body that he had previously left blank. He first tries various plant metaphors — including what may be his first sexually inflected use of the word *calamus* — but arrives at something different, a "tooth of delight." In its new position in the completed version of the poem, Whitman cleverly exploits various double entendres to position his "tooth" in a context that negotiates a furtively ambiguous — and at the same time quite vivid — erotic passage that preserves both his candor and his public poetic persona.

But Whitman was not yet done with the notebook. Still later, after the publication of the first edition, he turned to it once again for lines to use in his new poem, "Poem of The Road," which he first published in the second edition of *Leaves* in 1856 and to which he gave a new title, "Song of the Open Road," in 1867. In the lines he extracted for "I wander all night" the poet had abandoned the theme that had captured his interest months earlier, when he initially began writing in the notebook: the "efflux of the soul" behind the façade of everyday life, the hidden pulse of love that he saw in the workers on the street for whom he had such great affection and desire. In his original notebook writings he had disguised the gender of his love objects; by late 1855 or early 1856, when he began putting together

"Poem of The Road," he had developed confidence in a vocabulary to articulate his feelings for other men, and he returned to his reflections at the beginning of the notebook to find a way to finally express them in his work. In the "efflux of the soul" notebook he began by writing, "No doubt the efflux of the soul is ^comes^ through beautiful ₐgates of laws." In "Poem of The Road," at the turning point in the poem just before the stanzas beginning with the refrain "Allons!" that eventually conclude the poem, Whitman writes:

> Here is adhesiveness — it is not previously fashion'd, it is apropos;
> Do you know what it is as you pass to be loved by strangers?
> Do you know the talk of those turning eye-balls?
>
> Here is the efflux of the soul,
> The efflux of the soul comes through beautiful gates of laws, provoking
>   questions

Under the cover of "adhesiveness" Whitman is able to recuperate the phrase that captivated him when he first described the love that he found in the open air of Brooklyn, and he uses it again ten lines later when he declares, "The efflux of the soul is happiness." We have seen that he used the phrase "pennants of joy" for his "gay gang of blackguards" in line 41 in "I wander all night"; in "Poem of The Road" he uses the phrase again. In fact this time he creates an entire line by lifting that section of the notebook word for word to form "Why when they leave me do my pennants of joy sink flat and lank?" encoding his loss of sexual arousal into this poem as well. The "fisherman that [. . .] draws his seine by the shore" is recovered a few lines later, as are other lines, including the "melodious thoughts" that Whitman had previously described descending upon him from the trees. As much a "Song of the Open Road" notebook as it is a "Sleepers" notebook, "efflux of the soul" is mined for all it's worth even after the publication of his first *Leaves of Grass*, where he had already used the same material significantly for "I wander all night."

∾

With both the "efflux of the soul" notebook and the drafts of the "cow crunching" line in "I celebrate myself," the closer we examine the manuscripts, the more layers of revision are revealed and the more complex, mobile, and versatile Whitman's language appears. In "efflux of the soul" there is yet another revision of some of this material, where Whitman entirely rewrites his prose passage titled "The Poet." Later he extracts from this a passage that he used almost word for word as lines 35–41 of "I wander all night." Just as he did with his "tooth of delight" image, he seems to have frequently improvised notes and lists as fodder for his erotic writing. In what appears to be a lost manuscript described in *Notebooks and Unpublished Prose Manuscripts*, he drafted this list: "Loveaxles. / Lovepivot. / Sleepripples. / Love-ripples. / Lovejet. / Loveache. / Lovestring. / Glued with Love. / Tiller of Love."[33] Although none of these phrases made it into *Leaves of Grass* Whitman used similar conjugated phrases in "Song of Myself" and "I Sing the Body Electric" to describe male and female genitals.[34] In another manuscript he lists dozens of body parts, most of which were lifted intact and added onto "The bodies of men and women" from the first edition of *Leaves* to make up the 1856 and all subsequent versions of the poem eventually called "I Sing the Body Electric" (see figure 14). The manuscripts show that signifying the body, whether directly or through metaphor, was something Whitman took quite seriously, and his curious locutions for various parts of human anatomy were often drafted in lists on the versos of other manuscripts and later substituted into the poems in

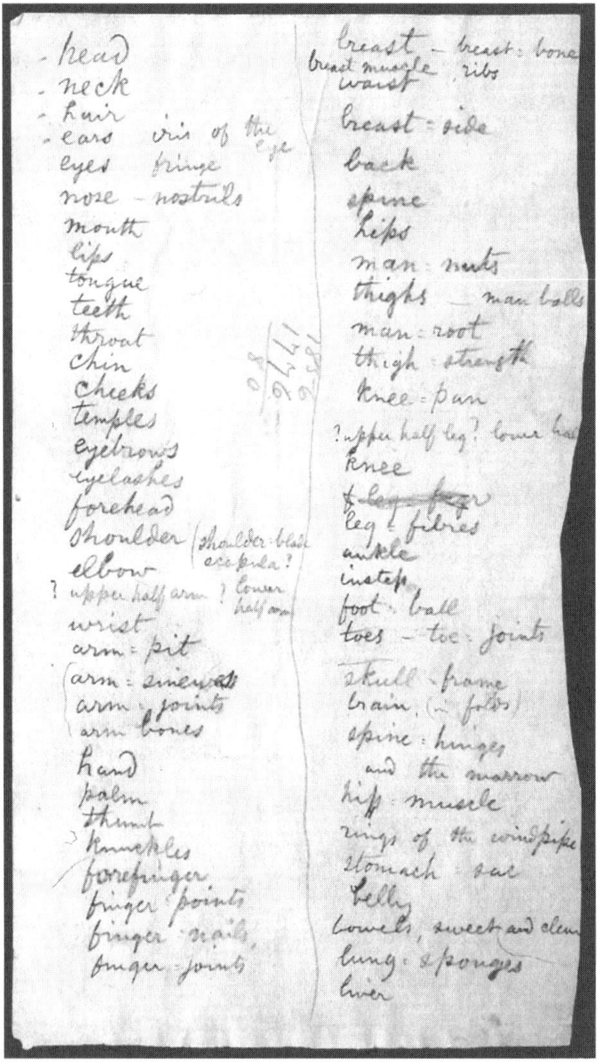
- head
- neck
- hair
- ears iris of the eye
eyes fringe
nose – nostrils
mouth
lips
tongue
teeth
throat
chin
cheeks
temples
eyebrows
eyelashes
forehead
shoulder (shoulder-blade scapula?
elbow
? upper half arm ? lower half arm
wrist
arm-pit
arm-sinews
arm-joints
arm-bones
hand
palm
thumb
knuckles
forefinger
finger-points
finger-nails
finger-joints

breast – breast-bone
breast muscle, ribs
waist
breast-side
back
spine
hips
man-roots
thighs – man balls
man-root
thigh-strength
knee-pan
? upper half leg ? lower half leg
knee
leg-fibres
ankle
instep
foot-ball
toes – toe-joints
skull-frame
brain (in folds)
spine-hinges
and the marrow
hip-muscle
rings of the windpipe
stomach-sac
belly
bowels, sweet and clean
lung-sponges
liver

FIG 14. Whitman's list of body parts for "I Sing the Body Electric." Trent Collection of Whitmaniana, Duke University Rare Book, Manuscript, and Special Collections Library.

which they eventually found a home. Whitman used lists similarly to enhance the specificity of his references to many other fields of knowledge, such as geography, history, anthropology, and world religions. These words and phrases that he transplanted from lists to lines represent the smallest units of text he mobilized to include in his published writing.

From simple words to entire poems, Whitman's arrangement and rearrangement of language took place in various scales of size and intensity as he worked toward publication. As we have seen in the "cow crunching" and "boss-tooth" passages, Whitman liberated fragments from both prose and poetry in his old notebooks, combining and disassembling them into various interim arrangements that often have just as much coherence as the published versions. Although we have only a few manuscripts that contain language later used directly in lines for "I wander all night," it is worth noting that the original sources for all of them were his prose.[35] Not a line of manuscript writing has survived to indicate that any part of the poem was originally written in verse; as far I can discern from the extant evidence, the poem he eventually called "The Sleepers" is essentially a pastiche of various prose works broken into lines and arranged to convey the poem's visionary sweep. We have considerably more manuscript evidence to assess the origins of "I celebrate myself," and these sources vary tremendously. Parts of the poem, such as the "cow crunching" passage, seem to have originated as lines, other parts as prose of various types, and still other parts from lists like those I have just described. Further complicating the poem's composition, the manuscript evidence suggests that considerable portions of the poem were derived and sometimes simply lifted from outside sources. In some cases Whitman's use of others' writing is so direct that he has been subject to charges of plagiarism; indeed one scholar, Esther Shephard, has argued that Whitman derived his entire persona as a poet from a character in George Sand's *The Countess of Rudolstadt* and that *Leaves of Grass* is therefore an elaborate fraud that only imitates instead of describes a mystical awakening. Shephard's judgment on Whitman's derivations is severe, and her claims regarding Sand's influence seems rather far-fetched in light of the tremendous variety of sources Whitman used to piece together his poems and his poetic identity.[36]

Gay Wilson Allen, Floyd Stovall, and others have documented Whitman's use of outside writing for his lines, and their findings show just how dynamic and far-ranging the poet's use of these materials was. In the previous chapter I described an appropriation that had not yet been noted, Whitman's use of an ornithological guidebook by J. P. Giraud Jr. called *The Birds of Long Island* (1844) to form lines 237–43 of "I wander all night." One of the least surprising of numerous examples that might be cited is Whitman's use of Emerson — or rather, what is surprising is that Whitman didn't make *more* use of Emerson, given Whitman's attitude toward authorship and linguistic propriety. I am referring to the poet's collage method of composition in his early poems, as opposed to the influence Emerson had on Whitman's ideas, which is pervasive and well-known. In terms of actual language, however, Whitman seems to have borrowed minimally from Emerson, and what he used was filtered through considerable paraphrase. The first and still one of the most thorough accounts of the similarities of phrasing between Emerson and Whitman is by William Sloane Kennedy, whose 1897 essay in the *Conservator* (a journal that was mostly devoted to the poet) enumerated some thirty-four parallels between *Leaves of Grass* and Emerson's essays.[37] The similarity between their ideas in these passages is striking and there are some echoes of phrasing, yet the language is never identical beyond more than a few words. In *The Foreground of Leaves of Grass* Stovall lists nearly as many parallels, though again, the similarities are indirect.[38] Perhaps Whitman realized the content of his writing was close enough to Emerson's that using his language would appear merely derivative, and so he was careful to cover his tracks. Or maybe he had so thoroughly absorbed Emerson that the ideas poured out of him naturally in his own language. The difference is important, though we can only guess at the nature of Whitman's actual practices. Perhaps the most authoritative reference we have in this regard is Emerson himself, who, though he expressed other reservations about Whitman's poetry, never seemed bothered by any such literary echoes.

Whitman made use of other writers, including the one Shephard outlines with such insistence, though again the similarities in actual language are minimal. Whitman does seem to have taken the title for one of his short poems in "Children of Adam," "O Hymen! O Hymenee!" from an "epithalmic song" in Sand's *The Countess of Rudolstadt*, and an important passage from the "Talbot Wilson" notebook that Whitman titled "Dilation" and from which he later extracted lines for "I wander all night" seems to have begun as a paraphrase from the epilogue of that same book.[39] Allen has shown that Whitman paraphrased some ideas from Jules Michelet's *The People* and used some direct material from *The Bird* for lines included in "To the Man-of-War Bird."[40] Whitman also collaged language from an anthology of German philosophers called *Prose Writers of Germany*, which was edited by Frederic H. Hedge, who in addition wrote the introduction and biographical notes for the book. As Sister Mary Eleanor Hedge first pointed out, Whitman drew on Hedge's comments on Hegel, Fichte, Schelling, Kant, and Herder for a number of passages in *Leaves of Grass*, and Stovall shows that he also used some material from the anthologized writing itself, including Hegel's "History as the Manifestation of Spirit," Fichte's "The Destination of Man," and Herder's "Love and Self."[41]

More vital to Whitman's collage-like writing process than any literary or philosophical writings were the various scientific, pseudo-scientific, and nonfiction sources from which he freely extracted material for his lines. The most famous example of this is his use of terms from the nineteenth-century pseudo-science phrenology, especially *amativeness* and *adhesiveness*, words he used for heterosexual and homosexual love, respectively. (More subtly he also developed a special understanding of the word *prudence* from phrenology, which he put to use in such poems as "Song of Prudence.") Other examples abound, including lines that Whitman derived from the giant scrapbook of nonfiction material that he assembled by taking apart various geographies and atlases and recombining them with blank pages so that he could paste relevant clippings near the maps to which they were related. These clippings, which were taken from newspapers and magazines that are difficult to identify due to Whitman's excerpting, address geography, anthropology, history, and travel. Whitman drew on these for the proper names of countless geographical features and other details mentioned in *Leaves of Grass*. They laid the groundwork from which he launched the visionary flights through time and space described in "I celebrate myself" and later in "Poem of Salutation" (1856), which he subsequently called "Salut Au Monde!" and later still in "Proto-Leaf" (1860), which eventually became "Starting from Paumanok." Whitman unpacked language from the scrapbook more substantially as well, mobilizing fragments of text larger than simple names. On some pages left from the original atlas in which he pasted his clippings, for example, he found a short history of Texas, including the story of the massacre of Colonel Fannin and his troops at Goliad.[42] Intrigued by the story, he decided to tell it in his poems, extracting the overall narrative as well as several phrases to form the passage in "I celebrate myself" that later became section 34 of "Song of Myself."

Many more documented examples could be cited, and more will surely be discovered as future scholars pore over Whitman's various sourcebooks and clippings. One of the more interesting of the developing discoveries is the work of Ted Genoways, who has found that Whitman also collaged from newspaper reports of Civil War battle scenes, using found language to help string together his lines in *Drum-Taps*.[43] Many more of Whitman's sources will probably never be known due to the ephemeral nature of some of the publications he perused and the difficulty of locating brief fragments in some of the dense tomes to which he had access. Also lost is the language he derived from conversation with local experts. The list of words related to human anatomy that I previously described, for example, may have been derived at least partially from such a conversation, as is suggested by a manuscript at Duke University in which Whitman reminds himself to "read the latest and best anatomical works" but also to "talk with physicians" so that he can write "a poem in which is minutely described the whole particulars and ensemble of a <u>first-rate healthy Human Body</u>."[44] There is nothing on the manuscript to help us date it, but this certainly sounds like the poem that begins "The bodies of men and women" (later called "I Sing the Body Electric"). From now forgotten conversations, from newspapers, magazines, and journals, from histories, atlases, and science books, from various continental poets, novelists, and philosophers, from all these and more Whitman unpacked text and mobilized it in his manuscripts to mold the linguistic contours of his *Leaves*.

For Shephard and others, Whitman's copious use of found language has sometimes seemed an artistic failing and even, as Shephard sees it, a façade that betrays a poverty of originality and imagination. At the root of this objection is what she regards as an essentially deceptive enterprise:

> There would be nothing wrong with his [use of Sand], but the fact that he spent the rest of his life artfully concealing the source of his inspiration argues him not a great man with confidence in his ability as a poet and belief in his message but a small man, willing to prostitute his honest feelings for the sake of personal fame. From the time of his Great Illumination Whitman became a poseur, always pretending to be what he was not, posing as a great religious prophet, "Hebraic and mystic," uttering Truth but actually being, in his character as seer, merely an artificer carefully concealing his secret sources.[45]

There is no doubt that Whitman was skilled at maintaining a public persona in both his life and his art, and his deceptions regarding how he presented himself to his peers have been thoroughly documented. But as we have seen, the extent and range of the sources go far beyond Sand, who emerges as a rather minor figure in the overall tapestry of his intellectual preparation. Moreover he used these sources the same way he approached *all* writing that he both found and wrote: he extracted phrases and lines that attracted him, and in the process of moving them from their initial sources into new contexts, he filtered and changed their tone and meaning. His appropriation of found text is not a weakness or a disguise; it is something essential to his writing process and reflective of his lifelong involvement with language: as a newspaper writer, a typesetter, an editor, a layman scholar and linguist, and a nomadic young poet who wrote while on the move. Whitman was not an "artificer carefully concealing his sources." He outlined his attitude toward language and his creative method a number of times both verbally and in writing, and he consciously theorized his ideas about creativity, originality, and the groundbreaking new poetic form that he brought to literature.

The question of originality in art was a problem Whitman deeply considered, and the attitudes that he expressed toward it were complex and illuminating. On the one hand, he vehemently decried poetic derivation, dismissing American poetry that preceded him as being too dependent on European models. He was clearly aware of his own artistic originality and boasted about it in his early self-reviews. He held the idea of poetic genius up to the highest standards, and originality, in a certain sense, was clearly a component of such greatness. What is less discussed is how Whitman also, in a different sense, denied the existence of originality and even discredited it as a concept that should apply to the greatest poets. In a manuscript first printed in Bucke's *Notes and Fragments*, which I have not been able to locate and may be lost, Whitman describes his own project in the third person:

> Philosophy of *Leaves of Grass*
> Walt Whitman's philosophy — or perhaps metaphysics, to give it a more definite name — as evinced in his poems, and running through them and sometimes quite palpable in his verses, but far oftener latent, and like the unseen roots or sap of trees — is not the least of his peculiarities — one must not say originality, for Whitman himself disclaims originality — at least in the superficial sense. His notion explicitly is that there is nothing actually new only an accumulation or fruitage or carrying out these new occasions and requirements. (*CPW* 9:12)

In this draft of a self-review or perhaps a note to a friend who was writing about *Leaves of Grass* Whitman explicitly rejects the idea of originality, at least in a philosophical or metaphysical sense. He seems to be thinking here of something like Ecclesiastes' claim that there is no new thing under the sun, an idea that is echoed and elaborated on by the German Idealists who had influenced him, especially Hegel. There are no new materials, only "new occasions and requirements" that "carry out" or bring to fruition that which already exists in more compelling and relevant ways. For Hegel this amounted to an ongoing historical pattern whereby a dominant paradigm engenders its opposite and progresses by way of an eventual synthesis with its antithetical complement. Whitman doesn't carry his analysis that far, but he does seem to be thinking in historical and ontological terms in his denial of originality — stating that "there is nothing actually new" — in favor of what seems to be a kind of recombinatory originality that is dependent on "occasions and requirements."

Still speaking of himself in the third person, he continues, "He evidently thinks that behind all the faculties of the human being, as the sight, the other senses and even the emotions and the intellect stands the real power, the mystical identity, the real I or Me or You" (CPW 9:12-13). This passage, which follows immediately upon the one quoted previously, may appear at first to be a digression. It might seem to anticipate the famous lines from "As I Ebb'd with the Ocean of Life" about the "real me" that stood "untouch'd, untold, altogether unreach'd" and mocked the poet with "distant ironical laughter." But this is a different "real me" from the one that mocked him in that poem; this one is more universal and, keeping with the earlier passage, "metaphysical." The "mystical identity" here seems more like the universal identity he elsewhere describes as underlying all humanity, and it stands in contrast to the "superficial sense" he described previously in which he "disclaims originality." The question of how exactly this "real power" that underlies personal emotions and intellect relates to "originality" goes unanswered in this passage, which seems cut off.

Another manuscript in which Whitman discusses his concept of originality helps to connect these ideas:

> The originality must be of the spirit and show itself in new combinations and new meanings and discovering greatness and harmony where there was before thought no greatness. The style of expression must be carefully purged of anything striking or dazzling or ornamental — and with great severity precluded from all that is eccentric.[46]

In this passage Whitman makes clear that real originality is for him an expression of the kind of underlying spirit he described previously, and further that it is, as with Hegel, something that will "show itself in new combinations." It stands in direct contrast to "all that is eccentric," because the eccentric is an expression of that "superficial" originality he disavows; that is to say, it is a narrow, limited, merely personal style, as opposed to a necessary central expression of "new occasions and requirements" that arise as a result of cultural and historical change.

The change that Whitman saw as necessitating his own writing was, of course, the rise of democracy and the establishment of the United States as its cultural and spiritual flag-bearer (or so he was able to see it then). Nothing preoccupied him more in the years leading up to the publication of his first *Leaves* than his passion to found a new national literature. Given his vision of America and its citizens, especially in his antebellum writing, it should not be surprising that he formulates his concept of originality as the process of "discovering greatness and harmony where there was before thought no greatness." The poet doesn't so much *make* something original as he *finds it*, and true originality in Whitman's view was a kind of spiritual vision or sensibility, as opposed to style. Too much pursuit of an original style leads to mere eccentricity, which dooms a writer to a marginal and ultimately ephemeral artistic existence. It is this kind of superficial, stylistic originality that he condemns in his manifesto of national poetics, the preface to the 1855 *Leaves*, declaring:

> The greatest poet has less a marked style and is more the channel of thoughts and things without increase or diminution, and is the free channel of himself. He swears to his art, I will not be meddlesome, I will not have in my writing any elegance or effect or originality to hang in the way between me and the rest like curtains. (LG 717)

By associating originality with the act of seeing (as opposed to making) and the function of the poet with being a "channel of thoughts and things" (as opposed to a stylistic innovator), Whitman lays a fertile conceptual groundwork for his own use of found text and collage method of composition. Because the originality of authorship is in his view artificial, there is little reason to avoid using text written by others, as long as it is recontextualized so that it can "show itself in new combinations." Whitman's grammar here renders his attitude toward the use of found text quite explicitly, for when he speaks of the poet becoming a "channel of thoughts and things without increase or diminution" he is speaking of the "thoughts and things" of others, which is why he augments his discussion with "and is the free channel of himself" immediately afterward. He is stating that the "greatest poet" must be a channel for a whole culture's "thoughts and things," including, but hardly limited to, those that originate from his own imagination. By mobilizing text from the various discourses of his day and age—narrative, journalistic, metaphysical, scientific—he becomes that cultural conduit.

In a statement made elsewhere Whitman is even more specific about the appropriation of cultural discourse in the making of major poetry. He took great interest in an essay titled "Thoughts on Reading" that was originally published in 1845 in the *Edinburgh Review*, and he highlighted parts he found important and jotted down various notes. His annotated copy of the essay is in the Trent Collection at Duke University; the most fascinating note is one that was written in response to a passage in which the author, whose primary purpose is to define and champion the reading of great works, bemoans the effect that reading second-rate literature has on the minds of typical audiences. Whitman seems generally in agreement with the author, but he pauses at one point to make this crucial exception: "Still all kinds of light reading, novels, newspapers, gossip, &c, serve as manure for the great productions, and are indispensable and ˄ or perhaps are premises to something better." In describing the material that went into the making of *Leaves of Grass* here as "premises," Whitman uses a logical term that loosely suggests his reading of the German Idealists, especially Hegel, a connection that is strengthened by the word's specific use in logic as "the two propositions from which the conclusion is derived in a syllogism,"[47] which, by suggesting a logical system in which two premises lead to a new conclusion, is reminiscent of Hegelian dialectical synthesis. His phrase "manure for the great productions" also recalls his love of composting, an interest that bore poetic fruition in his 1856 poem "Poem of Wonder at The Resurrection of the Wheat" (later called "This Compost"). Both the idea of "premises," which progress toward new and different logical conclusions, and "manure," which resurrects the wheat and the grass with its leaves (a word that always for Whitman carries the double meaning of foliage and paper in a book), suggest that Whitman sees his textual appropriations as something transformative. He may use "found text" for some of his lines, but his theorizing of the process emphasizes the final product, not the source material, at least in this particular statement.

Whitman continues in the same note, "The whole raft of light reading is ~~indeed~~ also a testimony in honor of ~~some~~ the original good reading which preceded it. — The thousands of common poets, romancers essayists and attempters ~~are so~~ exist because some twenty or fifty geniuses at intervals led the way before." This note, which he probably wrote considerably after the original publication of the journal,[48] defines Whitman's attitude toward the reading that informed the composition of his first *Leaves*. Concordant with his often expressed view that great poets are those who produce other writers, he takes a more charitable attitude toward "light reading" than the *Edinburgh Review* author, defining the "novels, newspapers, gossip, &c" that "serve as manure for the great productions" as part of an ongoing cycle of reading and writing. In Whitman's view this secondary writing is not only a "testimony" to the great writers who precipitated it; it is also a *continuation* of it: it could not exist without the "twenty or fifty geniuses" that are the true fountainheads of creativity. But because these geniuses in turn used the "light writing" as "manure" for their "great productions" — a practice that we know from manuscript evidence sometimes involved collage-like appropriations — the light reading is consequentially essential for the production of major works.[49] Like so much else in Whitman's thinking, the dynamic is cyclical and never-ending: the great writers compost the ephemeral secondary writing that preceded and surrounds them, transforming and recombining it into major art; this art in turn fosters all manner of secondary cultural discourse, which eventually serves as compost for another great writer whose genius transforms it. If we recall the quote in which the poet said "there is nothing actually new only an accumulation or fruitage or carrying out these new occasions and requirements," we can see that his idea of "genius" is a kind of "accumulation or fruitage" of this secondary writing, one that comes into being as a result of historical "occasions and requirements." Genius, for Whitman, was an expression of the culmination of cultural discourses as necessitated by time and place. Although active in the process of creation, the poet is also an agent for these larger forces. Using words like "genius" Whitman employs the vocabulary of his day, but his description of the process of the creation of major art is remarkable for how it anticipates recent ideas about creativity and language. Literary art is described as an expression of culture, not simply of an individual creator; rather than being a "spontaneous overflow of powerful emotions," writing is theorized as a crystallization and transformation of preceding text; literary writing is not a pure and rarefied use of language; rather, it partakes of popular culture and is endlessly open to appropriation and paraphrase, regardless of the literary merit of various source texts; and the production of major writers is itself meant to be stolen, appropriated, composted, and transformed in new, culturally defined occasions for future writing.

∾

We can see how Whitman's use of outside materials was deeply engaged with his overall thinking about the nature of creativity and discourse. In his overall approach to the use of his own previous writing in his notebooks we see the same kind of attitude. Whether they were originally written by himself or extracted from others, Whitman mobilized fragments of text, unpacking them from their original context and repacking them into a literary body where they are transformed by his own visionary (and revisionary) discernment. The result, in poems such as "I celebrate myself" and "I wander all night," is what R. W. French has called "a poem of fragments." French situates "Song of Myself" in terms of the major poems of high modernism, explaining that "*Song of Myself* is [not] difficult because it belongs to the nineteenth century; the problem is, rather, that the poem is difficult because it belongs more appropriately to the twentieth. Its analogues are not 'Dover Beach' and 'My Last Duchess' and *In Memoriam*, but *The Waste Land* and *Paterson* and the *Cantos*."[50] French is certainly correct in asserting that the poem's fragmentary structure anticipates many of the watershed moments of American modernist poetry. If he had described Whitman's collage-like writing practices, he could indeed have strengthened his argument by relating the poet's recycling of cultural and literary discourse to similar writing practices of Eliot, Pound, Williams, and Marianne Moore, as well as poets they influenced such as Charles Olson and George Oppen, and European poets who used collage and fragmentary structure such as F. T. Marinetti, Tristan Tzara, and Kurt Schwitters. The use of collage technique and fragmentary structure in literary writing is usually traced back to the visual art practices of Picasso and Braque, who directly influenced the European understanding of the possibilities of found material in the work of the Futurists and Surrealists. But as we have seen, we can trace the line of development further back to Whitman, who not only employed these practices but theorized them in his journals, notes, and marginalia. Although all of these poets were, to varying degrees, aware of Whitman, his influence, such as it may have been, was often indirect. Ironically, although Whitman directly anticipates modernist interest in collage and fragments, more often than not modernist poets who used collage-like techniques scorned or simply ignored Whitman, whose nationalist poetics and bardic stance seem to have obviated more direct engagement with his writing, especially in the sense of a writing *practice*.

Whitman of course could not describe his own work as *collage* because the word itself was not in use when he was alive. (The Oxford English Dictionary cites the occurrence of its first use as 1919.) The word comes from the French, where it literally means pasting or gluing — appropriately so, since Whitman often pasted together fragments of text in his notebooks and manuscript drafts to form his various sequences. Another recently developed term that we might consider when describing Whitman's technique is *montage*, a term used in discussions of film and television, where it indicates a series of contrasting images that unfold sequentially in time as a result of "editing and piecing together separate sections of film to form a continuous whole."[51] Recently, however, poets and critics have applied the term to literature, where its meaning has evolved. Although there is a good deal of debate about the specific differences between collage and montage techniques, most discussions seem to center on the degree to which the disparate materials are integrated into the artistic whole. The term *collage* is usually used to refer to works that are more fragmentary and where the different source materials stand in more stark opposition to each other. *Montage* in literary terms typically denotes a work in which the fragments have been worked over by the artist to form a more seamless and continuous whole. The poet and critic Pierre Joris writes:

> Much ink has also been shed trying to define exactly what the differences between the various words collage, montage, assemblage, are. . . . Gregory Ulmer suggests that "collage is the transfer of materials from one context to another, and 'montage' is the dissemination of these borrowings through the new setting," while Charles Bernstein sees montage as "the use of contrasting images toward the goal of one unifying theme" and collage as "the use of different textual elements without recourse to an overall unifying idea."[52]

Neither of these terms precisely describes Whitman's method in composing these poems, but both have some applicability. As with collage, Whitman "transfers materials from one context to another," and the results often display the jagged, fragmentary quality associated with the term. But like a montage his technique is also filmic in the way that one image follows another in the act of reading. This filmic aspect of Whitman's poetry has been noted by previous readers, such as Ben Singer, who compares his poems with the work of Dziga Vertov, whose breakthrough film *The Man with the Movie Camera* is seen as mirroring Whitman's cinematic imagery, as well as Lesli Anne Larson, who has argued that the imagery in "The Sleepers" was influenced by the distorted projections of camera obscuras.[53] Furthermore, if we take Bernstein's definition, these poems are also montage-like in the sense that they are unified by theme (though what the dominant theme might be is a subject for much debate, and in a poem as inclusive as "Song of Myself" it may not make sense to isolate a single overarching idea). Complicating the situation further, the majority of Whitman's work was pieced together from material he himself had originally written, for though we have many examples of material derived from outside writing and they make up a significant portion of his early poems, we have far more examples of fragments he extracted from his old notebooks that were originally composed in short bursts of his own creative energies. So although Whitman's creative practices resulted in a cultural collage of discourse, in his major early poems this pastiche is absorbed into a broader collage of himself.

Without recourse to terms like collage and montage, Whitman described what he had created using metaphors, which often compare the form and structure of his poetry to nature. Critical discourse has followed his lead, resulting in a substantial body of writing that discusses *Leaves of Grass* as a poem of "organic form." Indeed there has been so much scholarly work that partakes in what I am describing that one prominent Whitman scholar, M. Jimmie Killingsworth, has written a book on "the organic tradition in Whitman studies."[54] Killingsworth's subject matter goes far beyond the specific aspect of organicism that I want to explore now — which is a way of coming to terms with the structure that resulted from the poet's radical new writing process — to discuss the biographic and bibliographic background of *Leaves'* overall development. Nevertheless a trope that crops up repeatedly in the "organic tradition" of Whitman studies, the metaphor of a tree, is one I believe we must explore further in order to fully contend with what Whitman's notebooks and manuscripts have revealed about his early poems.

The use of arboreal metaphors to discuss *Leaves of Grass* has a long history, dating back to some of Whitman's earliest critics, such as Oscar Triggs, who in a 1902 essay described *Leaves'* development as having "the character of expansive growths, like the rings of a tree."[55] Comparing *Leaves* and its poems to trees has been repeated by others, such as Gay Wilson Allen, who elaborates and qualifies the metaphor:

> The metaphor of "growth" has often been applied to the work, and is perhaps the best descriptive term to use, but even assuming that many branches have died, atrophied, been pruned away, and new ones grafted on, the metaphor is still not entirely accurate — unless we think of a magic tree that bears different fruit in different seasons. . . . Not only by indefatigable revising, deleting, but also by constant re-sorting and rearranging of the poems through six editions did Whitman indicate his shifting poetic intentions. Thus each of the editions and issues has its own distinctive form, aroma, import, though nourished by the same sap.[56]

Allen's complication of the metaphor is instructive, and it is easy to agree with his assertion that every edition has its own purpose and that Whitman's revisionary practices are so intense that each edition forms, in a sense, its own unique structure. My focus here has been on the first edition, which has sometimes been called a sprout or seed from which the overall tree grew. James E. Miller, for example, writes, "*Leaves of Grass* grew, much of its own accord, like a seed that contains within itself all its potential of size and shape."[57] Whether viewed as a tree or a seed that leads to a tree, what is at stake in conceiving of *Leaves of Grass* in these terms, and how can we relate these organic metaphors to the writing process that led up to the poems' initial publication?

Ignoring for now the question of whether readers are well served by comparing the *overall* development of *Leaves of Grass* with that of a tree, I believe what we have seen regarding the fragmentary, collage-like nature of poems like "I celebrate myself" and "I wander all night" casts serious doubt on the accuracy of describing the first edition in these terms. Our look at the "cow crunching" manuscript from Duke University has shown that Whitman aggressively arranged and rearranged the fragments that compose his poems and that the lines of "I celebrate myself" can be shuffled into alternate poetic forms that make just as much sense as how they were eventually presented. The various manuscripts I have explored leading up to the sexually inflected passages from "I wander all night" demonstrate the radical mobility of these fragments: how they move from manuscript to manuscript, notebook to notebook, adapting and changing to different verbal contexts. The numerous fragments of discourse that Whitman unpacked from outside sources and collaged into the overall fabric of his design demonstrate the variegated nature of a poem peppered with fragments that originated from a hand besides the poet's own. If we are to conceive of the first *Leaves* as a tree or a sprout, what we have is a curious plant indeed. Structurally speaking, it has no central trunk to unify it, but rather a vast array of structural points of gravity around which the fragments cohered. This plant is also impermanent and malleable: its parts can and were rearranged numerous times, moving through linguistic environments startlingly different from where the parts eventually came to reside. It is also a plant onto which have been "grafted," to use Allen's word, parts from entirely different species, and which has absorbed them effortlessly, even from its most tender stages of development. If the first edition of *Leaves* is a tree, it is one from a different planet altogether.

Nevertheless I don't believe we have to abandon the use of organic metaphors entirely in coming to grips with the first *Leaves'* structure. Rather than compare it to a tree, we might compare the poet's approach to a forest, the way he himself did in the preface to his 1876 edition: "Poetic style, when address'd to the soul, is less definite form, outline, sculpture, and becomes vista, music, half-tints, and even less than half-tints. True, it may be architecture, but again it may be the forest wild-wood, or the best effect thereof, at twilight, the waving oaks and cedars in the wind, and the impalpable odor" (*PW* 2:473). Like a forest *Leaves of Grass* has many trunks and even many species, and like "the waving oaks and cedars" its parts are in constant motion. And though the roots of these trees are entwined, there is no central axis on which the parts are dependent, but rather a kind of underground matrix, suggestive of the countless notebooks and manuscripts from which the poems were derived. Whitman's use of the word "vista" in this passage is suggestive as well. The word connotes the sense of an expansive view from which the reader can take in the diverse parts, absorbing them in a panoramic expanse that can accommodate variance and diversity. It is perhaps in this sense that he uses the word to describe "the most fragmentary book ever written," his *Specimen Days*, which offers an equally broad and various perspective.[58]

We might also begin with the first edition's title, where the leaves are not those of a tree but of grass. Like the prairie grass that Whitman so loved, the fragments that make up the major poems of the first edition can be seen as independent and autonomous entities, but at the same time the grass is united at the roots in an interdependent totality that spreads without definite beginning or end. In a prairie or meadow there is no radial axis or trunk from which the overall design spreads, but the various sprouts of grass are linked in an underground matrix and depend on each other to prevent ground erosion and to resist being washed away in heavy rain. Conceiving of grass as a structural metaphor for the first *Leaves* also usefully calls to mind the subsequent structural poetics of poets such as Charles Olson, who proclaims in his essay "Projective Verse" that "any poet who departs from closed form . . . ventures into FIELD COMPOSITION — puts himself in the open."[59] Whitman's approach to poetic form may not have been as open as some of the work of poets like Olson, Louis Zukofsky, and Robert Duncan, but relative to his milieu it is open indeed, and he would surely have approved of the idea of an "open air" poetics that could provide the broad-ranging vistas he sought to evoke in his readers' minds. Although his lines are always justified on the left margin and are more dense than these later poets, Whitman's "field composition" also mobilizes fragments of text across the entire page, is unbound by conventional formalism, and dissolves hierarchical concepts of structure, where each part sits in what is meant to appear to be a fixed, preordained order. Whitman himself actually depicted language as a kind of irregular, grassy plant in the hand-drawn font he used for the cover

FIG 15. Whitman's hand-drawn cover lettering for the first *Leaves of Grass*. Walt Whitman Archive.

design of the first edition (see figure 15). Although it would have been impossible to spell "Leaves of Grass" using the realistic anatomical makeup of actual grass, this font, which Whitman himself sketched out, does suggest something similar to what I am describing here: a visualization of language as made up of multiple, interdependent, plant-like entities that are put together in an irregular, centerless, and asymmetrical structure.

Finally, if we are inclined to look outside Whitman's vocabulary to the tropes of recent critical theory, we might compare the poet's structural fragments to the rhizomes of Gilles Deleuze and Félix Guattari. The critical description is too complex to do it full justice in the scope of what I am trying to achieve here, but to describe it briefly, the rhizome is the primary trope of Deleuze and Guattari's theory of nomadology. In *A Thousand Plateaus* they offer a complex comparison of the stable, relatively symmetrical tree in opposition to the constantly moving and evolving rhizomes of numerous plants, including, interestingly enough, many kinds of grasses. A rhizome is a botanical term for the horizontal and usually underground stems of plants that send out various roots and shoots from their nodes. Plants use rhizomes to spread and grow through vegetative reproduction. Deleuze and Guattari use the idea of rhizomes to describe the structural thinking of nomadic cultures, where the image replaces the tree as the classical paradigm of the world. In contrast to trees, rhizomes have no central, radial trunk but rather various asymmetrical nodes that spread out and adapt to the contours of their environment. As we have seen in discussing its use as a metaphor for Whitman's poetry, the concept of a tree implies the existence of an underlying, hierarchical unity (from the trunk come branches, from the branches, leaves). With rhizomes the visible structures of plants (their shoots) appear in relation to the cartography and resources of their environment. As with Whitman's best early poems, the visible fragment of the entity is mobile and malleable; as with the lines of poems in his notebooks and the sequence of his poems in successive editions, the structure of his work was continually changing and adapting to its place and time.

Obviously I've only scratched the surface of the critical resonance of Whitman's writing process and the forms that resulted from it. In the most in-depth study so far of the rhizomatic qualities of Whitman's poetry, Eric Wilson goes into greater detail, including this felicitous description:

> Whitman's poem in content and form is literally a rhizomatic, nomadic field of grass, a sprawling evolving ecosystem in which parts and whole enter into perpetual and unpredictable conversation, its parts (cells and organs; tropes and figures) suddenly swerve into new combinations that alter the living currents of the whole (the abyss of life; the overall composition); this fresh whole in turn affects the dispositions of the parts, forcing them to leap into further novel forms that will again change the whole.[60]

This metaphor of the poem as a "rhizomatic, nomadic field of grass" is attractive in light of what is revealed by the notebooks and manuscripts. The Whitman who wrote these early poems was indeed something of a nomad, always on the move and adapting to new environments. Depending on where and how you look, you can find either the Whitman of symmetry and design or the Whitman of mobility and fragmentation, the poet of "form, outline, sculpture" or of "vista, music, half-tints, and even less than half-tints." Conceiving of *Leaves* in arboreal terms is probably an outgrowth of the structural priorities of a generation of readers who were mindful of different values and moved by other forms than the ones that I find most compelling. But something that I think fascinates almost all of Whitman's readers is how, as our predilections and fervors change, Whitman changes with us and seems, as he promised, to wait for us and our particular needs. Looked at formally, the most attractive Whitman so far has usually been the Whitman of inspiration, continuity, and architecture. But this same poet has anticipated recent approaches to art that embrace more of a sense of fragmentation, multiplicity, and linguistic freedom. Whitman's poems *are* inspired, and one of their greatest enthusiasms was, and is, their extraordinary way of coming into being.

3

Kosmos Poets and
Spinal Ideas

E ven as the nomadic Whitman of the early 1850s lived a life
on the go, moving from house to house and desk to desk
with his myriad notebooks and scattered drafts of lines,
he was also searching for threads of order in what he had
written, structures that would come to shape the poems of the first
edition of *Leaves of Grass*. Whitman liked to call these concepts his
"spinal ideas," a phrase that calls to mind not only a human body but
also a book, with its spine, holding its leaves together. The concept
was highly elastic, and he applied it in different circumstances to
mean different things. In this chapter I focus on the "spinal ideas"
that are most thoroughly worked through in the early notebooks:
concepts and themes that get fleshed out in actual lines, often in
repeated drafts. One of the most important of these, which Whitman worked out in the "Talbot Wilson" notebook, is his concept of
dilation, a principle involved in almost all of his first mature poems
and which the notebooks show him preoccupied with during the

early and mid-1850s. Related to his notion of dilation is his concept of the *kosmos,* another key expression that helps us to understand much of what Whitman seems to have intended with his early work. These and other "spinal ideas" form structural principles that allowed Whitman to organize his scattered drafts without sacrificing the fragmentation, multiplicity, and fluidity essential to his project. They constitute mobile centers of gravity that could absorb and structure his lines without subordinating them to predictable metrical, narrative, or rhetorical ideas of order — ideas that, in Whitman's estimation, were too closely tied to European conventions and that reflected a rigid and unitary outlook that was anathema to the poet's own. With "spinal ideas" Whitman discovered a way to allow meaning to resonate and accrete around important moments in his notebooks, without smothering them in artifice and convention.

As an experienced and versatile newspaperman, Whitman had considerable familiarity with the process of organizing disparate units of text. His nomadic lifestyle involved not only multiple moves from home to home, but from job to job as well. These jobs, which he referred to as "sits" (a term that held much the same meaning as the contemporary expression "gig"),[1] occupied him throughout much of his early life, commencing with an apprentice printing job for the *Long Island Patriot* in 1831. Whitman worked at different jobs as a printer and compositor until a tremendous fire in the printing district of New York turned him to a short-lived vocation as a schoolteacher in 1836. He returned to the newspaper business in 1838 and worked as a printer, writer, compositor, and editor at many newspapers until his last sustained job in the business, from the spring of 1857 to the summer of 1859, editing the *Brooklyn Daily Times.* He was only twenty-two when he got his first job as a head editor working for the *New York Aurora* in 1842. Other substantial jobs included writing regularly for the *Brooklyn Star* between 1845 and 1846 and a sit as editor for the *Brooklyn Daily Eagle* from March 1846 to January 1848. Under his leadership the *Eagle*, which was primarily a partisan paper supporting the Democratic Party, turned its attention increasingly toward literary and cultural affairs; it is this job that provided him with many of his most important lessons in self-education (and considerable fodder for his early notebooks), writing numerous articles and reviews on literature, opera, and the stage, as well as covering important cultural events at local museums and lecture halls.[2]

Whitman worked for several other papers during these years, including the *Evening Tattler, Democrat, Mirror,* and *Statesman*; his irregular, ever-changing employment was not uncommon for a journalist at the time. We get a sense of just how volatile his working life was — and also of how casually he accepted his lifestyle — in this notebook entry:

> Edited *Tattler* in summer of '42
>
> Edited *Statesman* in Spring of '43
>
> Edited *Democrat* in Summer of 44
>
> Wrote for *Dem Review, American Review,* and *Columbian Magazines* during 45 and 6 — as previously.
>
> About the latter part of February '46, commenced editing the Brooklyn *Eagle* — continued till last of January '48
>
> Left Brooklyn for New Orleans, Feb. 11th '48[3]

This offhand list continues later in the notebook; it accounts for only a portion of the poet's actual journalistic employment. His long and varied tenure as a newspaperman has been well documented by Whitman scholars, who have usually either emphasized correlations between the subject matter of his articles and his poems, or how his experience as a printer shaped his attitude toward the making of books in general and the personal role he played in creating the first edition in particular. Equally important, though less explored, are the connections between his newspaper work and his actual writing *practice*, including his understanding of the spinal ideas that came to structure his early lines.

The only detailed exploration of this topic so far has been by Simon Parker, who offers a number of fascinating suggestions about the influence of Whitman's professional writing and editing on his poetic composition. Of particular interest to a study of his notebooks is Parker's description of how Whitman's catalogs parallel the nineteenth-century editorial practice of situating the reporting of disparate events side by side in incongruent, even jarring sequences:

> In the newspaper, the obvious instability of the city's identity was represented in the mingling of a new and apparently chaotic range of material — trivial and sensational, highbrow and lowbrow. Verbatim reports of a sermon or committee meeting would sit next to lurid details of a murder or a scandal amongst the city's elite, and this would be next to (say) a report on the construction of street lighting, which would be next to classifieds advertising treatments of syphilis. This variety is echoed in Whitman's long poems; in what became Section 15 of "Song of Myself," for example, there is a mixture of the sensational ("The malformed limbs are tied to the anatomist's table, / What is removed drops horribly in the pail") and the mundane ("the signpainter is lettering with red and gold").[4]

Parker refers to an editorial practice unfamiliar to modern newspaper readers, who are used to cleanly delineated articles organized into neat sections (e.g., "Local," "Life," "Entertainment," "World"). In the newspapers of Whitman's day, especially the cheaper papers that crammed a lot of text into a small space, it was common practice for the editor to place succinct accounts of various unrelated events directly beside each other in parallel columns. Whitman certainly engaged in this practice. While editor of the *Brooklyn Daily Eagle*, for example, he dedicated most of the second page of each issue of his four-page daily to short, sometimes single-sentence descriptions of the day's news; an account of a suicide might sit next to a description of a new church, which is next to an editorial complaint about local rowdies, followed by an account of a recent congressional meeting. It seems likely that Whitman, who for years wrote the copy for these kinds of reports, must have been influenced by this jagged style of editorial presentation, and that this journalistic experience helps to account for his writing practice — so odd in the context of poetry — of juxtaposing radically different details in his catalogs and lists.[5]

Parker goes on to describe the technical process of newspaper creation in a manner that has striking relevance to Whitman's poetic creation: "As a printer, he had been trained to see language in terms of blocks of type and proofs to be arranged and edited rather than composed. Later, as an editor, Whitman would combine editorial statements with columns of short news items and clippings, advertisements, and commercial and personal announcements." He elaborates that the poet's notebooks "suggest that a similar conception of creativity — experiments with the layout of combinations of lists, notes, and brief verses or passages of prose — defined his early drafting of a poem."[6] Based on what the notebooks have shown us about his attitude toward language and originality, I think we can go further: just as his newspaper experience emphasized arrangement and editing in addition to original composition, so Whitman's poetic theory in the notebooks emphasizes *an overall attitude toward language* much like that required of an editor. We have already seen how the poet "disclaims originality" and describes instead an "originality of the spirit" that must "show itself in new combinations and new meanings" (*CPW* 6:12, 37). Likewise Whitman as editor was trained to see language as something "arranged and edited rather than composed," and he exercised this view daily, arranging and editing his and others' text into newspaper form. It would seem, then, that the seeds of his attitude toward language were planted long before he began to borrow and collage material for his poems. To see originality in language as primarily the "new combinations" that result from "new occasions and requirements" that "carry out" or bring to fruition that which already exists, is to see language like a newspaper editor, manipulating others' writing alongside one's own to form compelling new shapes and presentations (*CPW* 6:37, 12).

Even more salient perhaps than this conceptual influence on what constitutes originality, his experience as an editor is directly reflected in his manipulation of the notebooks. Then, as today, newspapers recycled each other's stories; as editor, Whitman would have been responsible for assembling these stories for the page. In his book-length study of Whitman's days at the *Daily Eagle*, Thomas L. Brasher describes his typical duties as an editor: "Besides preparing editorials . . . Whitman clipped items from exchange papers, wrote book and periodical reviews, arranged a literary miscellany for the first page, compiled a column or so of local news, and frequently did his own legwork on news stories in Brooklyn and across the East River in New York."[7] This description of an editor's job — combining "clipped items," "writing," "arranging," "compiling," and "legwork" — parallels what we have already seen in Whitman's process of poetic composition. He wrote his own lines and did his own "legwork," strolling the streets of Brooklyn; but he also "clipped" them (sometimes literally) from other sources and compiled, arranged, and rearranged these fragments in his notebooks. His years as a newspaperman constituted not only his vocation but also, unlike his college-educated literary contemporaries, the bulk of his early self-education. We shouldn't be surprised to find that these reading and writing practices formed the foundation for his approach as a poet, both in his theory of poetry and in his direct application of it in his discovery and arrangement of lines.

Some of his early manuscripts show Whitman going further and arranging his literary drafts in a manner that actually looks like the front page of a newspaper. Several notebook and manuscript examples have survived that show Whitman breaking up the page into lined, newspaper-like columns. One of the most telling is a large penciled leaf that is a part of the Trent Collection at Duke University (see figure 16). Here we find Whitman actively working out his ideas for the poem first published in the 1856 edition of *Leaves* under the title "Broad-Axe Poem," which received its final title, "Song of the Broad-Axe," in the 1867 edition. As in a headline, the poet has written the word "Broadaxe" in large underlined lettering at the top of the page. Following that is a short account of what he means to indicate by this title:

> First as coming in the rough and out of the earth. — then as being smelted and made into usable shape for working — then into some of the earlier weapons of the axe kind — battleaxe — headsman's axe — carpenter's broad-axe — (process of making, tempering and finishing the axe.) — inquire fully

In this passage we find Whitman working out the rough beginnings of the spinal idea behind his "Broad-Axe Poem" of 1856; however, it is clear that he hasn't quite arrived at it yet. Sounding like the journalist he was, Whitman exhorts himself to "inquire fully" into the subject; below this, in neatly lined columns broken up into sections

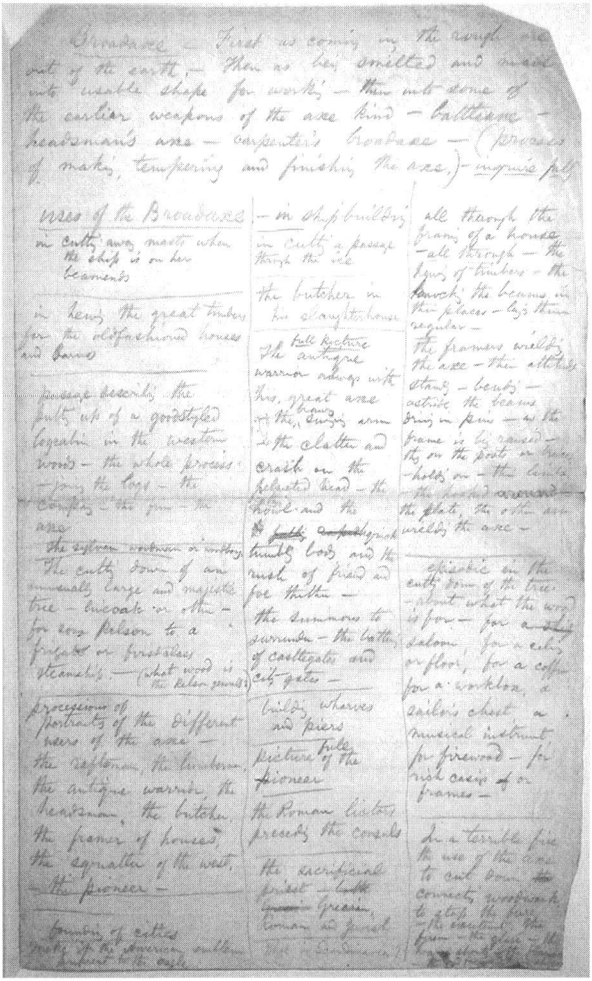

FIG 16. Newspaper-like manuscript for "Song of the Broad-Axe." Trent Collection of Whitmaniana, Duke University Rare Book, Manuscript, and Special Collections Library.

by irregularly spaced horizontal lines, he sketches out short accounts of various uses of the axe to be fleshed out later in the actual poem. A brief glance at this leaf reveals just how similar its visual layout was to that of a typical front page of a newspaper from his era.[8] The front page of a mid-nineteenth-century newspaper would have been larger and crammed more densely with text, but the essential layout is similar.

The short accounts of a broadaxe's uses in this newspaper-like leaf are described in one particularly telling note as "processions of portraits of the different uses of the axe." Clearly Whitman already has in mind his signature approach of using episodic and discrete units, each of which is itself a static "portrait" but which when read together form a dynamic "procession." If there were any doubt that Whitman himself was aware he was setting out to create a poem based on this kind of episodic structure, he dispels it with this comment from the same leaf: "episodic in the cutting down of the tree — about what the wood is for — for a ~~ship~~ saloon, for a ceiling or floor, for a coffin, for a workhouse [?], a sailor's chest, a musical instrument, for firewood — for rich casings ~~of~~ or frames." Just as he here plans a representation of the broadaxe based on a variety of snapshot accounts, so the newspapers of Whitman's day, especially the cheaper ones like the *Brooklyn Daily Eagle*, told the news in brief, offering accounts far shorter than the kind to which newspaper readers today are accustomed. Often these stories amounted only to a single sentence: "The returns of the late Virginia elections received this morning indicate that the democrats have elected ten members of congress, the whigs five" is a typical story, and there are countless other one-liners.[9] Sometimes these miniature articles describe sensational events, such as house fires, ship sinkings, and murders, while still keeping within one to three sentences, just as his poems

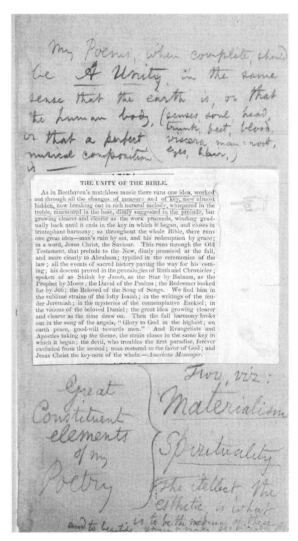

My Poems, when complete, should be *A Unity*, in the same sense that the earth is, or that the human body, (senses, soul, head, trunk, feet, blood, viscera, man-root, musical composition eyes, hair,) is

THE UNITY OF THE BIBLE.

As in Beethoven's matchless music there runs one idea, worked out through all the changes of measure and of key, now almost hidden, now breaking out in rich natural melody, whispered in the treble, murmured in the base, dimly suggested in the prelude, but growing clearer and clearer as the work proceeds, winding gradually back until it ends in the key in which it began, and closes in triumphant harmony; so throughout the whole Bible, there runs one great idea—man's ruin by sin, and his redemption by grace; in a word, Jesus Christ, the Saviour. This runs through the Old Testament, that prelude to the New, dimly promised at the fall, and more clearly to Abraham; typified in the ceremonies of the law; all the events of sacred history paving the way for his coming; his descent proved in the genealogies of Ruth and Chronicles; spoken of as Shiloh by Jacob, as the Star by Balaam, as the Prophet by Moses; the David of the Psalms; the Redeemer looked for by Job; the Beloved of the Song of Songs. We find him in the sublime strains of the lofty Isaiah; in the writings of the tender Jeremiah; in the mysteries of the contemplative Ezekiel; in the visions of the beloved Daniel; the great idea growing clearer and clearer as the time drew on. Then the full harmony broke out in the song of the angels, "Glory to God in the highest; on earth peace, good-will towards men." And Evangelists and Apostles taking up the theme, the strain closes in the same key in which it began; the devil, who troubles the first paradise, forever excluded from the second; man restored to the favor of God; and Jesus Christ the key-note of the whole.—*American Messenger.*

Great Constituent elements of my Poetry

Two, viz: { Materialism { Spirituality { the intellect, the esthetic is what is to be the medium

and to beautify

would, offering details in small unified divisions that abut each other but don't necessarily connect.

In other notebooks and manuscript fragments Whitman took his newspaper-like approach to composition a step further and pasted actual clippings onto a leaf with notes or lines. In one 1856 leaf, for example, he intersperses several registers of discourse: poetic theory sits near a newspaper clipping describing a Hungarian poet, between which is a list of qualities that seem to describe his own poems; below all this he draws a line and writes a brief reflection on Heinrich Heine's *Pictures of Travel*, a translation of which Whitman seems to have been reading at the time. Sometimes the notes seem more unified, as in the undated leaf shown in figure 17, which appropriately enough describes various takes on the idea of unity in poetry and in the Bible. He seems to have first pasted a newspaper or journal article to the center of the page, then filled in blank spaces above and below with related notes. This leaf contains important concepts related to a key spinal idea behind his *Leaves*. I'll explore these concepts shortly, but for now I would call attention to the small pointing hand just to the right of the clippings, directing us to an underlined passage. Anyone familiar with Whitman's notebooks has seen countless examples of these pointing hands, which the poet used to emphasize particularly crucial parts of his notes. His use of the hands was derived from newspaper conventions at the time, which used them primarily for emphasis in advertisements that were sold at a slightly higher rate than those without the hands. Even the conventions of advertisements were fair game to the omnivorously demotic Whitman, who was willing to absorb any approach that proved helpful to him, regardless of its origins.

Yet another way that his years as a newspaperman must have affected his writing process relates to the speaking position commonly adopted by mid-nineteenth-century journalists and editors. As the Whitman scholar and book historian Ezra Greenspan has described in greater detail, the form of address commonly adopted by Whitman and other editors of his milieu was one that might seem peculiarly intimate to twenty-first-century readers. In commercially motivated efforts to increase their publications' readerships, editors commonly sought to create a sense of personal familiarity, and hence loyalty, in their audiences:

> The journalistic style of intimate address to the reader was extremely common in the mid-century years, particularly in magazine journalism, where it became something of a literary convention. American magazine journalism had inherited the convention of the address to the "gentle reader" from the British; and as one might readily expect, that convention became gradually democratized as the American readership itself broadened and multiplied during the decades of Whitman's early manhood. Magazine editors regularly addressed their readers directly across the "editorial table" in caressing tones designed to cultivate a bond of familiarity between reader, editor, and journal — this, ironically, at the moment when the incipient age of mass circulation was actually putting distance between them.[10]

This style of address, which Greenspan argues was popularized by the nineteenth-century journalist and writer Nathaniel Willis, was an approach Whitman took up with particular vigor, both in his journalism and later in his poems. Just as Whitman the poet would address his readers as "Whoever you are holding me now in hand," so Whitman the journalist would call out to "Boy, or young man, whose eyes hover over these lines" in one of his columns.[11] This style of journalistic address, which would seem bizarre in contemporary writing, was used not only in editorials but also in straightforward reporting of the day's news. Guided by the need to portray a sense of impartiality, reporters now employ a more neutral style.

Whitman's move from being a newspaperman and practical printer to a major world poet has often been described by scholars as a "transformation," and there is obviously something transformative about his emergence as the author of *Leaves of Grass*, especially if we look primarily to the texts he published in his lifetime. If, however, we emphasize the notebooks as the yardstick of Whitman's development, the move might be better described as an "evolution" instead of a transformation. Despite some radical differences between the 1855 *Leaves* and almost everything he had previously published, there are numerous lines of connection between his practices as an editor and a poet. Like other writers and editors of his day, Whitman used the direct, personal style that had emerged as a successful strategy for getting and keeping audiences. He employed the visual and typographical conventions of newspapers, from smaller details such as his use of emphatic pointing hands to highlight important passages, to larger-scale appropriations such as the way he would sometimes create columns in the leaves in his notebooks to visually resemble the pages of a newspaper. His telegraphic style of presenting sequences of incongruent images and episodes is paralleled by the compact and jagged organization of the news in Brooklyn's "penny papers." Just as it is common practice among newspapers to reuse material from other papers, so Whitman used text from other authors and saw language not so much as personal property but as something liberally available for reuse. Related to this is his habit of rearranging clippings, both from his own writing and from outside sources, in various sequences until he found the order he desired. These last two aspects of his journalistically influenced writing practices relate most clearly to his manipulation of text in his notebooks, and these are the approaches that we need to pursue further as we explore Whitman's concept of the spinal idea and the manuscripts that put these ideas to use.

∾

One of the most revealing stories that helps to explain the origins of Whitman's poems comes to us by way of a transcription that one of his friends made of his 1887 conversation with the poet:

> He said an idea would strike him which, after mature thought, he would consider fit to be the "spinal theme" of a "piece." This he would revolve in his mind in all its phases, and finally adopt, setting it down crudely on a bit of paper, — the back of an envelope or any scrap, — which he would place in an envelope. After he had exhausted the supply of suggestions, or had a sufficient number to interpret the idea withal, he would interweave them in a "piece," as he called it. I asked him about the arrangement or succession of the slips, and he said, "They always fall properly into place."[12]

By the time Whitman made these remarks he was working primarily with notes that he himself had composed, collaging them together in sequences suggested by his spinal themes. As we have seen, however, there is no extant evidence to suggest that the younger Whitman even knew his life's work would be called poetry until 1853 or 1854, when he discovered his signature line and, subsequently, his broadly figured first-person poetic voice. Nevertheless the manuscript and notebook evidence suggests that as a younger poet Whitman employed compositional processes much the same as those he described in his old age to his inquiring friend. Many examples, such as the "crunching cow" passage, have survived that reveal the poet experimenting with radically different orders for his lines, rewriting them in successive drafts until they fell "properly into place" in their final published form. Even more in line with Whitman's 1887 comments, we have numerous examples of manuscripts that have been cut into strips and glued into sequences on another leaf. We don't know if he collected them in envelopes first, as Harrison says, but the results are the same: arranging clippings in the familiar manner of a newspaper editor, using scissors, pins, old notebooks, and multitudinous other source materials, Whitman unknowingly simulated a familiar word-processing technique, a literal cutting and pasting similar to the electronic kind that has become a widespread practice for users of computers.

Harrison's statement is one of dozens of examples in which Whitman used the metaphor of a spine to signify underlying structural principles. He discussed "A Spinal thought" for a "lecture on Religion" in which "man advances" and "God disappears," as well as a "spinal idea" that would unite all his planned lectures (though what this idea would be is not made clear; *NUPM* 6:2097, 2237). Whitman described "spinal and essential attributes," "spinal meaning," and "spinal requisites," as well as a "central, spinal reality," a "patriotic spinal element," and "spinal supports"—all in his published prose.[13] He referred to the "Spinal Idea of a 'Lesson'"—a phrase he used to mean didactic, instructional poems—with the immodest goal of "Founding a new American Religion" (*NUPM* 6:2046). In reference to specific poems, he directly stated the "spinal idea" for the poems "Passage to India" and "Song of the Redwood Tree," among others.[14] In addition he often remarked upon spinal ideas that underlie all of *Leaves of Grass*, though his accounts vary and sometimes seem contradictory. Furthermore these are only the spinal ideas that Whitman directly refers to as such; there are countless others that are not directly labeled, though they clearly seem to be spinal ideas. When Whitman used the phrase "spinal theme" to describe the underlying structural principles behind his process of composition, he was returning to a versatile trope that he had employed throughout his life and that he was comfortable using in personal and public address alike. Conceiving of such principles as a spine helped him to frame his writing process in organic terms, and this goal must surely have been on his mind as he described a process that risked appearing to others to be something methodic, artificial, and even, in the face of disciples who saw him as a mystically inspired prophet, uninspiringly mundane.

There is indeed a methodical quality to Whitman's 1887 description of his creative method, though the method also leaves room for spontaneity and inspiration. He describes a process that can be divided into four major components. First, an "idea would strike him," and he would turn that idea over in his mind, considering it in terms that his comments indicate were something of a testing process, subjecting it to more "mature thought" than his initial rush of inspiration allowed. If the notion proved worthy it made the transition to being a "spinal theme." As this comment suggests, the initial idea and the spinal idea were not the same. The spinal idea is one that has been tested for its worthiness and that he will "revolve in his mind in all its phases." It seems reasonable to assume that brief notes such as his isolated, two-word comment to himself, "Banjo Poem," would constitute a mere initial idea, whereas more extensively developed concepts, such as the paragraph that accompanies the underlined heading "Broadaxe," are "spinal themes" or ideas (*NUPM* 4:1328). These two steps in his compositional process are especially apparent in a notebook from the mid- to late 1850s, sometimes referred to as the "Dick Hunt" notebook, where we find dozens of examples of initial ideas noted as "Poem of _____," including "Poem of Precepts," "Poem of the Library," and "Poem of (after death)." In some cases these initial ideas are worked through to spinal ideas; others Whitman seems to have abandoned (*NUPM* 1:246–80). The third step in his writing process is the creation of actual lines and details that he would jot "down crudely on a bit of paper" and collect together "in an envelope" (in this case). The evidence shows that he would also collect such fragments in notebooks and even bundles pinned or tied together. Of the four stages, this is the only one described as involving actual writing, though we know his final step in the process — the interweaving and sequencing of the fragments — would usually entail the drafting of new material to help connect the pieces. So we have a four-step process that moves from inspiration to reflection, creation to arrangement, providing room for both the spontaneous and methodic sides of the poet's literary imagination.

Conceiving, testing, writing, and arranging — steps in a process that on the surface might not appear to be particularly unusual for a poet. After all, even a Romantic such as Wordsworth, who famously conceived of poetic creation as a "spontaneous overflow of powerful feelings," was driven not only by a sense of immediate inspiration, but also by larger unifying ideas. A book such as *Lyrical Ballads*, for example, is in one sense a conceptual project, benefiting from both the immediate flashes of creativity that led to specific lines and also from Wordsworth's overall predetermined goal to write a collection of poems that would challenge the prevalent taste of his day by investigating the question of how far the speech of the lower and middle classes could be suited to poetic composition. Likewise Yeats used the "automatic writing" methods made popular by Theosophists and other contemporaneous intellectual circles and also the carefully predetermined structural principles that inform a long poem such as "The Tower" and a sequence such as the Crazy

Jane poems. With few exceptions, such as the experiments of the early Surrealists and some of the jazz-inspired poems of the Beats, all poetry is motivated both by concept and immediate creation, notebook jottings and spinal ideas — and even the Surrealists and the Beats were following through with underlying conceptions of structure, even if such conceptions amounted to a prescribed goal of abolishing any sense of predetermined structure.

At the other extreme we find the highly programmatic work of poets involved with the avant-garde group known as the Oulipo, where, in an effort to critique what adherents see as the excessive emphasis on freedom in predecessors like the Dadaists and Surrealists, poems are created within the highly programmatic constraints of predetermined formulas.[15] Yet even with this group, which emphasizes the conceptual over the spontaneous, it is hard to see how poems get written without some sense of immediate inspiration, even if that inspiration only amounts to choosing words from another's text.[16] The Romantic movement may have swung the pendulum further toward emphasis on inspiration and spontaneity, but it certainly didn't set out to abolish conceptual structure (just as Classicism, as it has been understood, puts greater emphasis on overriding formal structure but finds room for immediate inspiration within such structure). With all poetry there is a gap between the intellectual formation of structure and principle and some kind of "spontaneous overflow" of creativity, and so it's a fair question to ask what makes Whitman's method particularly noteworthy.

Familiarity with his notebooks helps to answer that question, and what we find there is more than just noteworthy. First, as we have seen, Whitman specifically theorizes his work in a way that anticipates important subsequent poetic practices of others. The Beats found in Whitman a liberating example in his spontaneity and formal freedom;

through that inspiration poets such as Allen Ginsberg inaugurated a rebirth of Romantic ideals that have inspired countless young people in their writing and their lives. This inspired and spontaneous Whitman remains the prevalent public representation, but as we are beginning to see, the conceptual Whitman, with his critique of originality, his groundbreaking use of literary self-collage, and his spinal ideas holding the fragments together, offers us another model with relevance to aesthetic principles that oppose those emphasized not only by the Beats but by almost all biographical accounts of the poet. This Whitman anticipates other groundbreaking creative approaches, such as the collage-like presentation of text employed at times by Marianne Moore and William Carlos Williams; the methodic, recombinatory practices of Raymond Queneau, with his *100,000,000,000,000 Poems*; Brion Gysin and, shortly after, William S. Burroughs, with their infamous cut-up method; and occasionally John Ashbery, especially in *The Tennis Court Oath*.[17] These artists may not have been aware of Whitman's role in the development of such literary methods, but Whitman does anticipate them in important ways, often to the detriment of claims for their methods' novelty.

All poets strike some kind of balance between conception and execution, inspiration and predetermined ideal, but what sets Whitman apart and aligns him with later avant-garde ideas is not only that he consciously theorizes his practices, but also the relationship with language that engenders them. Partially as a result of his experience as a newspaper editor, Whitman came to see language in highly material terms, and this emphasis on language's materiality led him to see it as something that precedes his own creativity, as opposed to originating within himself and flaring up in inspired bursts. Or, more accurately, Whitman saw these moments of immediate inspiration as being contained within a larger vision of language, encouraging him to manipulate and restructure it in radical, even violent ways. Wordsworth had conscious preconceived ideals in mind for the poems in *Lyrical Ballads*, but the immediate act of writing was something sacred to him, and he enshrined his creativity in theoretic formulations that present poetic language as something that originates inside the poet and spills out in volcanic eruptions. He revised and sometimes rearranged his lines, but his sacralization of poetic language would never have encouraged him to cut up previously written material, stuffing the scraps in envelopes for safekeeping, and later arranging and rearranging the lines until he found the order he liked. It took a poet like Whitman, with his background as an editor and practical printer, to reconceive poetic language as a kind of movable type to be constantly toyed with and restructured—to see the role of the editor and the corresponding work of revision and visual arrangement of text as equally important to poetry as the immediate act of creation.

This materialist attitude toward language is reflected in the material nature of his manuscripts, not only in their cut-up structuring but sometimes even in the very paper he chose to write on. With an irony that Whitman himself may or may not have been aware of, he once jotted down a note on what Grier describes as "an irregular piece of floral wallpaper," the contents of which describe his notion of a "poet of materialism" (*NUPM* 1:198)! It is as if the very wallpaper he was writing on—the material oddity of which is difficult to ignore—is evidence of his own materialist attitude toward language and art. For Whitman any material, even a ripped-off hunk of wallpaper, is a suitable medium for his collage-like writing process. Another editor of Whitman's notebooks, his friend and literary executor Richard Maurice Bucke, commented further on the mongrel nature of some of his manuscripts: "The notes printed in this volume came to me in scrapbooks and in bundles. They are all on loose sheets and small pieces of paper of endless sizes, shapes, shades, and qualities, (some even written on the back of scraps of wall-paper!). Sometimes they are pasted in a scrapbook but more often they are stuck in loose, or (as said) tied in bundles" (CPW 1:xv). Neither was the variegated nature of Whitman's manuscripts lost on another of his early aficionados, William Garrison, who remarked not only on the poet's odd use of paper but on his use of ink and lead: "I have seen a manuscript, a part of 'November Boughs,' a single page of which was composed of at least a dozen kinds of paper, written in black pencil, blue pencil, black ink, and red ink. Some of the parts of this manuscript were written on bits of brown straw paper, others on manila paper, others on the blue paper that had once formed a part of the cover of a pamphlet, and each piece of a different size, shape, and color."[18] Whereas Romantics, as well as later, formally forward-thinking poets, would often make a kind of altar out of the blank page (think of Mallarmé's use of white space in *Coup de dés*), Whitman saw the page in the manner his professional background had trained him to see: as unformed bulk material, something to be manipulated, conserved, and recycled based on one's immediate practical and financial needs.

There are many extant examples of such manuscript panoplies, one of the most dramatic of which is a pasted-together assemblage of cut-up scraps that shows Whitman experimenting with lines used in his late poem "You Tides with Ceaseless Swell." This manuscript, which is currently on display at the Walt Whitman House in Camden, New Jersey, consists of no fewer than eleven separate fragments, thin, mostly one-line scraps of paper that are pasted on top of one another on a single 12¼-inch leaf (see figure 18). The manuscript reveals a particularly aggressive effort by Whitman to find an order

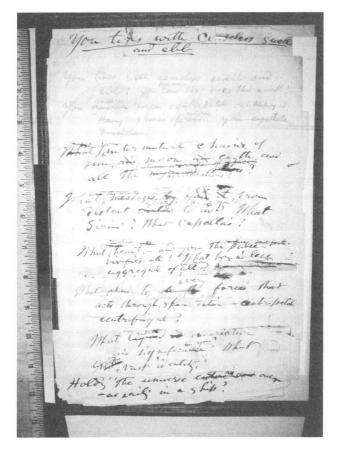

FIG 18. "You tides with ceaseless swell and ebb" manuscript. Walt Whitman House, Camden NJ.

for his fragments, manipulating them into place around the spinal idea of a poem relating the tides and the far-off gravitational forces at work upon them to the "fluid, vast identity" behind existence, "Holding the universe with all its parts as one" (LG 514). As with the manuscripts just discussed, Whitman recycled paper to form these lines, in this case from various letters sent to him between 1884 and 1878. However, unlike those manuscripts, this one shows Whitman layering draft upon draft, one over another, creating significant, even overwhelming difficulty for anyone trying to explore the development of his thornier drafts. Certainly the topmost layer of paper represents a later stage in the poem's development, but how do we assess the order of the drafts beneath? There is no way for us to know when he pasted one strip on top of another, so we cannot say exactly what alternative concepts of order he considered for these lines, nor how many. Was the uppermost layer of strips pasted down in order, from the top to the bottom of the page? Or did he paste them down bottom to top (or in some other pattern)? Did he first arrange and rearrange the lines without pasting them down, suggesting the possibility that each individual layer too might once have been sequenced differently? To begin to address these kinds of questions we need to be sensitive to details that are often not apparent in transcriptions, such as the small descenders of letters that are visible at the top of some of the cut-off strips, which at least help to illuminate one stage in his process of revision and recombination. Many such manuscript thickets will never be fully disentangled, a problem exacerbated by the self-contained nature of his lines — each framing a distinct unit of meaning — that offers us few semantic clues to base our arguments on.[19] As in the children's book game *Heads, Bodies, Legs,* where body parts from each section can be interchanged to form fantastic new combinations, there is no fixed order by which we can assume Whitman combined the pieces in his cut-up manuscripts.

Luckily not all of Whitman's spinal ideas met with such fractured, labyrinthine treatment. The majority of his earliest manuscript and premanuscript manipulations seem to have taken place by way of

126

rewriting the lines rather than cutting them up into individual strips. In such cases we can often tell from his cross-outs and insertions in what order he tried out variations. Because many of these earliest lines were originally written as prose, it would have been difficult for him to use his scissors and glue so prolifically; after all, with a poetic line one can simply make two straight cuts across the page to extract the line from an unwanted order. With prose such a process was made impractical, as he would have had to carefully lift a sentence from its source paragraph, cutting around the contours of the sentence instead of simply slicing up a discrete strip. Whitman's habit in such cases was to rewrite the prose as poetry, and such rewritings leave a more easily discernable trail of development. We can probably assume that in most cases a prose version of a given line precedes its existence in verse form. The material composition of a bound notebook offers us more clues to determine a chronology of drafts than does a palimpsest of disparate strips. Using one particularly important document, the infamous "Talbot Wilson" notebook, let's take a detailed look at Whitman's writing and editing process, tracing the development of a particularly telling spinal idea into actual lines eventually used in "Song of Myself."

The same Whitman who disassembled his old journals, tore apart history and science books, and cut and pasted together paper scraps from wherever he could find them is also the poet who staked his entire body of work on a metaphor for paper. It was one of the only things that remained consistent through his lifelong project: his title, *Leaves of Grass*, and accompanying statements such as his invitation to "read these leaves in the open air every season of every year of your life."[20] Whitman did not have a pious attitude toward the page in and of itself, but when the act of reading transformed paper into a medium joining writer and reader, it became something more. Grass too is transformed into something enigmatic and transcendent. As has been well documented, the "riddle of the grass," as George Hutchinson phrased it, would seem to be the central, abiding mystery of the first edition of his poems. The contention finds support in his early notebooks; after all, in what may be the earliest extant example of Whitman consciously writing his *Leaves of Grass* poems, the young writer instructs himself to "personify the general objects of the creative and give them voice . . . a leaf of grass, with its equal voice." And in what most scholars have regarded as the most important of his early notebooks he exhorts himself, "Bring all the art and science of the world, and baffle and humble it with one spear of grass." Whitman's leafy, grassy trope is vital to his intentions, and it forms a broadly relevant spinal idea in "Song of Myself." It is in fact so encompassing that it becomes difficult to approach by way of specific manuscript examples. To address such an inclusive concept, it seems practical to begin with more discrete principles when exploring the relation between his spinal ideas and his written lines.

The "Talbot Wilson" notebook provides a useful case study. In it are a number of important spinal ideas intersecting and evolving, as well as early attempts to present these ideas in actual lines. As we have seen, the literary contents of the notebook were probably written in 1854, a mere year before the publication of the first edition. Despite the short time span separating the notebook's contents from the first *Leaves*, Whitman never refers to a "leaf" or "leaves" of grass in the "Talbot Wilson" notebook, employing instead the more conventional phrase "spear of grass," which suggests that the idea of grass was important to him at the time but that he was still working through the question of how to present it. The notebook has long enjoyed pride of place among Whitman scholars as the "earliest and most important" notebook, and even if the first part of that description is untrue, a strong case can be made for the second.[21] Whitman himself once authorized the importance of this notebook, when he described it to Horace Traubel as expressing the "a b c" of *Leaves*: "'What has that particular book to do with *Leaves of Grass*?' 'Oh! everything! is full of its beginnings — is the a b c of the book — contains the first lisps of the song.'"[22] What then are these "a b c"s of his *Leaves,* these building blocks on which his first mature poems grew?

Whitman described the most important of these building blocks, his concept of dilation, in this helpfully titled notebook passage:

Dilation

I think the soul will never stop, or attain to any ~~its~~[?] growth beyond which it shall ^{not} go. ~~no further.~~ — ^{When} I ~~have sometimes when~~ walked at night by the sea shore and looked up ~~too~~ ^{at} the ~~stars~~ countless stars, and _^^I ^{have} asked of my soul whether it would be filled and satisfied when it ~~was~~ ^{should become} ~~a~~ the god enfolding [deletion, illegible] all these, and open _^ to the life and delight and knowledge of every thing in them or of them; and the answer was plain~~er~~ to ~~my ear~~ ^{me} — ~~than~~ ^{at} the [deletion, illegible] breaking water on the sands at my feet; and ~~it~~ _^^{the answer} was, No, when I reach there, I shall want ~~more~~ to go further still.

The passage is central to Whitman's future development in a number of ways. For one, it may be the earliest extant mature writing that describes the poet in what many readers have regarded as his most crucial natural environment: the shore, a setting Whitman mythologizes in such important poems as "As I Ebb'd with the Ocean of Life," "By Blue Ontario's Shore," and "Out of the Cradle Endlessly Rocking," to name just a few, and which eventually became the focus for entire clusters of poems, first in "Sea-Shore Memories" in the 1871 *Passage to India*, and later in *Leaves* as "Sea-Drift." More important here, however, this passage, which contemporary readers might regard as a kind of prose poem, shows Whitman defining a spinal idea that would remain crucial to him throughout his life and that is especially apparent in the early poems: the idea that the poetic soul craves limitless expansion, that even when it becomes "the god enfolding" the universe it "shall want to go further still." This concept of dilation crops up throughout *Leaves of Grass*, especially in the poem that eventually became known as "Song of Myself." It is an idea that appears under many linguistic guises and which, in its broader implications, undergirds the entire piece. To further understand what Whitman was describing, it helps to come to terms with his particular conception of the soul — that which becomes the "god enfolding" Whitman's cosmos — which reveals how the idea of enclosing, absorbing, and ingesting the world dominates his thinking throughout this crucial notebook.

Whitman was determined to convince his readers that the soul is something that should be understood not only abstractly, but also physically — that the body and the soul are harmonious coequals, intrinsically related to one another. Memorable formulations of this idea occur throughout *Leaves of Grass*, including in his declaration "I have said that the soul is not more than the body, / And I have said that the body is not more than the soul" and in his rhetorical question "And if the body were not the soul, what is the soul?" (*LG* 86, 94). Perhaps his most famous presentation of the body and soul becoming one is in section 5 of "Song of Myself," when body and soul are joined in erotic union, with the soul performing a kind of mystical fellatio upon the body:

I mind how once we lay such a transparent summer morning,

How you settled your head athwart my hips and gently turn'd over upon
me,

And parted the shirt from my bosom-bone, and plunged your tongue to
my bare-stript heart,

And reach'd till you felt my beard, and reach'd till you held my feet.

(*LG* 33)

Whitman also articulated body-soul union explicitly as a spinal idea in this notebook fragment: "My two theses—animal and spiritual—became gradually fused in <u>Leaves of Grass</u>, — runs through all ~~my~~ ᵗʰᵉ poems & gives color to the whole." He does something similar in the "Talbot Wilson" notebook, declaring, "The ₍effusion or corporation of the₎ soul is always under the beautiful laws of physiology." Even his choice of the word "dilation" as reference for spiritual expansiveness is involved in his efforts to define physical and spiritual equality, for as Webster's *American Dictionary of the English Language* and other contemporaneous dictionaries show, the word's primary use in Whitman's time was to describe physiological processes of the body, as in the dilation of the eye in the darkness or of the cervix while giving birth.

So we should not be surprised to find Whitman describing dilation, a concept crucial to his spirituality, in both spiritual and physiological terms. The physiological aspect of dilation is apparent in the 1855 Preface, where Whitman evokes the concept of the poet as dilator, following it up immediately with the very physical image of the eye as a peach pit capable of dilating to encompass the world:

The greatest poet hardly knows pettiness or triviality. If he breathes into
anything that was before thought small, it dilates with the grandeur and
life of the universe. He is a seer—he is individual—he is complete in

himself—the others are as good as he, only he sees it, and they do not. He is not one of the chorus—he does not stop for any regulation—he is the president of regulation. What the eyesight does to the rest, he does to the rest. Who knows the curious mystery of the eyesight? The other senses corroborate themselves, but this is removed from any proof but its own, and foreruns the identities of the spiritual world. A single glance of it mocks all the investigations of man, and all the instruments and books of the earth, and all reasoning. What is marvellous? what is unlikely? what is impossible or baseless or vague—after you have once just open'd the space of a peach-pit, and given audience to far and near, and to the sunset, and had all things enter with electric swiftness, softly and duly, without confusion or jostling or jam? (*pw* 438–39)

Whitman's presentation here involves several levels of physicality: the act of dilation is first described as a form of breath, followed by a comparison of the function of the poet with the general function of the eye in relation to the world; this metaphor of the eye is rendered even more physical in relation to the eye-shaped pit of a peach, which, once presented, immediately dilates to encompass all things "far and near," which enter poetic consciousness "with electric swiftness, softly and duly, without confusion or jostling or jam." The last word in this sequence may hide a sly double entendre, with its potential double meaning on the word *jam* as something stuck, as well as the *jam* made from peaches. Another crucial place where the poet presents dilation with bodily physicality is in the "Talbot Wilson" notebook's descriptions of food and eating:

I know the bread is ~~mine, I have not a~~ [deletion, illegible] ~~dime more~~ my bread, and ₍that on it must I dine and sup. ~~for the dime that bought it was my last.~~ I know ~~the~~ I may munch, ~~and never~~ and not grit my teeth against the laws of church or state. What is this then that balances itself upon my lips and wrestles ~~like~~ as with the knuckles of God, for every bite, I put between them, and if ~~I my~~ my belly is ~~the~~ victor, ~~it~~ my not will can't ~~not then~~ ~~so~~ ^even then be foiled, but follows the ~~crust~~ innocent food down ~~my throat~~ my throat and ~~is~~ makes it ~~like~~ ^turns it to fire and lead within me? — What [deletion, illegible] ^angry snake ~~that~~ hisses ~~hisses whistles softly~~ at my ear, ~~as saying deny your greed and this night your soul shall~~ O fool will you stuff your greed and starve your soul?

In this scene, which never made it into *Leaves of Grass*, Whitman describes something like the soul's conscience, which perches on his lips and follows his "food" into the stomach, turning "it to fire and lead" because the speaker is feeding the body, but not the soul. Ever the religious revisionist, Whitman toys with Christian ideas of communion and transubstantiation to critique a kind of deluded materialism that fails to acknowledge the spirit. The "Dilation" passage affirms the soul's hunger for limitless expansion and inclusivity; the draft above takes a negative approach to the same theme, depicting a speaker whose soul "wrestles ~~like~~ as with the knuckles of God" for that which is taken in by the body. Both passages portray the action of a hungry soul, one by way of rhapsodic celebration, the other by way of critical, moral allegory, and in both the soul's hunger is figured as an enfolding or ingesting of the world into the speaker's physical and spiritual horizons.

Elsewhere in the notebook the undesirable form of materialism critiqued in the previous passage is again framed in terms of eating and food, and here it takes on a decidedly political cast:

The dismal and measureless fool called a rich man, or ~~a~~ thriver, ~~What folks call a thriver or rich man is more likely~~ some dismal and measureless fool, who ~~leaves the fields~~ leaves untasted untouched ~~the~~ all the million [deletion, illegible] ~~part of~~ those countless and evenly[?] spread tables ~~tables spread~~ thick

~~with~~ in ~~the~~ immortal dishes, ~~every one~~ heaped with the meats and ~~thinks~~
~~h~~ drinks of God, and fancies himself smart because he tugs and sweats ~~in~~
~~the slush after~~ among cinders, and parings, and slush

Here the single meal portrayed in the "I know the bread" passage
becomes a banquet that remains "untasted ^{untouched}" by the "dismal
and measureless fool called a rich man." In some ways it is a familiar
lesson, criticizing how wealth blinds one to the spiritual feast that
surrounds us every day. This was a lesson that Thoreau tried to express
in *Walden*, Emerson in "Nature," and Whittier in "Snow-Bound:
A Winter Idyl," to mention just a few examples from Whitman's
milieu. The shallow materialism of the "fool called a rich man" is
impoverished beside the enlightened materialism of the poetic soul
that sees God's "immortal dishes" for what they are, a daily manifestation of the divine. Characteristically, however, Whitman has
rendered his lesson in more physical terms than his contemporaries
did. For Whitman it wasn't enough to merely become a "transparent
eyeball" before the wonders of nature; his poetic soul would devour
such wonders, ingesting and enfolding them in its limitless hunger
to dilate and include the world.

One of his mobile fragments of manuscript text, the "measureless
fool" appears elsewhere in the "Talbot Wilson" notebook in a passage that specifies more precisely the difference between spiritual
and capitalist modes of ingestion and enclosure:

The ~~measureless fool who fancies that~~ orthodox ~~who~~ proprietor says ~~t~~ This
is mine. I earned or received or paid for it, — and _^ by [deletion, illegible]
positive right of my own it[?] I will put ~~this~~ ^a fence around it, and keep ~~the~~ it
exclusively to myself

. . .

~~How can I be so~~ ^{that} dismal and measureless fool not to ~~understand~~ see the hourly lessons of [deletion, illegible] ~the one~ eternal law, ~which~ that he who would grab blessings to himself, ~and~ as by right, and deny others their equal chance — and will not share with them everything that he has

For Whitman the problem with "orthodox," materialist claims to reality is that such possession is exclusive, seeking to portion out and claim the world for oneself, and such exclusivity is not only elitist and restrictive in the sense that others cannot share in the world's wealth, but also spiritually restrictive because the soul's hunger is limitless. As the "Dilation" passage teaches us, the human soul will not "be filled and satisfied" even when it becomes a "god enfolding" the heavens; it "shall want ~more~ to go further still." Such complete inclusivity is impossible for the "dismal and measureless fool" because "orthodox" ownership can be only partial — one can never personally possess everything — and this undesirable form of inclusivity seeks to exclude others from what it believes it purchases, frustrating both its own and others' need to become a "god enfolding" its world. Likewise on the first surviving page of Whitman's writing in this notebook he describes "True noble expanded American character" as "accept[ing] nothing except what is equally free and eligible to every body else," and in the preface to the 1855 *Leaves* he writes, "The American bards shall be marked for generosity and affection and for encouraging competitors . . They shall be kosmos . . without monopoly or secresy . . glad to pass any thing to any one" (*PW* 446). In these kinds of passages Whitman's early politics, with its Locofoco emphasis on egalitarianism, comes together with his developing ideas of dilation and spiritual expansion.

Not surprisingly Whitman elsewhere specifies that such inclusivity relates not only to that which is conventionally regarded as good and beautiful, but also to the ugly and distorted. As in the passage just cited, he uses the image of a fence to describe spiritual enclosure. Here, however, his trope of dilation assumes a slightly different cast. In a passage that immediately precedes the "Dilation" passage he writes, "The universal and fluid soul impounds within itself not only all the good characters and heros but the distorted characters, murderers, thieves." Once again we have a description of spiritual expansion and inclusion; however, it is noteworthy that when the poet's soul is enfolding the stars, it is described as an act of dilation, but when it includes within itself "distorted characters, murderers, thieves" it engages in an act of "impounding." Today the verb *impound* is almost always understood pejoratively, as in having one's car impounded for illegal parking, and contemporary readers might assume that Whitman intended such a definition for this passage. But this definition presents an interpretation that is at odds with how Whitman otherwise describes the soul's relation with wicked or nefarious characters, a relation that is consistently affirmative and untroubled. After all, this is the poet who in "Song of Myself" proclaimed himself "not the poet of goodness only" and stated, "I do not decline to be the poet of wickedness also." Two lines below this he writes, "Evil propels me and reform of evil propels me, I stand indifferent" (LG 50). Given this attitude, why would it be necessary for him to *impound* "distorted characters, murderers, thieves"? And given that for Whitman the act of dilation is a desirable state of limitless spiritual expansion, one he advocates for all (including the wicked), why would the great "universal and fluid soul" engage in such a restrictive act to begin with?

The answer lies in how the meaning of the word has evolved. The verb *impound* seems to have had two dominant meanings in Whitman's time, the more common of which was positive in connotation and has by now faded from popular use. In addition to the word's contemporary definition as "to seize or secure by legal right," *to impound* was understood in terms of animal husbandry, where it was used to mean "to shut up (cattle) in an enclosure."[23] Although such enclosure was sometimes undertaken for legal reasons — and in this sense the word's meaning was similar to its contemporary use in reference to cars and other property — its more common usage was positive and indicative of healthy care for horses or livestock. The dictionary Whitman owned and likely used while composing his early poems, *The Original Webster's Unabridged Dictionary*, defines *impound* primarily as "to put, shut, or confine, in a pound or close pen; as, to impound unruly or stray horses, cattle, &c." Surely the poet had this definition in mind when he used the word in his description of spiritual dilation. Taken this way the passage presents the speaker more as a shepherd than a policeman; so viewed in its historical context, the line represents an instance of Whitman's religious revisionism, as he appropriates Christian imagery and themes to convey his own, more radical perspective. Like so much else in his writing, however, the line also allows for a more conventional interpretation if understood in the sense of "locking up" the evil represented by "murders" and "thieves," as the soul "apprehends" (both in the sense of "understanding and taking in" and in the sense of "catching" the "thieves") the world.

The theme of the soul's ingestion of the world is everywhere in the "Talbot Wilson" notebook, from the more realized scenes, such as those just described, to the particular details of scenes and images that are tangentially related to the idea. Sometimes Whitman's use of such details reveals his notion of dilation forming a bridge to other important concepts:

~~Shall we never see a being~~ Why can we not see ~~men~~ beings who by the ~~majesty~~ manliness and transparence of their natures, disarm~~s all criticism and~~ the

~~rest of the~~ entire world, and brings ~~them~~ one and all to his side, as friends and believers? — ~~W Are we never to~~ Can no father ~~and~~ beget or mother conceive ~~I would see that~~ a man child so entire and so elastic ~~tha and so free from all discords,~~ that whatever action he do or whatever syllable he ~~utt~~speak, it shall be melodious to all ~~men~~ creatures, and none shall be an exception to the universal and affectionate yes of the earth.

Without understanding the poet's preoccupation with the concept elsewhere in the notebook, this passage's relation to dilation might not be clear. It seems to be one of Whitman's many quasi-eugenic exhortations to bear a new and more evolved race, progeny who can realize his vision for humanity. Specifically Whitman asks for the idealized poet-interpreter figure apparent elsewhere in his early poetry who can be understood universally and who can unite and lead humanity. The "man child" described here is the same child described in his earliest *Leaves of Grass* notebooks, such as the "Med Cophōsis" fragment, where he first drafted the opening lines to the poem eventually titled "There Was a Child Went Forth," the published poem that most directly presents this concern. Here in the "Talbot Wilson" notebook this child is described as being empowered toward universal poetic utterance by his capacity for dilation: "a man child so entire and so elastic ~~tha and so free from all discords,~~ that whatever action he do or whatever syllable he ~~utt~~speak, it shall be melodious to all." Whitman's strange choice of adjectives to describe the poet-child, "so entire and so elastic," reveals his preoccupation with dilation and shows that here at least the elastic capacity for dilation, for including all within oneself, is the specific quality needed to produce the common language of fraternity.

Although the reference would be lost on most readers today, Whitman had a precedent for relating the word *dilation* to ideas of poetic speech. A connoisseur of dictionaries and himself an amateur lexicographer, he was likely aware of less common definitions of words that preoccupied him as intensely as the word *dilation*. Indeed early in his career he began making notes for a personal dictionary, which has survived in the Harned Collection of the Library of Congress and which demonstrates a deep and abiding interest in etymology.[24] So although the dictionary he most likely used when composing the first poems of *Leaves,* Noah Webster's American Dictionary of the English Language, does not contain this particular definition, it is reasonable to assume that he was familiar with an older usage of the word, which the Oxford English Dictionary defines as "to relate, describe, or set forth at length; to enlarge or expatiate upon." Although this definition is now considered obsolete, it was still in use during Whitman's time and was employed by authors with whom he was certainly familiar, including Charles Dickens, who is cited by the OED as an example of this usage.[25] The OED also includes a similar definition for the word's noun form, though here the reference is to a variant and now seldom used synonym, *dilatation*: "The action or practice of dilating upon a subject in speech or writing; amplification, enlargement, diffuse treatment." This understanding of *dilation* casts fresh light on Whitman's use of the term in such noted writings as the prose passage from "Talbot Wilson" to which he gave that title. Indeed this definition makes just as much sense in reference to that passage as does the word's use as a spiritual and physiological metaphor. Whitman's "child so entire and so elastic" that "whatever syllable he uttspeak, it shall be melodious to all" could be crudely translated as a "child so capable of dilation that he can dilate upon any subject and be understood."

With this in mind we can see how this passage links dilation to another of Whitman's most deeply considered spinal ideas: the concept of a personal spiritual idiom, a language of the individual soul. Elsewhere in the "Talbot Wilson" notebook he writes:

> Every soul has its own individual language, often unspoken, or lamely feebly ~~haltingly~~ spoken; but a ~~perfect~~ true fit for ~~[deletion, illegible]~~ that ~~a and~~ man, and perfectly adapted ~~for~~ to his use. — The truths I tell, you or any other, may not be ~~apparent~~ plain to you, ~~or that other,~~ because I do not translate them ~~well~~ right fully from my idiom into yours. — If I could do so, and do it well, they would be as apparent to you as they are to me; for they are ~~eternal~~ truths. — No two have exactly the same language, ~~but~~ and the great translator and joiner of ~~all~~ the whole is the poet

This passage has been highlighted by one of Whitman's more skeptical readers, Esther Shephard, who insisted that it was paraphrased from an 1847 translation of George Sand's *The Countess of Rudolstadt* and who uses this contention as the basis for her extended argument that Whitman's spiritual outlook is a pose derived from his reading, not the result of lived experience.[26] Similarities do exist between Sand's passage and Whitman's, and because subsequent scholars followed Shephard's lead, including Edward F. Grier (who refers approvingly to Shephard's argument in his notes to his transcription of the notebook in *Notebooks and Unpublished Prose Manuscripts*), the notion that Whitman stole this idea has become a critical commonplace. Yet a more comprehensive look at the notebook suggests otherwise, as we find Whitman working through the concept in repeated drafts, struggling to come to terms with it and relating it to other ideas important to him, such as his trope of dilation. For example, on the notebook page immediately preceding the aforementioned quote he writes, "Every soul has its own language, The reason why any truth [deletion, illegible] which I tell is not apparent to you, is mostly because I fail of translating it from my language into" — and then the

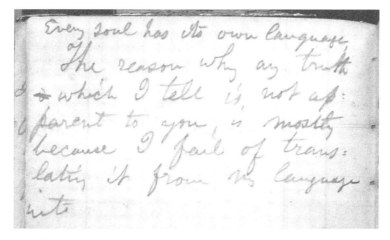

FIG 19. "Every soul has its own language" manuscript. Charles Feinberg Collection of Walt Whitman, Manuscript Division, Library of Congress, Washington DC (loc.00141.036).

thought is abruptly cut off, only to resume in extended form on the next page. A look at the actual manuscript leaf shows that he began with the phrase "The reason why any truth" and then added "Every soul has its own language" in the page's top margin (see figure 19). It seems improbable that Whitman would struggle in this way if he were merely paraphrasing Sand. What the notebook seems to reveal instead is a poet working to formulate something for the first time and revising it into a more finished and acceptable form, a possibility strengthened by the fact that, as we have seen, Whitman relates this idea to the "dilation" of a poet-child "so elastic" that "whatever action he do or whatever syllable he ~~utt~~speak, it shall be melodious to all," which would seem to demonstrate an abiding interest in the topic that goes beyond mere paraphrase. It is possible that he came upon the first inkling of his concept of an individual language for each soul by way of Sand; however, the evidence is hardly conclusive, and the notebook as a whole indicates a coincidental relation in which the poet was probably struck by the Sand passage because it reflected an idea that had already preoccupied him.

The problem of communication between souls, each speaking its "own individual language," obsessed Whitman during this phase of his composition of *Leaves*. The idea of a poetry that "speaks to the soul" is a rather trite cliché in our presumptively post-Romantic worldview, but for a poet of Whitman's grand ambitions in the years leading up to 1855 it was a tangible dilemma. If each individual's soul is subjectively and idiosyncratically expressive — a proposition that suggests a Babel of spiritual idioms — then there would seem to be no easy resolution for the poet who would be universally understood. Early in the notebook Whitman considers the problem from the audience's point of view: "A man only is interested in any thing when he identifies himself with it." To "identify" with something is not necessarily to dilate and spiritually ingest it, and considered in isolation this thought doesn't relate closely enough to dilation to reveal any specific intentions. In another pre-1855 notebook, however, Whitman is more explicit: "No one can realise anything unless he *has it in him* . . . . or has been it" (italics mine).[27] The idea of becoming that which one perceives was crucial to the Whitman of the early 1850s, and he presents the concept explicitly in the tenth poem of the first edition of *Leaves,* later titled "There Was a Child Went Forth":

There was a child went forth every day,
And the first item he looked upon and received with wonder or pity or love or dread, that object he became,
And that object became part of him for a day or a certain part of the day . . . . or for many years or stretching cycles of years.

As we have already seen, he was working out his concept of this child elsewhere in this notebook, and both the phrasing in that passage, "so entire and so elastic," and in the one just cited, "unless he has it in him . . . . or has been it," reveal how these ideas relate: to perceive something in the way Whitman envisions is to identify with and "realise" that thing (or, as he phrases it here, to become it). Once one has experienced this perceiving or becoming, the object of one's attention becomes a part of one, is *within* one. This, Whitman's notebook writings suggest, is the process of dilation, and only when the poet dilates to become "so entire and so elastic" that he contains his world does "whatever action he do or whatever syllable he ~~utt~~speak" become "melodious to all ~~men~~ creatures." It is, however, a reciprocal process, for as he also notes, "A man only is interested in any thing when he identifies himself with it." For the communion of souls Whitman envisions to be complete, not only must the poet dilate to include the reader, but the reader too must dilate to become and include the poet: only then will the true idiom of "souls" be understood.

"Song of Myself" begins with the assumption that the speaker has already experienced the kind of complete inclusion and becoming that the soul requires, and the work the poem would achieve is to help its audience become and include that which it names (or, put another way, to "assume" what the poet "assumes," beginning with the poet himself). If we take seriously Whitman's comments in these early notebooks, this kind of dilation to include the world would be a prerequisite to read this work in the way that is required. Thus his emphasis on mutual identification in the opening lines of "Song of Myself": "what I assume you shall assume, / For every atom belonging to me as good belongs to you." Sometime during the complicated process of his creation of the first *Leaves of Grass* poems he developed a special meaning for a word that would describe someone who had expanded to include and realize the world within him or her, much as he had with the word *dilation* as a reference for this overall process. For Whitman this evolved, inclusive individual was called a "kosmos," as in the famous line "Walt Whitman, an American, one of the roughs, a kosmos."[28]

Another key spinal idea, Whitman's kosmos beings were the spiritual and poetic progeny he imagined creating, the prophesied result that would fulfill the promise of his *Leaves*. It was a term Whitman used with such strange insistence and implied specificity that he was mocked for it by some of his early readers, such as Charles Eliot Norton, whose 1855 review wittily chided him about the line just cited: "That he was one of the roughs was . . . tolerably plain; but that he was a kosmos, is a piece of news we were hardly prepared for. Precisely what a kosmos is, we trust Mr. Whitman will take an early occasion to inform the impatient public."[29] Whitman did indeed "inform the impatient public" what this word meant for him in an 1860 poem that reads as such a direct and literal act of definition that it could be a personal response to Norton:

KOSMOS.

Who includes diversity and is Nature,
Who is the amplitude of the earth, and the coarseness and sexuality of
    the earth, and the great charity of the earth, and the equilibrium also,
Who has not looked forth from the windows, the eyes, for nothing, or
    whose brain held audience with messengers for nothing;
Who contains believers and disbelievers—Who is the most majestic lover;
Who holds duly his or her triune proportion of realism, spiritualism,
    and of the æsthetic, or intellectual,
Who, having considered the body, finds all its organs and parts good;

> Who, out of the theory of the earth, and of his or her body, understands
> by subtle analogies, the theory of a city, a poem, and of the large
> politics of These States;
> Who believes not only in our globe, with its sun and moon, but in
> other globes, with their suns and moons;
> Who, constructing the house of himself of herself, not for a day, but for
> all time, Sees races, eras, dates, generations,
> The past, the future, dwelling there, like space, inseparable together.

Although it contains a number of superfluous flourishes ("Who is the most majestic lover"), this poem presents essentially the same definition of the word that he was working with when composing his pre-1855 poems and that is suggested in the poem's first line, "Who includes diversity and is Nature." The poem's conclusion sheds further light on Whitman's vision of kosmos and dilation, suggesting, through his choice of the present-progressive "constructing," that the process of becoming kosmos is a sustained, self-conscious activity. His use of the metaphor of a "house of himself" echoes the phrase "Song of Myself" and may relate to his early unpublished poem "Pictures" (which represents perhaps his first sustained interest in the catalog style of presentation), in which he compares his brain to a house (or gallery) populated by myriad images traversing space and time.

Long before the 1860 "Kosmos" poem he defined the term explicitly in his "Words" notebook, demonstrating that he was using the word with care and specificity in his 1855 references in *Leaves*: "Kosmos, noun masculine or feminine, a person who[se] scope of mind, or whose range in a particular science, includes all, the whole known universe" (*DBN* 3:369).[30] We can be relatively certain that this particular definition is Whitman's own, for there is no known precedent for his application of the word to refer to an individual human being, though there is a precedent for his unusual spelling. The Oxford English Dictionary cites *kosmos* as an alternate of *cosmos* and reveals that the word's meaning has remained consistent with today's definition as "the world or universe as an ordered and harmonious system."[31] Whitman, who may have first come upon the word *kosmos* in his readings of the German Idealists and their contemporary Anglophone popularizers, seems simply to have taken the conventional definition and applied it to people — or his idea of people — who had dilated to include the cosmos as the word was conventionally understood.[32] He describes his vision of kosmos poets repeatedly in the 1855 preface, employing the phrase three times in this capacity, beginning with his claim, "The American bards shall be marked for generosity and affection and for encouraging competitors . . They shall be kosmos . . without monopoly or secrecy . . glad to pass any thing to any one . . hungry for equals night and day" (*PW* 15). As with the "orthodox proprietor" passage described previously, this passage links Whitman's spinal ideas about dilation and ownership, but here it is the hoarding of poetic riches that is declaimed. The implication is that his poetic progeny, like Whitman himself, will not monopolize their poetic gifts through private or esoteric acts, but instead will create a poetry that is of use to others, even (or especially) their poetic competition. As his notebook writings indicate, this is the only attitude toward poetry possible for the poets he envisions, poets who have dilated to include, identify with, and realize others so that they can speak to them, soul to soul, and encourage their own audiences to do the same, extending the cycle in perpetuity.

Consistent with his overall emphasis on orality and physicality, the dilation that Whitman and his poetic kin would deliver arrives by way of the mouth, not the pen. Also from the Preface, he envisions this for the kosmos-poet's role: "The greatest poet hardly knows pettiness or triviality. If he breathes into anything that was before thought small, it dilates with the grandeur and life of the universe" (PW 438). This in itself is not an unusual apologia for literary greatness. The statement echoes the conventional Romantic attitude toward the function of poetic imagination as an instrument for perceptual amplitude. Returning to the "Talbot Wilson" notebook, however, we find the trope of dilation through poetic "breath" worked out in startling fashion. In two places in the notebook Whitman drafts separate versions of what would become lines 1008–20 of the first poem of the 1855 *Leaves*. Here is the initial, aggressively revised version:

> I am the poet of ~~s~~Strength
>   and Hope
> ~~Swiftly pass I~~
> Where is the house of
>   any one dying?
> Thither I speed and ~~raise~~
>   turn the knob of the door,
> ~~Let~~ ~~And Let~~ ~~t~~The physician and the
>   priest ~~stand aside,~~ timidly withdraw,
>   That I seize on the ~~despairer~~ ghastly man
>   and raise him with
>   resistless will,
> O ~~ghastly man~~ despairer! ~~you~~
>   ~~shall~~ I say tell you, ~~you~~
>   shall not ~~die~~ go down,
> Here is my ~~hand,~~ arm ~~sick~~
>   press your whole
>   weight upon me,

[page break]

~~In my~~ ~~Lo!~~ with O With tremendous ~~will~~ breath,

    I force him to dilate,

~~I will not~~

~~Doubt and fear~~

~~With Treading~~

~~Baffling doubt and~~

~~I will~~

~~Doubt shall not~~

Sleep! for I and they

    stand guard

    this night,

And when you rise

    in the morning you

    find ~~that I told~~ the[e?] what I told you is so.

In this remarkable passage Whitman conflates physical and spiritual health to vigorously present himself as a kind of doctor for the sick soul. He frames the scene as metaphor with his opening claim, indicating that what follows will illustrate him to be "the poet of strength and hope," yet as the metaphor realizes itself with such purpose and immediacy, the physicality of the scene asserts itself and nearly displaces its metaphoric relation. Many are familiar with this passage from its published version in "Song of Myself," where the essential components are preserved and the speaker "dilates" the patient with "tremendous breath." Contemporary readers unfamiliar with Whitman's nuanced development of the concept of dilation might naturally interpret the images of his breathing into a dying man as a depiction of mouth-to-mouth resuscitation. However, mouth-to-mouth resuscitation was not practiced when he drafted these lines, for at the time doctors believed that there wasn't enough oxygen in exhaled air to support life.[33]

If Whitman wasn't thinking of mouth-to-mouth resuscitation when he wrote this passage, what was he imagining? It's possible that he may have been envisioning what was then considered the medically unsound biblical practice of something similar to mouth-to-mouth resuscitation from the Book of Kings (II, 4:34), where Elisha revives a dead boy by warming his body and "placing his mouth over his." Or he may have been creating a metaphor that wasn't intended to depict a recognized practice at all, but simply a physical gesture embodying his notion of dilation as the poet's invigorating act, similar to his claim in the preface that if "he breathes into anything that was before thought small, it dilates with the grandeur and life of the universe" (PW 438). Such a reading is strengthened by the fact that Whitman first described dilating his patient with force of "will," which was later overstruck and changed to the physical "breath," suggesting that the image of the poet breathing into the patient was an afterthought to his overall designs. Even if Whitman's physical gesture here is not meant to portray any particular known act or practice, readers are left with some lingering questions: Who exactly is this "ghastly man," and even more puzzling, who or what are the "they" that suddenly appear toward the end, and why would they need to "guard" the dilated patient?

A broader look at its place in the notebook helps to illuminate some of these issues. On the leaf immediately preceding the one just cited Whitman drafted these lines:

I am the poet of the body
And I am the poet of the soul
~~The~~ I go with the slaves ~of the earth ~equally with the ~~are mine, and~~
    the masters ~~are equally mine~~

And I will stand between
    the masters and the slaves
~~And I~~ eEntering into both, ~~and~~
      so that both shall understand
      me alike.

Previous readers have noted the audacity of Whitman's claim in this passage to "stand between the masters and the slaves."[34] Equally audacious is the subtle cogency of his theory of dilation, kosmos, and poetic speech being realized in his description of "Entering into both" master and slave "so that both shall understand" him. As we have seen, Whitman's theory of the idiom of souls hinges on his belief that "No one can realise anything unless he has it in him . . . . or has been it." Thus the true kosmos poet must not only dilate to include the world but also enter into his audience so that they too shall dilate and "realise" him, assuming what he claims to assume, which is nothing less than the totality of being. Whitman's use of anaphora in the repeated "I am the poet" construction connects this with the passage that begins "I am the poet of sStrength and Hope." Indeed this deathbed scene is revealed to be a direct continuation of the masters and slaves passage, for here Whitman explicitly "enters into" the "ghastly man" to dilate him "With tremendous ~~will~~ breath." Whitman's patient, then, seems to be a runaway slave, hounded toward his physical grave as well as his soul's despair, but saved by the poet, whose breath is life. This would explain why the speaker promised to "stand guard" over him, protecting him from capture while he rests. Seen in this light, the draft on these leaves presents a cogent sequence in which the poet first claims that he is a poet capable of "entering into" slaves and then presents a scene in which he does so, transforming the gesture into a metaphor for physical and spiritual healing.

Later in the notebook he revised the passage, making the relation between characters in the scene clearer by replacing the anonymous "they" with "armed men":

> I dilate you with tremendous
>   breath, [deletion, illegible]
> I buoy you up,
> Every room of your house do
>   I fill with armed men
> Lovers of me, bafflers of hell,
> Sleep! for I and they staynd
>   guard ~~all~~ this night
> Not doubt, not fear, not
>   Death shall lay finger
>   upon you

In these drafts Whitman gives dramatic body to his claim to "enter into" the slave, but what of the master he also promised to "enter into"? Has that claim been dropped, knowing as Whitman did that both his immediate audience in the North and his projected, spiritually realized audience of the future would find the poet's assumption of the role of master repugnant? And from a dramatic standpoint, how can the speaker assume the position of the master from whom the slave flees, even as he promises to "stand guard" over him?

In a savvy move Whitman indeed enters into the master in this revision's next two lines, transforming the role of slave master into that of a loving God:

~~God and~~ I have ˄embraced you, and
    henceforth possess you
    all to ~~our~~myselves,
And when you rise in the
    morning you shall find it
    is so.

Although edited out, we can see that Whitman initially drafted this passage so that it equated his own role with that of a greater "master," who, having "embraced" the runaway slave/patient, is described as the slave's new owner, one who "possesses" the slave "all to [himself]." Yet this form of possession is far different from that of a southern slaveholder. Immediately following the preceding passage Whitman positions himself as a master who dilates and heals the slave/patient and then stands guard with "armed men" to protect him from those who would return the slave to an oppressed condition. He is a master who would "buoy up" the downtrodden rather than maintain subjugation. Further he enters into the role of master by way of physical intimacy: first inviting the slave to "press [his] whole weight upon [him]," then breathing into him and dilating him, and finally embracing him. The romantic association of possession with the beloved was surely not far from Whitman's mind as he fulfills his promise to enter into both master and slave so that he might be understood by both. Thus by disassociating the master's role from that of oppressor (and possessor) to that of lover, healer, and caretaker the poet rescues a form of masterly being that is amenable to his poetic conception. For Whitman the southern slave master could be "master" in name only, since he was the ultimate possessor, one who worked on the assumption that humans could be owned, could be one's personal property, an idea that is the very antithesis of dilation. By entering into the master, Whitman dilates the very notion of "master." In retrospect the passage assumes an aura of ironic prophecy, since Whitman went on to play a similar role, "buoying up" countless dying soldiers and playing the roles of both doctor and priest in the hospitals of the Civil War. That he could not have known he would ever do so when he wrote these lines renders them that much more remarkable.

With this extensive notebook background in mind we can better understand Whitman's most prominent use of his spinal idea of dilation in the first *Leaves of Grass*. Early in its opening poem he offers this rather cryptic tercet:

> I chant a new chant of dilation or pride,
> We have had ducking and deprecating about enough,
> I show that size is only development.

This key statement occurs in one of the crucial moments of the poem, following five lines after one of his most famous assertions (which was also drafted in the "Talbot Wilson" notebook), "I am the poet of the body, / And I am the poet of the soul." Yet the passage has not received much critical attention, and the only sustained analysis of it is from a brief 1974 essay by P. Z. Rosenthal, who offers a semantic analysis of Whitman's terms that emphasizes his struggle to find "new potentialities of speech," as Whitman put it.[35] Rosenthal doesn't get very far in his assessment, concluding that Whitman "takes words that describe the physical world and re-defines them so that they dramatize the possibilities of the human soul."[36] Our exploration of the poet's nuanced development of this spinal idea and its co-relations allows us to go further. His "chant of dilation" is of course *Leaves of Grass*, especially the immediate poem that he eventually titled "Song of Myself." It is a "chant of dilation" because that is the effect Whitman intended for his audience: to be dilated by their engagement with his poems so that they may include others in themselves, realizing them in sympathy and understanding. Doing so his audience becomes kosmos, spiritually evolved beings capable of speaking soul to soul with humanity. Thus Whitman's "chant of dilation" posits a new spiritual idiom, assertive and transformative, that is the vehicle by which he must be understood.

This passage contributes a new element to our understanding of the process, for it is not just a "chant of dilation" but of "dilation *or* pride" (italics mine). This locution implies that "pride" is not something he chants *in addition* to dilation, but rather that his song is of something that can be one or the other. "Pride" does not supplement dilation; it is an alternative form of its presentation. A consistent joiner of what are conventionally conceived as disparate elements, Whitman conflates two seemingly unrelated terms, forcing us to come to grips with his special definition not only of dilation but, apparently, of pride as well. The challenge is complicated by conventional understandings of pride, which usually associate it with a narrow egotism. Like his view of egotism, however, his conception of pride is expansive, not contractive, as is suggested by a phrase from the second poem of the first edition of *Leaves*: "the endless pride and outstretching of man."[37] This view of pride is reinforced by a phrase from the fifth poem of the first edition: "the fullspread pride of man."[38] Nevertheless this concept of pride only partially helps us to see what the poet had in mind by conflating the term with dilation.

Again the notebooks and manuscript fragments offer assistance. In this fascinating single-leaf manuscript Whitman outlines a meta-physical purview in which "dilation or pride" occupies an even more prominent position than as a descriptor of his flagship poem in the phrase "chant of dilation or pride":[39]

My ~~Soul~~ ˰Spirit ~~was [illegible] back to the~~

    sped [illegible] ˰back to the [insert below:] ~~beginning~~

    times when the earth was forming mist

[inserted below, among the lines] the aft forming the mist

And peered ~~beyond~~ aft, and could see Concord beyond

    the beginning;

And brings ~~me~~ word that ~~Goodness is the~~ Dilation or Pride ~~is a~~

    ~~perpetual Mother~~ father of Causes,

And ~~that the Father~~ a Mother of Causes is ~~Love~~ ~~Dilation~~

    Goodness or Love. — or ~~Pride~~.

And ~~the~~ ˰that[illegible] they are the Parents ˰yet and witness and

    register their [~~illegible~~] amours eternally;

And devise themselves to ~~this~~ [illegible] These States and this hour.

And Again ~~But yet still~~ my ~~Soul~~ Spirit was curious and travelled ahead

And pierced the ~~black~~ stern firm hem of ~~darkness~~ life, ~~death~~ and went

    fearlessly through,

And came back from the grave with serene face,

And said ~~to me~~, It is well I am satisfied,

I behold the causes yet [illegible] ~~the same that are eternally fresh~~ —

I beheld Love also in the ~~darkness~~,

I beheld ~~Goodness~~ ˰~~Dilation Pride~~ Dilation just the same ~~in the grave~~ after-

    ward —. and concord ~~just the same in the grave~~ afterward. —

I behold Love also in the darkness.

Here Whitman describes his spirit's journey to the beginning of the universe and then to what lies after death, where it beholds the primeval forces of creation: the "father of causes" and "mother of causes," who "witness and register their amours eternally." As with the passage just discussed, "Dilation" and "Pride" are presented interchangeably, as alternative words for the same cosmic force. In this passage, however, we are also presented with the complementary opposite of "Dilation or Pride": "Goodness or Love," another conflation of terms, which here is posited as the "mother of causes," presenting a kind of dual creative God. This ontological dynamic offers crucial clues to Whitman's understanding of underlying creative principles. Subverting Judeo-Christian formulations of a singular and paternal creator, he presents God as a family as opposed to an individual. Because, as the original manuscript image shows, the poet struggled with the question of precisely which force, "Dilation or Pride" or "Goodness or Love," to present as father and which as mother, the specific gender of each side of the equation seems less important than the effort to present them as harmonious coequals. Either "Dilation or Pride" or "Goodness or Love" could have been mother or father of creation. What seems important is the effort to present the godhead not as the all-male, patrilineal cast of Father, Son, and Holy Ghost, but as an eternal and loving embodiment of both masculine and feminine creative principles.

The idea of goodness and love as interchangeable forces is less difficult to reconcile than Whitman's presentation of "dilation or pride," and this may help us to understand what he had in mind by joining these two seemingly disparate terms. That goodness and love are essentially the same is a conventional notion, reflecting the belief that love is the force behind good acts and deeds; the love of a mother for a child, for example, is intrinsically regarded as good, just as God's love for man is seen as the source of human goodness in Judeo-Christian traditions. It is a basic humanistic understanding to regard love as the source of all that is good, and by presenting dilation and pride in this same manner Whitman capitalizes on this fundamental belief and invites us to regard these forces similarly.

Part of the challenge in doing so, however, relates to the fact that in conventional understanding pride is regarded negatively. Pride, after all, is the first of the deadly sins and is often said to be the sin from which all others arise. Whitman's conflation of dilation and pride is a part of his ongoing effort to rescue pride as a positive and essential value in his new American cosmology. He distinguishes an expansive understanding of pride from a narrow one that we might equate with mere vanity. Both pride and vanity are expressions of self-love, and whereas his Christian contemporaries held both to be constrictive, isolating the individual from a proper recognition of the grace of God, Whitman positioned a healthy form of self-love as the foundation of creation itself, as well as humanity's necessary attitude toward it. By loving ourselves we reflect the love that created us and grow closer to that divine creation, becoming expansive in our knowledge that to love ourselves is to love God because we are in fact a part of God. Pride for Whitman is interchangeable with the idea of spiritual expansion, because it is through a correct understanding of self-love — through "celebrating ourselves" — that we can begin to include others within us, allowing for a more direct and loving intercourse that is the origin of true poetic utterance and the kosmos engendered by it.

The passage just discussed was never used directly in *Leaves of Grass*. Perhaps Whitman, poet of "faint clues," obliquity, and necessary textual wrestlings, came to regard his metaphysical presentation as too explicit. He did, however, revise and greatly condense this passage in another notebook, where it is reduced to this formulation: "There are two ~~attributes~~ ? of the soul, and both are illimitable, and they are its north latitude and its south latitude. — One of these is Love. The other is Dilation or Pride." As with the previously discussed manuscript, Whitman again presents a dualistic divine principle, which posits "Dilation or Pride" as a complementary attribute to "Love" (though in this second passage he does not conflate love with "Goodness"). Whereas the first manuscript emphasizes a cosmic creative principle, the second emphasizes its outcome in the human soul. The poet's allegorical drama, in which his spirit journeys to the beginning and ending of life, is replaced with a more direct assertion. But though more straightforward in its presentation this second passage is actually less explicit in meaning, as there is less context present to illustrate what the poet had in mind. It is this stripped-down rendition of his cosmic principle that Whitman felt comfortable publishing in 1860 as a line in the fourth of his "Chants Democratic" (later titled "Our Old Feuillage"): "Encircling all, vast-darting, up and wide, the American soul, with equal hemispheres — one Love, one Dilation or Pride."

Through this extended analysis of Whitman's development of some of his crucial spinal ideas we can better understand not only the local meaning of some of his most important published lines, but also his creative process and the imaginative workings behind it. As the notebooks demonstrate, Whitman seems to have developed his spinal ideas in isolation from one another, but when put to use they spawned immediate relations, suggesting a cohesive underlying vision of the world. When we compare seemingly disparate concepts from the notebooks — such as his ideas of kosmos, dilation, and the language of souls — we discover a network of associations binding the ideas together and enriching them through their interplay. Specific scenes from poems, such as the sickroom passage that would become lines 1008–20 of the first poem of the 1855 *Leaves,* reveal important subtexts lost in their final presentation, such as the fact that the patient in this scene was, at least in its original form, a runaway slave. The notebooks also demonstrate that the significance of such underlying details can be easily misunderstood, since the poet's choice of representing a slave and a master in this passage seems less important to him politically or ethically than portraying the range of humanity he is capable of dilating to include.

The spinal ideas I have examined have in common their involvement in the poet's ongoing struggle to come to terms with (and to find terms for) a consistent spiritual cosmology that obsessed him throughout the mid- to late 1850s. Whitman's linguistic wrestlings — bending words toward references that they did not previously signify — suggest that his spiritual vision was less derivative than has often been thought. There is little in the notebooks to suggest that he paraphrased these ideas from others, such as Emerson, Sand, or the German Idealists. After all, if his spinal ideas were derivative, why would he need to work his way toward a new vocabulary for their expression? A new style, as opposed to lexicon, would suffice for such an enterprise. My exploration validates Whitman's assertion from *An American Primer*:

> Of words wanted, the matter is summed up in this: when the time comes for them to represent any thing or state of things, the words will surely follow. The lack of any words, I say again, is as historical as the existence of words. As for me, I feel a hundred realities, clearly determined in me, that words are not yet formed to represent.

Whitman clearly saw himself as the catalyst for the poetic realization of these hitherto wordless realities, and perhaps this is what he had in mind many years later when he referred to *Leaves of Grass* as "only a language experiment." Viewed in this light the passage above seems as much an ars poetica as part of a linguistic inquiry, and the poet's spinal ideas are revealed not only as the gravitational centers of his poems, but also as limbo spaces in the evolution of wordless realities into worldly (and worded) art.

4

Poems of Materials

In July 1855 two events occurred that must have profoundly affected Walt Whitman: in the beginning of the month the first edition of *Leaves of Grass* was made available to the public, and only a week or so later his father succumbed to a prolonged, debilitating illness, passing away in his home on July 11.[1] Whitman spoke little about his father's death, and we can only speculate about how it must have affected him. In fact there is not a single mention of his father in the notes that survive from this period. What we find instead is a poet intensely preoccupied with his fledgling book. Previously Whitman seems to have worked wholly without recourse to other readers, and the responses he began receiving in July 1855, first in the famous letter from Emerson and days later from the first of his early reviewers, Charles A. Dana, contributed to an obsessive self-consciousness toward his own artistic production. Lacking the stability of a book to contain his ideas, he had previously worked intuitively, cobbling together the scattershot materials that would compose the first edition with only the most fluid of notions of what it would add up to and how it would all fit together. Now, with the tangible reality of a book in hand, his critical attention began to shift from abstract conceptions of the figure of "the poet" to more concrete assessments of his actual poetic product.

As Whitman grew more self-conscious of his literary output, his writing technique began to evolve in significant ways. As we have seen, much of the text comprising the poems of the first *Leaves of Grass* already existed in various forms before Whitman discovered his signature line and began to collage this text together to form his first major works. These poems frequently reversed the conventional relationship between conception and composition: the language in these poems often existed long before the conceptions that shaped their published forms were discovered. In subsequent poems Whitman continued to implement previously existing language in his new poetic concepts, but increasingly he began to develop these "spinal ideas" in anticipation of the language that would embody them. This evolving approach toward his creative process, combined with the confidence he gained from Emerson's enthusiastic response, led, in the best of his new work, to a focus and cogency not found in the grand sprawl of "I celebrate myself."[2] At the same time as his creative method became more focused, his concepts for poems grew more diverse and numerous. His notes from the years just after the publication of the first *Leaves* reveal a poet bursting with spinal ideas, only a small number of which he seems to have followed up on. In just a single notebook from this period he uses his titling convention from the second edition of *Leaves* to describe more than a dozen nascent spinal concepts, including a "Poem of Prophecies," a "Poem of (after death)," a "Poem of Wise Books," a "Poem of American Names," and a "poem of the ~~Indians~~ aborigines," to name only a few examples.[3]

These spinal concepts seem to be notes for individual poems, but Whitman also made plans for new sequences of poems and other major projects, such as the one suggested by this manuscript fragment:

The Great Construction of the New Bible

Not to be diverted from the principal object — the main life work — the Three Hundred & Sixty five — (it ought to be ready in 1859. — (June '57)

This note is perhaps Whitman's most critically remarked upon unpublished statement from the years immediately following the publication of the first edition. It is a central piece of evidence in discussions that describe *Leaves of Grass* (especially its 1860 edition) as Whitman's effort to create a new American Bible. He seems to be exhorting himself to remain dutifully focused on expanding *Leaves* into a work patterned after the calendar, with a poem for each day, a structure echoing lectionary prayer books such as the widely read Elizabethan Book of Common Prayer.[4] The situation is uncertain, however, as he would be drastically overestimating his poetic output over the next two years, and lengthy pieces such as the poem eventually known as "Song of Myself" would certainly stretch the notion of the poem as a daily lesson.[5] Possibly Whitman was thinking of restructuring his book into more discrete sections, or perhaps this note doesn't refer to *Leaves of Grass* at all, but a speculative new project, such as the book of "lessons" he seems to be describing elsewhere in his notes.[6] Other statements do clearly indicate that Whitman thought of his early poems as fulfilling a religious purpose in American culture; however, there is little to suggest anything specifically biblical in the conceptual underpinnings described in his working notes from this period.[7] The idea of *Leaves*-as-Bible seems to articulate a broad conception of how Whitman hoped his audience would receive his work, as opposed to a specific, creatively generative spinal idea.

However, another concept more prevalent in his notebooks and manuscripts was a fundamental motivating force behind specific major poems from this period. In this chapter I track the origins of this critically neglected idea, Whitman's concept of the "poem of materialism," from an early conversation he had with his first readers, through his notebook elaborations, to its results in published poetry, especially his 1856 works "Poem of The Sayers of The Words of The Earth" and "Broad-Axe Poem." To understand what Whitman had in mind we must better come to terms with his approach to language: his emphasis on its *materiality*, by which I mean to indicate both his emphasis on the material nature of words on the page and the idea of words as materials, the building blocks, for Whitman, of both poems and people.

Although Whitman liked to portray himself as indifferent to the opinions of New England's intellectual circles, he did actually solicit their advice. He recorded three of these conversations in what reads like a journal entry:

Feb. 25th '57 Dined with Hector Tyndale

Asked H. T. where he thought I needed particular attention to be directed for my improvement — where I could especially be bettered in my poems — He said — "In *massiveness*, breadth, large, sweeping effects, without regard to details, — as in the "Cathedral at York" (he said) "I came away with great impressions of its largeness, solidity, and spaciousness without troubling myself with its parts"

Asked F. Le B. same question viz: *What I most lacked* — He said — "In euphony — your poems seem to me to be full of the raw material of poems, but crude, and wanting finish and rhythms."

Of others the answer has been —
"You have too much procreation"[8]

It is difficult to gauge how Whitman responded to these remarks, though he was likely most sympathetic with Tyndale's rather counterintuitive objection. (Whitman has seldom been faulted for lacking "breadth" or "sweeping effects.") Some of the qualities Tyndale describes as lacking in *Leaves of Grass* were things Whitman valued — "largeness, solidity, and spaciousness" — although elsewhere Whitman critiques the idea of an architectural model for poetry, writing that a poem "may be architecture, but again it may be the forest wild-wood, or the best effect thereof, at twilight, the waving oaks and cedars in the wind, and the impalpable odor" (*CPW* 2:473). He surely dismissed the piece of advice regarding procreation, and his curt description may indicate a degree of sarcasm or derision. His reaction to the second comment, which may have been offered by one M. Le Baron, an acquaintance from a pub the poet frequented, is the most difficult to assess.[9] If "finish and rhythm" was intended to mean "rhyme and meter," the comment was unlikely to have found a sympathetic ear. There is evidence, however, that Whitman may have taken the remark as an unintentional compliment, for around that time he was very interested in the idea of a poem offering "raw material," as further investigation of his notes from this period reveals.

In a neglected manuscript housed in the Trent Collection at Duke University there is a loose leaf (apparently paper stock from

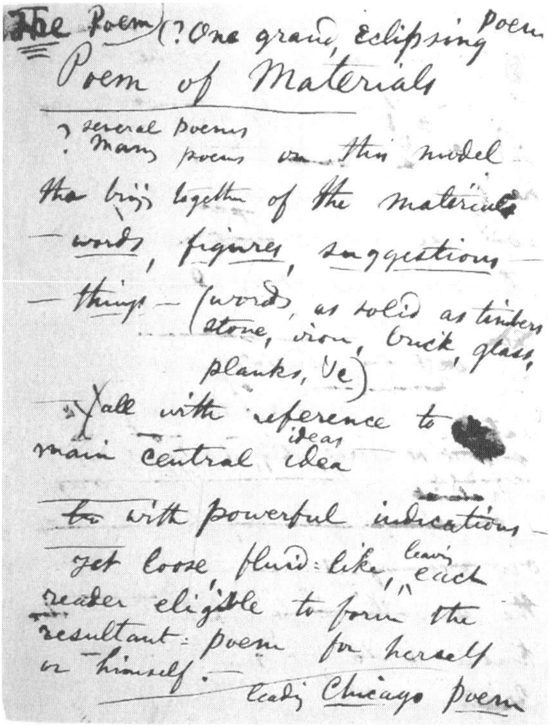

FIG 20. Whitman's theory of the "poem of materials." Trent Collection of Whitmaniana, Duke University Rare Book, Manuscript, and Special Collections Library.

the wrapper of the first edition of *Leaves*) on which Whitman has left comments fundamental to his poetic project as it was evolving during those years (see figure 20):

THE Poem) (? One grand, Eclipsing poem
Poem of Materials
   ? several poems
Many poems on this model —
the bringing together of the materials

—<u>words</u>, <u>figures</u>, <u>suggestions</u>—

—<u>things</u>—(words, as solid as timbers

stone, iron, brick, glass,

planks, &c)

—all with reference to

main central idea ^{ideas}—

~~br~~ with powerful indications—

---

yet loose, fluid-like, _^^{leaving} each

reader eligible to form the

resultant-poem for herself

or himself.—

---

    leading <u>Chicago</u> <u>poem</u>

Here Whitman makes plans for a major work important enough for him to envision it "Eclipsing" the rest of his poems. He is unclear whether the projected project will become "THE Poem"—perhaps replacing the poem eventually known as "Song of Myself" as the centerpiece of his next *Leaves*—or a cluster of "several poems" that will become central to his next edition. His idea here was no passing fancy. He returned to the notion repeatedly in his contemporaneous notebooks and manuscripts, developing it in meaningful ways. Unlike his comments regarding a "New American Bible," the concept of a "poem of materials" has been overlooked by Whitman scholars, who seem to have assumed, perhaps because no poem with a similar title ever emerged, that Whitman dropped the idea to pursue other projects. The manuscript catalog for the collection containing this leaf notes that Whitman does refer specifically to a "poem of materials" in "Proto-Leaf" (later known as "Starting from Paumanok"); in another 1860 poem, number 16 of his "Chants Democratic" (later "Mediums"), he seems to make a related remark.[10] The fact that Whitman, who continually experimented with his works' titles, didn't actually publish a piece called "<u>Poem of Materials</u>" does not mean that subsequent work wasn't shaped by the idea; as I hope to demonstrate here, this spinal idea is related to several works from this period, most importantly the 1856 "Broad-Axe Poem" (later titled "Song of the Broad-Axe"), an underestimated poem that takes the notion to extraordinary lengths. Before approaching the manuscript and published versions of "Broad-Axe Poem," however, we need to understand the theoretical underpinnings expressed by Whitman in this note.

When Whitman's friend "F. Le B." commented that his work was "full of the raw material of poems," he implied that the poems were unfinished and distressingly crude. As the note just cited suggests, however, the idea of work "full of the raw materials of poems" was a concept that Whitman meant to achieve in his writing. His comments in this note reflect his way of describing poetry in the immediate period after publishing his first edition of *Leaves*. As with the poems in the 1856 edition, he uses the "poem of _____" formulation as a placeholder for his ideas; however, unlike the lengthy assort-ment of *topical* spinal ideas in the notebook described previously, his thinking here provides a *model* for how any number of poems might unfold structurally. A "Poem of American Names," for example, can also presumably be a "poem of materials," providing the "materials" or building blocks described in the note. The methodical approach he advocates seems to reflect aspects of his work already apparent in the first *Leaves of Grass,* especially his catalogs, which offer readers inventories of "<u>words, figures, suggestions</u>," all "with reference to main central ideas." In part, then, Whitman appears to be coming to a more self-conscious understanding of an approach he had already employed intuitively in his prior work. Perhaps motivated by the prodigious goals he had set for his own poetic output, he distills an approach that was already working for him into a clearly defined methodology for replicating his success in subsequent projects.

In addition to formalizing a creative method the note establishes an underlying goal behind his model: "leaving each reader eligible to form the <u>resultant</u>-poem for herself or himself." He doesn't define precisely what he means to suggest by the phrase "<u>resultant</u>-poem," but his syntax offers some clues. The "<u>resultant</u>-poem" is presented as something separate from his own poem but built from the "materials" that poem provides. This poem is the result of the reader's interpretive engagement, the imaginative synthesis of the writer's "loose, fluid-like" offering of "<u>words, figures, suggestions</u>," presented, it would seem, without an overall guiding metanarrative, but nevertheless forcefully, with the poet's "powerful indications" intended to provoke readers to complete their own "<u>resultant</u>-poems." Again the thinking here seems to be an elaboration on ideas he had already set in motion. In a very early manuscript in which he drafts sentences for the 1855 Preface he makes a remark directly related to his "<u>Poem of Materials</u>" note.[11] Speaking of "the poet" he writes, "He does not give you the usual poems and metaphysics. — He gives you the materials for you to form for yourself ~~the~~ poems, ~~and~~ metaphysics, ˏpolitics, behavior, ~~and~~ histories, ~~and~~ romances, ~~and~~ essays and every thing else." The clear parallels between this comment and those in the "<u>Poem of Materials</u>" note suggest that the concerns had been brewing in his mind for some time, and apparently he was driven to formulate his ideas more clearly to help guide his subsequent writing.

For whatever reason, Whitman later chose not to include these remarks, but in the actual preface he writes, "A great poem is no finish to a man or woman, but rather a beginning." Unlike his unpublished comments just discussed, his remark here does not echo the "<u>Poem</u>

of Materials" note in its diction. There, as in the "Poem of Materials" note, he is critiquing the idea of literary authority. He goes on to ask, "Has any one fancied he could sit at last under some due authority, and rest satisfied with explanations, and realize, and be content and full? To no such terminus does the greatest poet bring—he brings neither cessation nor shelter'd fatness and ease. The touch of him, like Nature, tells in action." Whitman's poems of materials will embody the values expressed in his preface statement. The model precludes the possibility of conventional "due authority" by eschewing the notion that what the poet presents and the reader ultimately engages should even be the same text at all. As in recent theoretical models, Whitman conceives of the reader-writer relationship as involving two texts: the physical text produced by the writer and the abstract text produced by the reader engaged in a creative act of interpretation.

Whitman's comments in this note also seem to reflect a certain anxiety in relation to his chosen artistic medium. The poet's "materials," he realizes, are by necessity words, and the phrase "poem of materials" carries a double meaning. A "poem of materials" is a poem that not only offers readers the "material" to create their own readings—in effect, for Whitman, their own poems; it is a poem that also conceives of words themselves as "material" objects. Attempting to exemplify what he means by "materials," he begins with this list: "words, figures, suggestions." Apparently unsatisfied with the abstract nature of how these terms are conventionally understood, he then attempts to define them more concretely by interjecting the word "things" between em dashes. Simply labeling the abstractions "things" doesn't satisfy him, so he immediately includes this parenthetical aside: "(words, as solid as timbers stone, iron, brick, glass, planks, &c)." Returning to the fundamental "material" of his poems—words—he posits a series of common physical materials familiar to him from his background in carpentry. Words,

Whitman implies, must offer readers the same solidity and utilitarian purpose as the materials one uses to construct a home. Distressed by the intangibility of language, he searches for a way of seeing words as raw material building blocks like bricks and boards.

Whitman's conflation of language and material objects in this note is a tactic he uses elsewhere. In the 1855 Preface he asserted, "The United States themselves are essentially the greatest poem," and he promises his readers that if they live correctly, their "very flesh shall be a great poem." In his 1856 "Poem of The Sayers of The Words of The Earth" (later "Song of the Rolling Earth") he takes the conflation of language and material reality as his poem's central device:

> Earth, round, rolling, compact — suns, moons, animals — all these are words,
>
> Watery, vegetable, sauroid advances — beings, premonitions, lispings of the future — these are vast words.
>
> Were you thinking that those were the words — those upright lines? those curves, angles, dots?
>
> No, those are not the words — the substantial words are in the ground and sea,
>
> They are in the air — they are in you.

This poem, Whitman's most sustained poetic enactment of his concept of language, presents one of his most elaborately developed conceits: an extended metaphoric argument binding words to things in an effort to challenge his readers' assumptions about language and meaning. Where the "Poem of Materials" note engages the idea in simile, here he is less equivocal. Words are not simply *as* solid as material objects; in this poem he maintains that material objects *are* words. His insistence is so direct and matter-of-fact that he forces us to confront an essentially metaphoric assertion as if it were a literal truth. "Air, soil, water, fire, these are words," he instructs his readers, and as the poem develops we engage the concept of the universe as a linguistic system, in which each of its elements, gross and finite, are constituents in cosmic conversation. Humanity, by the nature of its very existence, is a part of that conversation, and poets are those beings capable of apprehending this grammar of empirical relations: "The workmanship of souls is by the inaudible words of the earth, / The great masters, the sayers, know the earth's words, and use them more than the audible words." Whitman's "great masters" may use the language of being more than they do "audible words," but as poets they must also "echo the tones of souls and the phrases of souls." Ultimately, the poet admits, these "sayers" must work with the shadow reality of ordinary language and provide, as he claims his own poem does, "hints of meanings" rather than the true meanings themselves.[12]

"Poem of The Sayers of The Words of The Earth" is intended to be a celebration of the limits of language, an affirmation of Whitman's belief that "what is better than to tell the best . . . is always to leave the best untold." It is also, however, an enactment of a crisis of meaning:

> When I undertake to tell the best, I find I cannot,
> My tongue is ineffectual on its pivots,
> My breath will not be obedient to its organs,
> I become a dumb man.

Whitman's resolution to the crisis is to enact new criteria for effective speech. It is futile, he implies, to attempt to communicate ultimate truths. The function of poetry is to prepare the way for others to discover such things on their own. All language is limited, but all language is not the same. Both this poem and his "Poem of Mate-rials" note indicate that effective language must be "grounded" in empirical reality. Human beings are not sayers of words but "sayers of the earth":

Say on, sayers of the earth!

Delve, mould, pile the substantial words of the earth!

Work on, age after age! nothing is to be lost,

It may have to wait long, but it will certainly come in use,

When the materials are all prepared, the architects shall appear,

I swear to you the architects shall appear without fail! I announce them and lead them!

Here again language is a material. The seeming futility of communication — its inability to get at essentials — is only an evolutionary stage. As we "Work on, age after age," not so much communicating as we are "piling" words, we are also preparing the materials for poetic redemption by "the architects" who "shall appear." Whitman's own role is to announce and pave the way for these redeemers by providing his readers with the materials to speak "the substantial words of the earth."

In the poem's complex skein the project announced in the "Poem of Materials" note emerges as a crucial thread. In both documents language is presented as material, that is to say, both as something conceived of materially and as the raw material or building blocks for his readers' linguistic engagements. In a related comment from a notebook he used to draft parts of "Song of the Broad-Axe," Whitman echoes this latter emphasis, broadening his intentions from those listed in the "Poem of Materials" leaf, so that the idea becomes implicated in his entire body of work:

Gist of my books

To give others, readers, people, the materials to decide for themselves, and know, or grow toward knowing, with cleanliness and strength.

Whitman made many such sweeping declarations of his artistic goals, no single one of which overrides the others. Nevertheless his repeated emphasis on offering materials to his readers at the very least indicates that this was a strong and abiding concern. His development of the idea in the poem just discussed shows how this material-providing enterprise hinges on his success in enacting a new and more material conception of language. There he defines himself as language's redeemer, a catalyst for the reengagement of words with their empirical roots. Only after this empirical, materialist emphasis on language is established does Whitman describe language "saying" as the preparation of "materials" for poetry's audience.

Involved in this is Whitman's preference for language that arises from native origins, both in the sense of regional or native English vernacular and of words derived from the language of America's original natives. Another of his references to a "poem of materials" stresses this latter point:

poem of the ~~Indians~~ aborigines
— introducing every principal aboriginal trait, and name

_____

🖎 bring in ~~Indi~~ aboriginal traits in poem of (American) Materials

"Aboriginal" traits and names appear to have been an important component of the materials he sought to provide his readers. This note also indicates that at the time of its composition Whitman was considering multiple poems of materials, one of which would focus explicitly on American productions, and it underscores that the key material was language. His emphasis on using Native American rather than European-derived names for things highlights the privilege he attributed to language arising from original perceptions over secondhand language imported from foreign origins. Whitman stressed this preference repeatedly in his notes on language, including his posthumously published "Primer of Words," in which he pondered the "strange charm of aboriginal names" (DBN 3:729). As with his affection for vernacular and slang words, he embraced aboriginal names for the North American landscape because he saw them as "words of the earth," arising directly from perception of the world.

Whitman's writing process reflects this preference. His early notebooks, most of which are small enough to easily fit into a shirt pocket, are filled with references to things going on around him as he composed. In one particularly striking example he kept extensive notes of several games of Twenty Questions that he apparently played with his companions while riding on the omnibus and ferry. The clues he left there indicate that many of the objects described in these games, such as the old Hotel Broadway on Twenty-second Street in New York, were seen on various bus routes he took at the time.[13] Interspersed between these games of Twenty Questions are various notes for poems and drafts of lines to be used in future poems, many of which reflect the sights and sounds of his immediate environment. His friend and early biographer Richard Maurice Bucke described Whitman's creative attraction to language of direct perception: "Early in 1855 he was writing *Leaves of Grass* from time to time, getting it in shape. Wrote at the opera, in the street, on the ferry-boat, at the sea-side, in the fields, sometimes stopped work to write. Certainly no book was ever more directly written from living impulses and impromptu sights, and less in the abstract."[14]

As his notebooks suggest and Bucke's comment reaffirms, Whitman's work habits reflect his desire to write directly from "living impulses" — to have his words reflect immediate perceptions of the world, as opposed to the isolated imagination. In the "Poem of The Sayers of The Words of The Earth" we have observed how Whitman suggests that language as it is conventionally received is incapable of relating our most fundamental truths. His emphasis on writing poems from a language of direct perception betrays a similar preoccupation with language's limits: words, he knew, are a static, limited approximation of what they signify. The situation cannot be wholly undone, but it can be mollified somewhat by basing creative language on immediate sensory engagement. Though still an imperfect reflection of the world, such language is at least closer in spirit to the world than language derived from memory and books while sitting at one's desk. Of course, as we have seen, Whitman *did* collage scenes from books, relying on the perceptions and imaginations of others, so he was hardly a purist when it came to the notion of empirically derived language. At the same time, the creative method prevalent throughout his early notebooks reveals a poet engaged in an ongoing hunting and gathering mission for snippets of poetic utterance derived from his time spent "at the opera, in the street, on the ferry-boat, at the sea-side, [and] in the fields," as Bucke put it. Whitman continued to emphasize a language of direct perception throughout his Civil War years, until illness debilitated him, severely limiting his access to the outside world.[15] Likewise his implementation of text derived from others continued.[16] These dual strands of his creative process — his collage-like appropriations of outside text and his juxtapositions of snippets of language based on immediate and direct sensory perception — coexist despite any apparent contradictions.

These contrasting approaches to language are particularly apparent in his catalog presentations of people and places, where far-flung, exotic examples sit beside domestic scenes glimpsed during his everyday life. Throughout his early poems Whitman proffers catalog images that were impossible for him to witness directly and by necessity had to have been collaged, paraphrased, or otherwise imaginatively reproduced. At the conclusion of these catalogs he returns to himself, the perceiving subject, in various present-tense declarations that locate poetic agency in the individual. The cycle of fanning oneself out into an amalgam of observed and collaged details, then coalescing the myriad particulars unto oneself, "consigning them," as Whitman once put it, "to the personal critter," is one of the central structural patterns of his major early poems.[17] This pattern represents his solution to an uneasy paradox in his creative method: while presenting himself as a poet who will help his readers to "no longer take things at second or third hand, nor look through the eyes of the dead, nor feed on the specters in books," Whitman himself fed upon such specters and used the language he found in his reading in his own poems. It is a paradox that, when later discovered by scholarly readers, has led some to regard him as a fraud.[18] As we have observed, however, Whitman's notebooks indicate that his appropriation of materials derived from his reading was not so much an act of self-conscious deception or duplicity as a predictable reflection of his general attitude toward language—the approach of a former newspaperman whose job involved recycling others' stories into a coherent textual whole. Although for financial reasons he did become concerned about the proprietary use of books by those who would profit from pirated editions, with regard to smaller units of language—phrases, sentences, even paragraphs—Whitman felt no such compunction. He regarded individual writing as involved in a linguistic activity larger than that of any one author. This transpersonal attitude toward language is reflected in his acceptance of the recycling of outside text as part of a natural evolutionary process, an aspect of the preparation of materials described in "Poem of The Sayers of The Words of The Earth."

In his published poems Whitman's linguistic borrowings found their most comfortable home in his catalogs and lists. Part of the reason for this may simply be a matter of convenience, for the paratactic structure of such lists, with their discrete, self-contained lines, allowed him to insert derived fragments of language with little need to smooth them over to meet the grammatical or stylistic priorities of more involved and elaborate syntactical structures. An autonomous, end-stopped line can absorb disparate forms of discourse more easily than the complex, interlocking syntax typical of his poetic contemporaries. At the same time the catalogs worked to resolve the apparent paradox between his belief in a language of direct perception and the secondhand nature of language stolen from outside material. In central early poems, such as the works later known as "Song of Myself" and "The Sleepers," he presents himself as a visionary witness to this spectral, secondhand language, standing apart from the staccato snapshot scenery of his catalogs, observing it with us, his readerly intimates, and allowing the scenes temporary autonomy from himself, the ostensibly perceiving subject, so that both poet and reader move out into the panorama and become lost in the expansive imagery. Eventually the centrifugal motion out from the self reaches its zenith, and our attention snaps back to the perceiving subject, as the poet offers a summarizing response to the preceding catalog that is sometimes thematic and, at least in his early work, invariably affirmative. This centripetal and centrifugal pattern relates to Whitman's nuanced concept of dilation. The centripetal motion is a paradigmatic example of how dilation is manifested in his published work; the centrifugal motion, in turn, is often a return to one of his spinal ideas.[19]

There are many instances of this pattern in the early poems. For example, the first sustained catalog that occurs in the 1855 version of the poem later known as "Song of Myself" is preceded by a line that firmly anchors us in the poet as witness—in this case, a witness to an immortality that all possess but that the poet alone sees: "I am the mate and companion of people, all just as immortal and fathomless as myself; / They do not know how immortal, but I know." The poet then offers a brief preliminary list of the diversity of mankind this entails, followed by a thematic development of his position as witness:

> Who needs be afraid of the merge?
> Undrape . . . . you are not guilty to me, nor stale nor discarded,
> I see through the broadcloth or gingham whether or no,
> And am around, tenacious, acquisitive, tireless . . . . and can never be
> shaken away.

Elaborating on his theme of immortality he describes death in sexual terms as a final "merge" with all humanity, and he develops his claim as poetic witness through the trope of nakedness, claiming to see a deeper self than is apparent in the superficial trappings posed by conventional understanding. This is followed by the poem's first real catalog, a nineteen-line assemblage of the diverse gestures of humanity, ranging from the gravity of a suicide to the ordinary pleasures of sleigh rides and snowball fights. Whitman himself becomes temporarily absorbed by this parade of sights and sounds, "merging" with it in his centrifugal motion outward. The catalog concludes with a statement returning us to the poet as witness: "I mind them or the resonance of them . . . . I come again and again." In lines simple in expression but complex in connotation, Whitman acknowledges both the direct perceptions that inform his poem and the secondhand images derived from others — the things themselves and "the resonance of them." The second half of the sentence reinforces his position as a witness who does not discriminate or judge, but who is "tenacious, acquisitive, tireless," returning "again and again" to both the harsh and pleasant aspects of the human parade.

This pattern establishes two registers of discourse: the beginning and concluding personal statements, which frame the catalog, and the catalog itself, presented as something apart from the poet, objects and scenes of a world that he is witness to but not creator of. Ultimately these details become absorbed in the poet's subjectivity, but it is important to Whitman that they first be seen as objective. The movement to dilate and include the world, after all, cannot be meaningful if the world itself is only a projection of the human imagination. Once absorbed these materials are both a part of and separate from the poet, which is not, as it might appear, contradictory, since Whitman's concept of identity is not singular. "I resist anything better than my own diversity," he says, and "I am vast, I contain multitudes." The contents of Whitman's multitudinous self are presented in his catalogs and lists, but these parades of materials have linguistic as well as personal significance, which helps to explain why he seems to have found no contradiction between a language of direct perception and one derived from others. In the dynamic he establishes the content of these lists is specifically intended to be things he witnesses and includes, not things he creates or projects. They constitute objective, not subjective materials. By disavowing authority over the objects of his catalogs Whitman also disavows the language that evokes them, obviating the conventional prerogative that requires original writing in a literary work. In the context he intends Whitman is the witness, not the creator, of the language of his visionary catalogs. The materials they offer are meant to be as much ours as his.

∽

I have argued that Whitman's concept of a "poem of materials" holds twofold significance, suggesting a poem that offers readers material for their own lives and works, as well as a poem constructed of language that stresses its status as a material. As we have seen, Whitman worked through the former of these meanings while completing the preface to the first *Leaves of Grass*, and the concept informs his use of catalogs and lists in many poems of the first edition, especially the works later known as "Song of Myself" and "A Song for Occupations," which provide the poetically realized "materials" for one's identity and job, respectively. Sometime between the publication of the first and second editions of *Leaves* Whitman developed the concept more specifically, giving it the actual title "Poem of Materials" in a note written on wrapping paper left over from one of the first edition's various printings. This note indicates that Whitman's idea related to no single poem but rather to "several poems" — that he hoped to write "Many poems [based] on this model." In the second edition there are indeed a number of new poems that seem to be poems of materials, including "Poem of Salutation," a work constructed almost entirely of catalogs, as well as more structurally complex poems such as "Poem of The Sayers of The Words of The Earth" and "Broad-Axe Poem," both of which also use lists to present readers with the buildings blocks to construct a new vision of the world. Furthermore, with Whitman's addition of a thirty-six-line pseudo-anatomical catalog to the untitled fifth poem of the first edition, the second edition revision of this piece — there titled "Poem of the Body" and known now as "I Sing the Body Electric" — is to some extent reenvisioned as a poem of materials as well, one providing the poetically vitalized building blocks of the human form.

The second aspect of Whitman's concept of the poem of materials, its emphasis on the physical materiality of language, is more difficult to locate specifically in his work. To a large extent it would seem that use of "words, as solid as timbers stone, iron, brick, glass, planks" would be a matter of choice of diction (choosing words with heft and physicality) and syntax (employing direct and muscular grammatical constructions). Again the catalogs, the paratactic structure of which emphasizes nouns and resists subordinating language in complex clausal relations, seem the most prominent vehicle for the poet's intentions. Nevertheless, because the idea of using words as material things seems to relate primarily to discrete linguistic choices, it would appear to be a rather diffuse concept, one that broadly informs Whitman's poem-making process as opposed to a specific strategy that can be discretely located in individual works. There are, however, certain moments in his early writing in which Whitman emphasizes the material nature of language in a focused, strategic manner, forcing his readers' attention to the actual page at hand, to the leaf that is his words' vehicle and physical presentation of type on the page.

One of the most important of these moments occurred for readers of the first edition before they encountered a single line of his poems. Confronting the original book cover of the 1855 *Leaves of Grass* Whitman's audience was greeted with a strange and striking material presentation of text in the form of Whitman's lettering for his book's title. Using this lettering as a case study, let's now take an in-depth look at Whitman's manipulation of the material qualities of the printed word. The plant and page metaphor suggested by the dual meaning of the word *leaves* is given physical embodiment by the hand-drawn gold-stamped letters formed from images of plants shaped to form the words of his title. The general idea of using plants to spell a book's title on its cover wasn't in itself an unusual concept when Whitman employed the technique. Typographers refer to this style of presentation as "floriated lettering," and it was a fairly common convention for books published during Whitman's time. Whitman was surely aware of fellow New England journalist Fanny Fern's commercially successful *Fern Leaves from Fanny's Portfolio* (1853), the spine and frontispiece illustrations for which may have provided the poet with the original idea for his own floriated lettering for *Leaves of Grass*.

If Fanny Fern was Whitman's first inspiration, his actual execution of the cover lettering was uniquely his own (see figure 15). Although we don't know for certain who drew this design, it is usually assumed to have been Whitman himself. It fits with his way of working — taking control of book production to the greatest extent possible — and we know with certainty that he drew the font design for the spine of the second edition because he left behind a drawing modeling these letters, an image of which was published in Joel Myerson's 1993 bibliography.[20] We don't have such concrete evidence that Whitman himself sketched out the lettering for the first edition; however, what we know about him suggests that he would have, and at the very least we can be certain that he approved of it. This highly distinctive lettering calls attention to the material presence of text before readers even opened his book. Compared to the floriated lettering common for books at the time, Whitman's design was extraordinarily detailed and complex. It was unusual for such lettering to be composed of multiple species of plant, as this design appears to be, but stranger yet is the fact that the foliage completely overcomes the letters constituting his title's central word, *of*, which is rendered almost completely unintelligible by the design's vegetal profusion. To viewers who hadn't seen the lettering on the spine, the book's title must have seemed to be "*Leaves . . . something . . . Grass,*" and it is easy to imagine those early readers squinting to make out the book's title. By severely obscuring his letters' linguistic clarity, the poet forces us to focus on their material presence in an effort to interpret them.

Another unusual and striking detail is the group of root-like structures dangling beneath the letters, some of which might be shoots or tendrils, or perhaps the Spanish moss that Whitman must have encountered on his trip to New Orleans. Previous readers have interpreted this lettering as being "rooted" in the book itself, suggesting a language emerging as naturally from the text as grass. Technically, however, this is incorrect; rather than language rooted in the cover of its book the roots seem to be floating in air. The images are reminiscent of pictures in botany books and science textbooks, where live plants are rendered as if planted in transparent soil. Those presentations are motivated by scientific realism, but here that is not the case. The letters seem to represent an amalgam of various realistic plant features, but no one specific plant seems to be depicted. The botanist Diana Horton has noted that some of these species — those adorning the *L*, the *of*, the *G*, and the final *s* — do seem to share a fibrous monocot type of root system similar to the roots of various species of grass.[21]

If we study the letters more closely we can discern further signifi-cance in Whitman's effort to focus attention on the material pres-ence of the text of his cover design. After examining this unusual floriated lettering, early readers were greeted by another striking presentation of text when they opened the cover and came upon the book's title page. Covering nearly the entire oversized leaf, these gigantic letters seem at first glance to be as different as possible from the ornate organicism of the letters on the cover. The type shown here is a classic example of the Scotch Roman face, and the contents of the book are printed in this type as well.[22] According to a book often referred to as the "bible of typography," Alexander Lawson's *Anatomy of a Typeface*, the term "Scotch face" was "first given to a type cut by [Alexander] Wilson and the S. N. Dickinson foundry in Boston about 1837." The actual design originated with a font called Pica Roman No. 2, which was first cut in 1809. Imitations of this font style were popular in the United States throughout the 1820s, 1830s, and 1840s; Whitman's font for the first edition of *Leaves* is one of them, a variant from the Bruce foundry in Williamsburgh.[23] The oversized type of this title page would have been more commonly used for commercial than literary purposes. It represents a conventional face but an unusually large choice of font (72 point for the word *Leaves* and 108 for *Grass*). With its boldness, its hard-edged clarity, and its commercial applicability, this typeface seems a far cry from the lettering on the cover. This striking contrast between the living letters of the cover and the "cold type" of the title page seems to have been intentional.

There is, however, a deeper connection. Closer comparison between the cover and the title page reveals that the floriated cover lettering is based on the same font as the title page (see figure 21). The letters' apertures are nearly the same, and although the letters are overgrown with foliage, you can recognize the same ball terminal at the end of the *r* and the *s*. The fat vertical right-side stroke of the capital *G* is paralleled in the plant lettering, as is the crossbar and the v-shaped opening at the stroke's bottom. We find the same exaggeration between thick and thin strokes in the lowercase *s*, the lowercase *v*, even the *e* and *a*. There is vegetation growing from the thin strokes, but if you were to strip it away it would be the same thin, elegant style of the letters in the title page. There are some obvious connotations to

this observation. For one, the parallel reveals something of Whitman's book-making process for the first edition. Because the cover lettering is based on the title page font, it seems likely that the cover design, like Whitman's addition of the 1855 preface, was a last-minute idea.[24] It would appear that sometime after he began to help print the contents of his first book, he sat down with his freshly printed leaves and, using the printed type as his foundation, sketched out the model for his cover's floriated lettering.[25]

The parallel between the title page font and the gold-stamped lettering also holds connotations for the intentions behind Whitman's emphasis on the materiality of the text on his book's cover. For one, it suggests a reason why the *of* on the cover is illegible. In imitating the title page design, Whitman rendered the *of* on the cover in a smaller scale, and in the scenario portrayed on the cover the letters of this *of*, because they are so much smaller than the rest, were simply the first to be overcome by foliage. The parallel also explains why the plant-encrusted *of* on the cover is set at an angle. As the *o* especially makes clear, the *of* on the cover is based on an italic type, paralleling the *of* on the title page. Another parallel involves that curious blob of plant matter after the final letter *s*, which is actually a period. Including a period at the end of the title was a common convention for title pages, but not for covers. Whitman himself didn't use periods at the ends of his titles on the covers of any subsequent editions of *Leaves of Grass*, though he did in all of his title pages right up until the 1881 edition, when the period vanishes. This isn't the first time he made interesting use of a period at the end of a title. As Ed Folsom has noted in a recent monograph, Whitman added a tail to the period on the title page of the 1860 edition of *Leaves of Grass*, turning it into what appear to be sperm.[26] The period on the cover of the 1855 edition is also symbolically generative, suggestive of botanical instead of human reproduction. Whitman's overall cover design, however, evokes both botanical and human fertility, for the foliage that adorns the type is itself sexual, stylized into bulbous, testicular protrusions fleecing the letters. Furthermore the italicized *of* in the cover design is distinctly phallic, a fact that Whitman, who had the phallic bulge of his trousers enlarged in successive printings of his frontispiece image, was surely aware of.[27]

In addition to explaining why the *of* in "Leaves of Grass" is illegible on the first edition's cover, the parallel between the title-page font and the cover lettering helps resolve another mystery: why the roots of the letters are ungrounded, floating in space. The plant life on this lettering isn't growing from the book; it is growing from the letters themselves. Beneath the foliage lies the more conventional and typographically uniform font of the title page, but fleecing it are various forms of plant life, transforming the font into organic material from the inside out. Whitman's strong opinions about language — and about American uses of it in particular — help explain why he gave these letters roots in the first place. Had the letters lacked them, he would have presented language cut off from its source, a rootless language that can no longer grow, a form of language analogous to how Whitman saw the poetry that preceded him in the United States; rooted in conventions from Europe, it was a poetry cut off from its own soil. It doesn't seem unreasonable that Whitman, basing his design on a typeface that originated in Europe, wanted to depict the letters as being transformed into something alive and indigenous to where they are found—that he wanted to depict a natural and, as he liked to phrase it, "autocthonic" portrayal of language in line with the views described in his various notebooks. He certainly knew the name of this type of font, as his notes regarding the typefaces of the 1860 edition demonstrate (*NUPM* 1:419–21). The Scotch Roman face possessed a title that referred to two distinct European heritages. So it might have been especially tempting for Whitman to portray this particular font as being transformed by its living surroundings. The design suggests a language reborn in its new climate—and a literature reborn in the newly established nation of its writers.

If we imagine the foliation as emerging from the font itself, as opposed to from the cover of the book, the symbolism of the lettering shifts. A book that sprouts its own title on its cover presents itself symbolically as a generative, organic entity. But if it is the *font* of the book that is sprouting and growing, then the emphasis turns to language itself, as opposed to the artifact of the book. It suggests a language that starts as the kind of "cold type" that Whitman elsewhere says "chilled" him, and that he transforms into something vital and living.[28] The fact that the roots of this language float suspended on the book suggests that they will take root elsewhere, perhaps in the hearts and minds of their readers. Such an outlook parallels the spermatic symbolism of the title-page font of the 1860 edition, where the spermatic rendering seems to suggest that his words are intended to impregnate his readers' imaginations. Another noteworthy feature of the floriated gold-stamp lettering is that none of the letters touches another. Despite their highly ornate vegetation, which sprouts in all directions and sends out shoots and roots that are longer than the letters themselves, Whitman was careful to ensure that not a single point of contact existed. They are ultimately unique and independent entities, thriving in close proximity to their neighbors but self-reliant and autonomous in structure and presentation. This combination of independence and living harmony is reminiscent of his vision of democracy, a vision that starts with the isolated self, independent and egotistically unique, but that through the course of his book dilates to include others in a larger totality.

Before discussing further examples of Whitman's use of the material presence of text, I want to return to an observation made previously: the fact that there are a number of species of plants represented by these letters (even if the species themselves are fanciful). The variety of plant types used in the gold-stamp lettering depicts a unity in diversity with revealing implications. On the one hand, this portrayal is suggestive of Whitman's vision of democracy and the evolving dream of American integration. The symbolism resonates with his antebellum optimism about his country's destiny. As I have suggested, however, the direct symbolism of this lettering is of a representation of language, and the resonance in this regard is equally rich. As his notes from this period indicate, Whitman delighted in the idea of American English as an inclusive and absorptive medium. He loved bringing together words of disparate origins, as is demonstrated by his idiosyncratic use of foreign-language terms in his poems. This fascination with bringing disparate parts into a whole is strikingly revealed in his approach to the language in his notebooks, and this representation is suggestive of the creative process Whitman was engaged in when the lettering was designed. Just as his title letter-ing brings together different species of plants, his notebooks and manuscript drafts reveal his bringing together different specimens of discourse in his poems. Although the symbolism in this regard may be unintentional, it does at least emphasize his pervasive inter-est in inclusive diversity.

The title *Leaves of Grass* and the first edition's gold-stamped cover lettering and title page anticipate numerous other instances of Whitman's meaningful emphasis on the material presence of text and the artifact of the book. In his early poems Whitman repeatedly calls readers' attention to the book they are holding, creating a sense of immediacy as well as a direct connection to the reader by way of the shared presence of *Leaves of Grass*. Sometimes he refers to the book directly;[29] in other instances, such as in the poem eventually titled "Whoever You Are Holding Me Now in Hand," he equates the presence of his book with his own physical presence. In this poem Whitman's speaking position seems to vacillate between his physical self and the book he has created. In one line he refers to his body in the first person, telling readers, "let go your hand from my shoulders," but in the very next line he seems to be speaking as his book: "Put me down and depart on your way." A few lines later he declares, "And in libraries I lie as one dumb, a gawk, or unborn, or dead." Elsewhere in the poem he sexualizes the presence of the book: "Or if you will, thrusting me beneath your clothing, / Where I may feel the throbs of your heart or rest upon your hip" (*LG* 116). The book was a particularly important material for Whitman, and his various strategies of focusing readers' attention on it form the basis of this poem.

Another crucial poem embodying this aspect of the "Poem of Materials" note is the second untitled work from the first edition of *Leaves*, which Whitman eventually titled "A Song for Occupations." In the poem's opening lines Whitman problematizes his notion of the book as a conduit between writer and reader:

Come closer to me,
Push closer my lovers and take the best that I possess,
Yield closer and closer and give me the best that you possess.

This is unfinished business with me . . . . how is it with you?

I was chilled with the cold types and cylinder and wet paper between us.

I pass so poorly with paper and types . . . . I must pass with the contact of bodies and souls.[30]

Even as Whitman's tone and address here imply closeness with his readers, he acknowledges the limits of such intimacy, expressing frustration with the limits of his chosen artistic medium. The passage deconstructs one of his primary artistic devices: the intimate speaking position so central to his poems, the mode of address by which he implies that he is at his readers' side while we read his work. As in "Whoever You Are Holding Me Now in Hand," where he concludes by asking his readers to "release" the poet-as-book and "depart on your way," in this poem also Whitman suggests that readers must move beyond the book itself toward his desired end. "Come closer to me" acknowledges the irony behind the fact that even as he implies intimate and often physical contact with his readers, in reality his readers are reading alone, interpreting the "cold type" of his text rather than making actual physical contact with another human being.

It seems unlikely that Whitman had these specific poems in mind when he documented his concept of the poem of materials; however, both his note from 1856 and the poems I have just quoted do reveal his preoccupation with the material nature of literary media. When he expresses his desire to set down "words, as solid as timbers stone, iron, brick," he also expresses anxiety that his chosen role as poet by necessity involves the production of the least physical material of potential artistic production: words. A sculptor, for example, would not be compelled to produce sculptures "as solid as timbers stone, iron, brick," but a poet who is so compelled is engaged in a quixotic enterprise. After all, even the striking material qualities of aspects of his work such as the floriated gold-stamp lettering on the cover of the first *Leaves* are subverted by the fact that the act of reading, as it is conventionally understood, involves only the most minimal engagement with the physical presence of text. Language is usually conceived as a window into the meaning it would evoke, whereas in other prevalent arts, such as painting, sculpture, and dance, meaning is found in the art object itself, whether a human body or a painted canvas. This is what we mean when we describe painting, for example, as a "plastic" and language as a "transparent" medium. Influenced by his background as a printer and newspaperman, in which he held language in his hands as metal type, Whitman broke with this conventional understanding to exploit the physical presence of the book and of type on the page to achieve some remarkable effects. Thus Whitman's poems of materials offer both the materials for readers to construct their own worlds and the material of literature as a physical presence.

These two qualities of Whitman's poem of materials come together in his most complex and accomplished poem in this mode, his 1856 "Broad-Axe Poem" (retitled "Song of the Broad-Axe" in 1867). "Broad-Axe Poem" was composed during Whitman's most prolific and arguably most successful period of writing, the phase immediately following the publication of the first *Leaves of Grass*. Of the major poems written during this time, it is the poem for which the most extensive proportion of manuscript sources have survived in relation to the poem's final length. Indeed it is one of the few poems for which traces remain of all four of the steps in Whitman's creative process: conceiving, testing, writing, and arranging. Even more than "Poem of The Sayers of The Words of The Earth," "Broad-Axe Poem" is Whitman's most clear and effective culmination of the ideas he had been working through in the profuse amount of poetic theory he was composing in his notebooks of the mid-1850s, especially his twofold notion of poetic materials. As I hope to demonstrate here, the dual aspects of the poem of materials are fused in this poem's central moment, one of the most provocative and conceptually advanced gestures in all of Whitman's writing.

The first inkling of Whitman's "Broad-Axe Poem" is suggested in the bottom portion of a loose leaf housed in the Trent Collection at Duke University. The leaf is composed of two pasted-together scraps of lined paper with penciled text. The top portion contains what appears to be a note not unlike many found in the "Dick Hunt" notebook describing the physical and personal qualities of one of Whitman's friends or acquaintances. The bottom portion, which is partially bracketed and overstruck with twin vertical lines, reads:[31]

— The Broad-axe — the axe of the headsman

First as the axe of the headsman — and what was done with it for a thousand years — then as the carpenter's broad-axe, and what is done with that now

The resultant poem is more complex than this brief note would suggest, but Whitman's comment here does reflect one of the work's basic devices: the emblematic comparison of Old and New World uses for the axe, so that its outmoded use in warfare becomes associated with European antiquity and contemporary, commercial uses of the axe come to represent Whitman's vision of American material achievement. Most critical readings of the poem emphasize this theme, though other thematic developments have been stressed, including another important idea in the poem, Whitman's humanist assertion that a city's greatness lies not in its "wharves, docks, manufacturers" or its "tallest and costliest buildings or shops selling goods from the rest of the earth," but rather that "A great city is that which has the greatest men and women." Both ideas are important to the poem, as Whitman negotiates the apparent contradiction between a work championing commercial production and one that devalues the results of such production as inferior to the human spirit that gives rise to them.

If the manuscript fragment just cited represents the conceptual seed of Whitman's spinal idea for the piece, another leaf, also at Duke, offers one of the clearest extant examples of his testing phase in his compositional process (see figure 16). This page, described in the previous chapter as exemplifying how Whitman's background as an editor organizing text into columns for newspapers affected his writing process, provides a record of his thinking as he turned the initial spinal idea over in his mind, brainstorming various uses of "the carpenter's broad-axe" described in the previous note, sketching out ideas for episodic, axe-related scenes, and making notes about research he intended to complete to fill out his understanding of how the axe is created and employed. Although his unusual layout of text on this leaf renders it difficult to accurately reproduce, this transcription provides a rough idea of the poet's method in this phase of his compositional process:

> The cutting down of an unusually large and majestic tree — liveoak or other — for some kelson to a frigate or first class steamship. — (what wood is the kelson generally?)
>
> ────────────
>
> processions of portraits of the different users of the axe — the raftsman, the

lumberman, the antique warrior, the headsman, the butcher, the framer of houses, the squatter of the west, — the pioneer

_____

founding of cities

_____

make it the American emblem preferent to the eagle

_____

— in ship building

_____

in cutting a passage through the ice

_____

the butcher in his slaughterhouse

_____

full picture
The antique warrior always with his great axe
— the ₍brawny₎ swinging arm
— the clatter and crash on the helmeted head
— the ₍death₎howl and the [illegible] ~~falling raped~~[?] quick tumbling body and the rush of friend and foe thither — the summons to surrender — the battering of castlegates and city gates —

_____

building wharves and piers

_____

full picture of the pioneer

_____

the Roman lictors preceding the consuls

_____

the sacrificial priest — ~~both Grecian~~ Grecian Roman and Jewish

_____

What in Scandinavia?

As Whitman tests his knowledge of the broadaxe, sketching a skeletal list of images to be poetically elaborated upon, he also notes absences in his understanding that he returns to later in his preparatory research. In another notebook he reminds himself of some reading that he needs to brush up on to enrich his poem with accurate historical details: "For ~~battle-a~~ broad ax — See acct of the sack of Rome in 1527 'sweeping on with that horde of Spanish bigots and German unbelievers and Italian brigands to the sack of the old great city.'" The source of this account has not been identified, so we do not know how Whitman may have used the material he found there in his published poem. We do know, however, that as Whitman moved beyond this phase in his compositional process and began to gather and compose actual text to include in his published poems, he collaged text not only from outside sources like the one just mentioned but also from his own rudimentary notes for the poem. We hear echoes of the text just cited in these lines: "The sack of an old city in its time, / The bursting in of mercenaries and bigots tumultuously and disorderly."[32] And from his earlier, preliminary notes composed in newspaper-like columns, he also extracted material. In fact the majority of these notations, even the least developed, find their way into "Broad-Axe Poem" in one form or another. His reference to "the butcher in his slaughterhouse" reappears verbatim in line 41; the "the brawny swinging arm" he referred to originally in reference to his "antique warrior" is transferred onto modern workers with their "brawny young arms and hips." His "antique warrior always with his great axe" also returns, as an "antique European warrior with his axe in combat," as do his "Roman lictors preceding the consuls," which appear in the line just preceding his warrior. Even his more abstract comments to himself are collaged, including his "processions of portraits of the different users of the axe," which transforms into

"The shadowy processions of the portraits of the past users also." Of the dozens of notes related to "Broad-Axe Poem" that have survived, Whitman repeated or paraphrased nearly every word somewhere in its published form. Far from the organic and spontaneous creative process he sometimes described for himself, his notes for "Broad-Axe Poem" reconfirm how elaborate and methodic the poet's preparation for composition often was.

At some point Whitman must have sat down and actually begun assembling his notes and drafted lines into a final order. When he did so for "Broad-Axe Poem" he made a highly unusual decision regarding how to begin the published product. For the first time in all of his *Leaves of Grass* writing he decided to include language that not only rhymed (which itself would have been a first) but is also in meter:

> Weapon shapely, naked, wan,
> Head from the mother's bowels drawn,
> Wooded flesh and metal bone, limb only one and lip only one,
> Gray-blue leaf by red-heat grown, helve produced from a little seed
>   sown,
> Resting the grass amid and upon,
> To be lean'd and to lean on.

There can be no doubt that Whitman was aware of just how violent a break from the rest of the language in *Leaves* this opening amounted to, and he surely expected that readers of his day — more so than many of today's readers, desensitized to what was once an assumed meaningful relation between poetic form and content — would ask why this poet of such bold and startling free verse would choose to interject a sestet of such chiseled formality. We do not know how his first readers responded. Of those who have published responses

in more recent years, some, such as David S. Reynolds, have argued
that the poem's formal opening was simply an effort to "make small
concessions to popular tastes."[33] If so it would seem to be a very
small concession indeed, given that nowhere else in the second
edition does Whitman write in either rhyme or meter and that
"Broad-Axe Poem" itself proceeds to include some of the most formally transgressive of all of Whitman's writing, including a passage
with fifty-three consecutive nouns separated by nothing more than
commas. It's difficult to imagine that a reader expecting traditional
formal verse would be comforted by the brief nod to formality at
the start of the poem.

Gay Wilson Allen, looking as I have to Whitman's working notes,
has speculated that Whitman was trying to reproduce the sound of
rain with his trochaic opening meter, basing his suggestion on Horace
Traubel's transcription of an early manuscript draft:[34]

> The irregular tapping of rain off my house-eaves at nightafter the storm
>   has lulled,
> Gray-blue sprout so hardened grown
> Head from the mother's bowels drawn
> Body shapely naked and wan
> Fibre produced from a little seed sown.[35]

Allen argues that the initial long free-verse line of this leaf describing
the "irregular tapping of rain" was "probably the subject, not a line
for a poem," and maintains that the lines that follow, which were
indeed revised and reordered to form part of the opening of "Broad-
Axe Poem," show that Whitman "was apparently trying to imitate
the sound of rain drops."[36] Allen's argument, however, is based on a
faulty assumption, since the free-verse line here was in fact used by
Whitman in line 27 of "Broad-Axe Poem": "The irregular tapping of

rain down on the leaves, after the storm has lulled."[37] Moreover the original manuscript, to which Allen apparently did not have access, suggests that, if anything, Whitman's unusual rhymed opening to "Broad-Axe" was associated in his mind with sex, not rain — though this too is speculative, as the association could be coincidental.[38] This manuscript alone does not provide enough information regarding why Whitman chose to include these rhymed and metered lines. We must look elsewhere, in addition to this manuscript leaf, if we want to understand what motivated him in this poem's idiosyncratic opening.

If Whitman was trying to be sonically imitative, a more likely aural analogue would be one related to the poem's central trope, such as the sound of wood being chopped (or perhaps the rhythms of sex). These suggestions, like Allen's, are of course hypothetical, and Whitman may not have had such mimetic intentions at all. What the opening sestet of "Broad-Axe Poem" presents us with most clearly is, I would argue, literally a riddle, though the situation is complicated by the fact that Whitman presents the answer to the riddle in his poem's title. If, however, we reconsider these lines as if we didn't already know what they were describing, then their resemblance to a riddle becomes more apparent. As with a riddle, the lines offer a series of abstract descriptions that conform to the object described, but that seem intentionally enigmatic and ambiguous: "Weapon shapely, naked, wan, / Head from the mother's bowels drawn, / Wooded flesh and metal bone, limb only one and lip only one." As was conventional with riddles in Whitman's day, these lines rhyme and follow a simple meter, and, as is still conventional with riddles, the lines present what at first appears to be fanciful (only a single "limb" and "lip"?) but that seems logical when we know the riddle's answer. Whitman himself enjoyed riddles and loved sharing them with his friends in

Brooklyn around the time he was composing this poem, as well as later with soldiers whom he cared for during the Civil War.[39] In fact in the extant notebook containing the most extensive notes and drafts of lines related to "Broad-Axe Poem" he jotted down dozens of riddling lines related to games of Twenty Questions that he played with his friends in the neighborhood. Interspersed between these games are lines from several poems, including "Broad-Axe Poem," and it is easy to imagine Whitman poring over the notebook for material and being inspired by these games when he conceived of his riddling introductory sestet.

In a good riddle the effect of each successive line is to provide clues that bring the reader or listener closer to the riddle's answer while still offering enough resistance to evoke a sense of mystery and suspense. In "Broad-Axe Poem" the effect is the opposite because the riddle's answer has been provided in the poem's title. Instead the successive lines here create a sense of distance from the object, defamiliarizing it, so that in its newfound strangeness we can begin to see the object afresh. The first question asked in a game of Twenty Questions is traditionally "Animal, vegetable, or mineral?" Here Whitman breaks the broadaxe down to its constituent materials as well, to the iron that is "by red-heat grown" and the wood "produced from a little seed." The purpose of his defamiliarizing riddle and reductive materialism is to set the stage for the axe to be reborn in his readers' imaginations. Thus shortly after the opening he draws us through a short catalog of "lands," concluding with "Lands of iron! Lands of the make of the axe!" Later in the poem he details the actual creation of the axe:

> The forger at his forge-furnace, and the user of iron after him,
> The maker of the axe large and small, and the welder and temperer,

The chooser breathing his breath on the cold steel and trying the edge
   with his thumb,
The one who clean-shapes the handle and sets it firmly in the socket.

Appropriately for this poem of materials, the poet not only takes as his central trope a tool that is a primary shaper of a key material of industry, but he also breaks that tool down into its own material basis and reconstructs it for us anew.

Whitman's rebirthing of the broadaxe is established as an idea at the poem's very outset. The phallic depiction of the axe in the first line ("Weapon, naked, shapely, wan") is continued in the second line, which suggests both sexual intercourse and the process of childbirth ("head from mother's bowels drawn"). The poem invites us to consider the withdrawal of the penis from the vagina and the emergence of a child during birth in the same poetic gesture. Whitman's phallus/child symbolism here parallels his interest in the broadaxe as an instrument that shapes the material from which it is derived. An axe requires wood for its existence, but once it exists, it acts upon the thing that created it in what Whitman portrays as a positive creative gesture. His anthropomorphic symbolism continues in the next line: "Wooded flesh and metal bone, limb only one and lip only one," where the presence of the "limb" continues the phallic connotation, and the "lip" suggests both the vulva and also hints at another emerging strand in the poem: Whitman's ongoing interest in language, that which emerges from the lips of humanity. The next line's "Gray-blue leaf by red-heat grown" is literally a description of the axe's head, but alert readers may also associate "leaf" with *Leaves of Grass*. The resonance here is suggestive: just as the axe is a thing made but also a maker of things, so a leaf in a book is a thing made and a maker (and container) of things. The second part of the line, "helve produced from a little seed sown" — a description of the axe's handle — again suggests the poet's fascination with an instrument designed to shape the material from which it is made. "Resting the grass amid and upon" is a particularly riddling line, one that picks up on threads of meaning suggested by the earlier "lip" and "leaf." On the most obvious level it is the axe that is resting "amid and upon" the grass, an image rejoined later when the poet describes "The log at the woodpile, the axe supported by it." However, the line's odd grammatical construction puts pressure on the phrase, teasing out sound associations and the idea of the poet "wresting" his (*Leaves of*) grass as the axe-like shaper of his own poems. The sestet's final line conveys something of the new role Whitman envisions for his emblematic broadaxe: its passiveness here hinting at the axe's withdrawal from its status as a weapon and its new function as an instrument of construction we depend on in our modern industrial society.

Nearly all of the poem's most important ideas are subtly compressed into these dense, tightly formed opening lines. At its most fundamental level Whitman's broadaxe is a symbol of the intersection between human agency and the materials with which it interacts, as well as about the resulting "Strong shapes, and attributes of strong shapes" suggested by catalogs presenting the "Long varied train of an emblem." Just as Whitman's opening conflates the axe with the form of the human body, "Broad-Axe Poem" ultimately conflates the creation of objects by the axe with the creation of human types by the poet. This move from the utilitarian instrumentality of the axe to the cultural instrumentality of art is indicated by the poem's second stanza, where we move from the axe and its resultant shapes to "dabs of music, / Fingers of the organist skipping staccato over the keys of the great organ."

Whitman also slyly hints at this aspect of his poem in a rather incongruous line inserted into a catalog in stanza 4: "The loose drift of character, the inkling through random types, the solidification." This line is followed by a catalog of various workers occupied in their trades, emphasizing that one's job forms or "solidifies" human character. More subtly, however, the word "types" recalls the poet's personal work-related experience with the types used in letterset printing, a suggestion reinforced by the echo of "inking" we hear in "inkling."[40] Interpreted this way, the line suggests something of the character-making power the poet claimed for his poetic enterprise — how the inking of type, such as that used to print his poems, leads to the solidification of individual selfhood. Printing itself at this time was the business of machines that were, like the axe, a fusion of wood and metal: the wooden handles on the iron press, the wood frames holding the lines of metal type.

The poem's third stanza, which may have been suggested by a pamphlet Whitman read containing the text of a speech by the ironmaster and philanthropist Abram S. Hewitt, returns us to the "mother's bowels" from which the axe is drawn, the "Lands of iron! Lands of the make of the axe!"[41] From the birthplace of the axe we move to the birthplace of the poem itself, which presents the poet contemplating the sound of "the irregular tapping of rain" as he stares from his "hut" at the "log at the wood pile" and "the axe supported by it." The noise of the rainstorm leads the poet to contemplate "The thought of ships struck in the storm" by lightning — and also by axes as gales necessitate "the cutting away of masts."

These thoughts lead Whitman to contemplate other users of the axe, from "wood-boys and wood-men" to the "butcher in the slaughter-house" to "lumber-men in their winter camp." Embedded in this catalog is a narrative in miniature, tracking the poet's imagination of the founding of the United States, from "The remembered print or narrative, the voyage at a venture of men" to "The voyage of those who sought a New England and found it" to "The settlements of Arkansas, Colorado, Ottawa, Willamette." Whitman's fancy alights upon "The house-builder at work in cities or anywhere," and, having been a carpenter himself, he lingers there for over a dozen lines, as he envisions the varied processes involved in the building of a house. His sustained interest in this passage holds more than just biographical significance, as a crucial thematic shift in the central portion of the poem turns our attention to the constructed results of the axe's labor: from the houses and other buildings produced by carpenters and their fellow laborers to the cities that these houses occupy and compose. After championing such material production in his descriptions of the axe, Whitman uses the platform he has established to push his inquiry further and challenge readers' assumptions about materiality and how we value cultural production. What, he asks, is the true underlying material of a great civilization? His epigrammatic answer marks an important shift in the poem: "The greatest city is that which has the greatest man or woman, / If it be a few ragged huts, it is still the greatest city in the world." For a "Song of the Broad-Axe" this might seem to be an incongruous assertion, but Whitman's broadaxe represents the intersection between raw materials and active human agency. It is a poem as much about the shapers as the shapes they produce.

Just as the axe is a tool that shapes the material from which it is made, so too human society shapes the people it comprises. From its direct assertion of the primacy of humanity over its inert products, "Broad-Axe Poem" proceeds with a reflection on the shaping power of the social forces of morality, art, labor relations, and politics:

Where thrift is in its place, and prudence is in its place,
Where behavior is the finest of the fine arts,
Where the men and women think lightly of the laws,
Where the slave ceases, and the master of slaves ceases
Where the populace rise at once against the audacity of elected
　　persons

Here and in the lines that follow in this stanza Whitman outlines his ideal for American society: an Emersonian delineation of power maintaining the centrality of the self-reliant individual, a site "Where outside authority enters always after the precedence of inside authority." Whitman champions the power of ordinary individuals over what he regards as the ephemeral cultural productions of unrealized imaginations: "How beggarly appear poems, arguments, orations, before an electric deed! / How the floridness of the materials of cities shrivels before a man's or woman's look!" Yet he maintains his own revolutionary role by distinguishing a superior form of being that not only shapes but transforms cultural materials:

All waits, or goes by default, till a strong being appears;
A strong being is the proof of the race, and of the ability of the
　　universe,
When he or she appears, materials are over-awed,
The dispute on the soul stops,
The old customs and phrases are confronted, turned back, or laid away.

This is Whitman at his most Nietzschean, privileging an Übermensch-like role for a "strong being" who transcends the conventional behavior of humanity and plays a radically transformative cultural role. There is no longer a need for "dispute on the soul" (presumably because of this being's capacity to comprehend and indicate truth), and the "customs and phrases" that remain of older times are "confronted" and "turned back" by this individual's transformative vision, a process not unlike Nietzsche's descriptions of the destructive use of the will to power. Whitman was an ardent democrat, but his egalitarian attitude coexisted with an equally fervent belief in the cultural exceptionalism of certain historically determined "strong beings."

Lest there be any doubt that Whitman regards himself as filling this role, the poem's mode of address shifts to an aggressive query targeted directly at the reader:

> What is your money-making now? What can it do now?
> What is your respectability now?
> What are your theology, tuition, society, traditions, statute books now?
> What are your jibes of being now?
> What are your cavils about the soul now?

The Whitman of these early visionary poems is not content to present a symbolic drama of historical change. His "Broad-Axe Poem" would enact that change, as he works to transform its central symbol from a trope to a tool—that is to say, from a representation of cultural definition and change to an actual catalyst for that change, born in the minds of responsive readers. The effect resembles another key moment in one of his 1856 works, his "Sun-Down Poem" (later retitled "Crossing Brooklyn Ferry"), where he interrupts his reflections with a direct address, asking the reader, "We understand, then, do we not? / What I promised without mentioning it, have you not accepted?" Both "Sun-Down Poem" and "Broad-Axe Poem" attempt to realize one of the inexpressible understandings that the poet confronts in "Poem of The Sayers of The Words of The Earth." Whitman views these "unspoken meanings of the earth" as something "print cannot touch," and so, to offer such "hints of meaning" as are possible, he employs what he elsewhere describes as an "indirect mode."

Whitman describes this strategy in the very same notebook in which he drafted lines for both "Sun-Down Poem" and "Song of the Broad-Axe": "Convey what I want to convey by models or illustrations of the results I demand. — Convey these by <u>characters</u>, selections of <u>incidents</u> and <u>behaviour</u>. This indirect mode of attack is better than all direct modes of attack."[42] Having already presented such "<u>characters</u>, selections of <u>incidents</u> and <u>behaviour</u>" — the material building blocks for his readers to reimagine their lives — Whitman confronts the reader in an assured yet intimate tone that implies an immediate connection between poet and reader. Sometimes this sense of immediacy is achieved with statements implying that Whitman is present to hear his readers' answers ("We understand then, do we not?"); often, as with his more aggressive querying in "Broad-Axe Poem," he employs a repeated emphasis on "now," creating the sense of a continuous present enacted in the exchange of meaning produced by language.

In both "Sun-Down Poem" and "Broad-Axe Poem" Whitman strives to create a connection across time with his readers, using "models and illustrations" of the foreseen results of his poem in combination with his intimate, direct address. Both poems also work to bridge time and place with an emphasis on the shared materiality of the world, "similitudes of the past and those of the future."[43] In "Sun-Down Poem" he stresses the shared material of water in the river and, more problematically, the ferry he used to cross it.[44] In "Broad-Axe Poem" he emphasizes the wood and iron ore that are the materials composing the axe:

> — A sterile landscape covers the ore — there is as good as the best, for all the forbidding appearance,
> There is the mine, there are the miners,

The forge-furnace is there, the melt is accomplished, the hammers-men
    are at hand with their tongs and hammers,
What always served and always serves, is at hand.

Although both poems are similar in this aspect, in "Broad-Axe Poem" Whitman pushes further in his effort to form a connection with readers across time. The imaginative bond advanced in "Sun-Down Poem" ultimately depends on the power of poetic description to convey the similitude between the world Whitman perceived and the one he believes his audiences will. "Broad-Axe Poem" makes a similar gesture by emphasizing the sameness of the basic materials used in the productive operations of human society, but here Whitman seems less confident relying on description as a means of forming a connection with readers. As with his use of the shared presence of the physical artifact of the book in a poem like "Whoever You Are Holding Me Now in Hand," in "Broad-Axe Poem" he relies on descriptions of objects in the world, but also on his readers' perception of the actual text before them as a binding force in his work.

After retiring his "European headsman" — symbol of the Old World and its militant heritage — and watching "the headsman withdraw and become useless," he witnesses "the mighty and friendly emblem" that the axe has become in his poetic revaluation. His symbolic transformation achieved, the poet claims his axe and offers a self-qualification, followed by an extraordinary enactment of his poetic axe at work:

America! I do not vaunt my love for you,
I have what I have.

The axe leaps!
The solid forest gives fluid utterances,

They tumble forth, they rise and form,

Hut, tent, landing, survey,

Flail, plough, pick, crowbar, spade,

Shingle, rail, prop, wainscot, jamb, lath, panel, gable,

Citadel, ceiling, saloon, academy, organ, exhibition-house, library,

Cornice, trellis, pilaster, balcony, window, shutter, turret, porch,

Hoe, rake, pitch-fork, pencil, wagon, stuff, saw, jackplane, mallet,
    wedge, rounce,

Chair, tub, hoop, table, wicket, vane, sash, floor,

Work-box, chest, stringed instrument, boat, frame, and what not
    (*LG*, 1856, 153–54)

When the new American "axe leaps!" what the "solid forest" issues aren't felled trees but "fluid utterances," and Whitman launches into one of the most unique and provocative passages in all his writing: a list of fifty-five unadorned words, a self-consciously antilyrical passage that might seem to justify for some readers the complaint heard from critics from 1855 until today that this writing "isn't poetry" (that is, doesn't meet aesthetic preconceptions). As an early critic complained, "According to Whitman's theory, the greatest poet is he who performs the office of camera to the world, merely reflecting what he sees — art is merely reproduction."[45]

Keeping in mind that this poem begins with six lines of rhymed iambic meter and was preceded by years of language study and the compilation of countless lists in his notebooks, we can be sure that the inclusion of this prosaic list was neither an accident nor a failure of lyric propensity. Indeed in an aside just before this list Whitman makes sure we are aware he knows what he's doing, when he says, "America! I do not vaunt my love for you, / I have what I have." What he has is language, and what his unvaunted list is doing is calling attention to itself as a presentation of language on the page. His phrase "The axe speaks!" emphasizes that what follows are in fact words — words representing the material productions of the New World broadaxe, but words nevertheless, the actual shapes of letters on a leaf of paper. Punctuating this material emphasis on language, the commas between each of these words become the linguistic chop marks left by the symbol/tool of the axe, each mark slashing out a new object on the page.

Moving from the tightest formal writing in all of his mature published poems to the opposite extreme — *Leaves of Grass*'s loosest and, literally and intentionally, most artless linguistic sequence — establishes a powerful and instructive structural tension in the poem. Here Whitman demonstrates just how capacious his concept of a poem has become. The same artistic vehicle that employs the sculptured and intricate musical and metrical detail of his opening sestet can also, in his conception, include a nearly formless assemblage of bare words, united only by their characteristic as products made from wood. To make such a gesture is to offer a powerful critique of the underlying nature of poetry. Whitman rejects any criteria based on form and structure, emphasizing only his art's foundational *material* as a viable defining quality.

Certainly there is bravado in such an audacious and aggressive dismissal of generic conventions, but there is also, as we have seen in exploring his notebooks, a self-conscious theoretical foundation informing his poem's formal statement. This climactic moment in "Broad-Axe Poem" is the culmination of years of aesthetic and linguistic inquiry, manifesting many of the ideas we have explored, especially his concept of the poem of materials. At the same moment that he presents the "shapes" hewn by a broadaxe acting on the base material for (and from) which it was made, he also breaks down the shape of poetry into *its* base material of language. This simultaneously creative and destructive gesture demonstrates both qualities described in his "Poem of Materials" note. He offers his readers two kinds of poetically reimagined materials—language and the productions of the axe—and at the same time stresses the material nature of his art form as his broadaxe "speaks" its "words of the earth," leaving its chop marks in the form of commas, which are the only syntactic device shaping these lines at all. By presenting his artistic material as poetically "over-awed" even in its presentation as a mere list, Whitman demonstrates how the "old customs" of poetic conventions "are confronted, turned back, or laid away."

In the poem's denouement Whitman offers a litany of the shapes that arise from his country's cultural and industrial materials. Echoing the three-word exclamation that introduced the previous passage, "The axe speaks!" Whitman introduces each of these catalog stanzas with the repeated refrain "The shapes arise!" These catalogs include a broad range of material productions, from "Shapes of factories, arsenals, foundries, markets" to "the coffin-shape for the dead to lie within in his shroud." Twice the poet lingers on the production of a particular object. First he devotes a stanza to the production of a ship: an important symbol for Whitman and the source of a crucial image he had already developed, "The live-oak kelson" he envisioned in asserting that "a kelson of the creation is love."[46] He also dwells on the shape of a door on a house, an image he uses as a transition to describing the human beings that emerge from it: first "Her shape arises!" in the form of his ideal model for American womanhood, and then her counterpart, "His shape arises!" Whitman's description here of perfect femininity is the poem's most disappointing moment. In contrast with his masculine ideal, "she" is a generic abstraction, her most noteworthy quality being her purity in the face of "the gross and soiled" thinking of base men, their "quarrels, hiccuped songs, smutty expressions." This passage was originally drafted in Whitman's "Crossing Brooklyn Ferry" notebook and appears to have been composed with another poem initially in mind. Defined by her response to men, "she is possessed of herself," but she is also "silent," a moderately more confident echo of the passive and "pure" historical feminine ideal.

Unsurprisingly Whitman seems far more interested in his ideal man, a more complex and developed paragon based on Whitman himself. His portrayal here is reminiscent of descriptions from the poem eventually called "Song of Myself," a figure "Arrogant, masculine, naive, rowdyish [. . .] / Of pure American breed" and "reckless health." This stanza presents one of Whitman's more earnest uses of the pseudo-science of phrenology in his description of his masculine American ideal as "corroborating his phrenology," followed by an amalgam of personal characteristics, some phrenological, some more general. More interesting than his self-portrayal is the passage's compositional history, part of which can be traced back to one of his self-reviews of the first edition of *Leaves*, a short biographical sketch originally published in the *Brooklyn Daily Times* as "Walt Whitman, a Brooklyn Boy."[47] Whitman extracted large sections from his review and used them intact, including "Of pure American breed, free from taint from top to toe, free forever from headache and dyspepsia," a passage repeated verbatim, the only difference being his addition of the phrase "clean-breathed" to the line's end. There are other substantial appropriations from his self-published review, and he appears unconcerned about the possibility that anyone would notice. (In fact he directly confronted early readers of "Broad-Axe Poem" with his appropriations from his self-review by including this very same review in an appendix to the 1856 *Leaves*!)[48] Such nonchalance suggests that Whitman's review, despite its ostensible anonymity, was not intended to deceive its readers, a suggestion reinforced by the fact that the review contains facts about Whitman's person that would have been impossible for anyone but Whitman or an intimate friend to know. An experienced journalist like Whitman surely knew how odd it was for a review to contain such details about its subject as "six feet high, a good feeder, never once using medicine, drinking water only—a swimmer in the river or bay or by the seashore [. . .] ample limbed, weight one hundred and eighty-five pounds." Appropriately for a review emphasizing the virtues of the author's egotism, Whitman defies conventions of self-modesty that discourage the idea of such "vanity reviews." Furthermore this appropriation leaves a clear window for readers to ascertain a glimpse of the poet's collage-like creative method and appropriation of outside text. Whitman didn't disguise his love of recycling previously published language; in some cases, as here, he actually flaunted it.

A poem of materials is a poem of and about the parts that make up a whole. At the beginning of this chapter I noted the remarks of one of Whitman's friends who, after the publication of the first *Leaves*, advised Whitman to create a poem like a cathedral, leaving readers "with great impressions of its largeness, solidity, and spaciousness without troubling [them] with its parts." Whitman, however, did trouble himself with "parts," both of the world and of his poems, methodically deconstructing and reconstructing the objects around us so that they respond to our most vital sensitivities—furnishing these "parts toward the soul," as he once famously phrased it.[49] Although many of his early poems are so motivated, "Broad-Axe Poem" is special for how it engages the process as a self-conscious theme. His visionary "axe leaps" so that the militant, feudal "axe sleeps" and the industrious New World "axe speaks," articulating the necessary shapes of cultural materials and of the people that produce and are produced by them. At the same time his poem presents words as materials. In lieu of a language that can bring its readers into direct engagement with the world, the poet brings his readers into a more direct engagement with language. The site of reading becomes an analogue of the reality that words portray but cannot deliver.

5

Whitman after Collage /
Collage after Whitman

After Whitman discovered his groundbreaking approach to literary composition he struggled with how to define and describe it, even in his notes to himself. The word *collage* had not yet been invented; nor did Whitman have recourse to related terms such as *pastiche*, *montage*, or *found art*. Lacking a critical lexicon for his creative method he worked with the tools at his disposal.[1] In an early notebook often described as a kind of homemade dictionary he offers this puzzling definition for the Italian *rifacimento*: "riffacciamento-rumble (sort of mosaic work mixture mess." The word, which Whitman likely encountered in reference to operas, refers to a modernization of a musical or literary artwork, and Whitman's misunderstanding (there is no intrinsic mosaic-like quality to rifacimentos) seems to reflect his preoccupation with his evolving creative process.[2] Introducing his prose collection, *Specimen Days*, he described a creative backstory in which he would "go home, untie the bundle [of notebook fragments], reel out diary-scraps and memoranda, just as they are, large or small, one after another, into print-pages, and let the melange's lackings and wants of connection take care of themselves." It's difficult to imagine a better description of collage making, and the result, Whitman unabashedly announced, was "the most wayward, spontaneous, fragmentary book ever printed" (*PW* 1).

Having invented a form of composition so novel that no vocabulary existed to describe it, Whitman was forced to torque the meaning of the approximate language that did exist in order to indicate his intentions. Fortunately for his twenty-first-century readers, a substantial amount of writing and thinking has been subsequently applied to the kind of artistic production he envisioned and made. Part of my purpose in this coda to my exploration of the poet's creative process is to take advantage of this emergent body of thought so that we may better understand what Whitman accomplished. Although literary collage has recently evolved into a widely discussed aspect of modern and postmodern writing, collage has evoked an even more substantial record of critical thought in the visual arts, where the term was originally coined to describe certain Cubist practices of Picasso and Braque, and developed further in discussions of work associated with Surrealism and Dada. More specifically I hope to illuminate Whitman's achievement by way of another peerless innovator, Marcel Duchamp, whose relation to the visual arts significantly mirrors Whitman's relation to literature. In addition to Duchamp I consider the work of some who interpreted him, relying especially on thinking associated with conceptual art. My argument is that Whitman created an art of ideas that few have recognized and of which even fewer have understood the implications. Like some protean miasma pooled beneath the surface, certain of his most radical ideas underlie those of conceptual art, and only now are we prepared to see how. So advanced were some of these ideas that to understand their significance we must read *back* to them through the lens of what we now know. The ensuing conversation flows both ways: just as subsequent art forms help us to understand Whitman, so Whitman too sheds light upon his heirs. Whitman anticipates those later movements that worked to consign the existing world around them to their own artistic ends, and so, far from representing a failure of imagination, his appropriations are inseparable from his originality.

What follows is both an interpretation of these ideas and an argument for their creator's innovation. The importance of Whitman's *influence* on subsequent artists throughout the world is no longer in question, and studies of this influence on specific individuals are legion. My argument is different. I am not arguing for his influence, but for his *precedence*. Although I touch upon the writing habits of certain subsequent poets and writers, I am more concerned with coming to grips with the implications of Whitman's writing than I am with the specific ways artists themselves processed his work. These implications have taken many generations to tease out, and now that we are finally in a position to assess them other innovations have emerged that obscure our view of Whitman's. They have emerged in ways Whitman himself could never have anticipated, and their practitioners, aware of Whitman but not of those aspects of his work most salient to them, have often made neglectful claims for their own inventiveness or have turned to more immediately attractive innovators (such as Duchamp) to define the lineage of those artistic concepts most vital to them. My claim is to have identified a genuine breakthrough in artistic modes of expression, a breakthrough that generates much that is radical and exciting about modern and postmodern art, and a breakthrough that we can now see Whitman accomplishing first, so that even artists who may themselves have failed to see his radical acts are nonetheless profiting by them, developing formal and conceptual practices that Whitman initiated, even as they may be oblivious to his precedence. We must either recognize Whitman's role in the creation of these ideas or continue to propagate falsehoods about their history.

∽

The term *collage* derives from the French *coller* ("to glue") and was originally coined by a viewer at an exhibit of the work of Picasso and Braque. Both of those artists adopted the term to describe their latest productions, in which, working in close cooperation, they had developed a technique that introduced everyday objects onto the painted canvas.[3] These innovations, which occurred simultaneously around 1912, are thought to represent the origins of collage as a concept and practice in Western art, and it should be noted that my claims for Whitman are prescribed by this specific context.[4] Picasso's and Braque's experiments in this mode were relatively brief, but the technique was adapted vigorously by Futurists, Surrealists, and Dadaists. Where Cubist experiments were restricted to paper and paint, with the occasional real-world object implemented to portray a pictorial concept or philosophical view, these later experiments branched out significantly. Futurists incorporated varied scraps of typography, often for political purposes, sometimes adding found objects to relate art to the outside world. Dadaists continued the use of collage for explicitly political ends, but they broadened the palette of collage technique as well, targeting other subjects by creating aggressive, absurdist anti-art collages from various, mostly two-dimensional media.[5] Surrealists adapted collage to their more Freudian enterprise, juxtaposing bizarre image combinations in an effort to evoke the uncanny.

All of these uses of collage were considered radical to varying degrees and were largely rejected at the time by critics and popular audiences. As visual artists found increasing use for collage-like techniques throughout the twentieth century, including such noteworthy practitioners as David Hockney, Robert Rauschenberg, and Jonathan Talbot, the idea of collage was mainstreamed first into critical and then into popular discourse. At the same time, collage as a creative paradigm was disseminated throughout the arts, playing an important role in nearly every form of art in the twentieth century, from T. S. Eliot's appropriations of classical texts in *The Waste Land* in 1922, to the emergence of sampling as a musical technique pioneered by Lee "Scratch" Perry in 1968, to Colin Rowe and Fred Koetter's influential architectural propositions in *Collage City* ten years later.[6] It is this prevalence of collage throughout the arts that has led to such sweeping claims as Donald Barthelme's infamous statement, "The principle of collage is the central principle of all art in the twentieth century."

Obviously this brief history elides many important artists and hardly does justice to the importance of collage as a concept in twentieth-century art. What I hope it emphasizes, however, is the prestige that found art and collage have come to enjoy. Indeed it has become almost a cliché to claim, as Barthelme did, that collage is the defining art form of the twentieth century, and though the assertion is reductive and homogenizes a remarkably diverse creative output, enough truth resides in it that the claim has seldom been challenged. What started as a very specific practice—affixing paper and other objects to a painted canvas—has developed into a creative paradigm that has proven remarkably serviceable in mapping artistic production. Thus *collage* has developed two primary meanings: one, related to its original use, as "an artistic composition of materials and objects pasted over a surface," and another, broader definition as "a work, such as a literary piece, composed of both borrowed and original material."[7] It is the latter of these two meanings that provides the more important starting point to examine Whitman's contributions; however, the former meaning, meant to describe the conventional visual arts application of collage, also finds parallels in the poet's creative process.[8]

Having already explored Whitman's use of paper clippings (and sometimes glue) in his creative method, we can see how, to some extent, his literary technique actually resembles later collages in its physical embodiment. There are countless examples of the poet's word collages in his notebooks: leaves spackled with pasted-on snippets of text, some derived from his own hand, some extracted from outside sources such as newspaper articles and science books. The mobile fragments of text I explored in chapter 2 find their collage-like origins in these composite manuscripts. Traces of Whitman's cutting and pasting in his manuscripts remain apparent in the published products. As we've seen, there are elements akin to the jagged disjunctive quality of paper collages in his catalogs and lists: abrupt fits and starts, rough edges intact, with little or no effort to smooth together transitions, and catalog items, framed by self-contained lines, for which the only grammatical ligature is a comma.[9] Modern word processing has transformed the phrase *cut and paste* from a literal description into a convenient metaphor. Thus this phrase that originated in reference to visual arts collage has now come to signify textual applications; however, if we probe the history of visual arts collage, we find that Whitman's *literary* technique actually antedates visual collage. Ironically Whitman's creative process, which actually involves cutting and pasting of text, resembles the modern meaning of *cut and paste* far more than the technique to which it originally referred.

It is, however, the second dictionary definition that provides the more fertile launching point to delineate the poet's relation to his heirs. The dictionary's compact phrasing, "composed of both borrowed and original material," hides a provocative body of critical concerns, many of which can be traced back to the work of Marcel Duchamp. Picasso and Braque may be responsible for introducing the collaging of found materials as a viable creative *method* in Western art practices, but it is Duchamp who unveiled the method's profound and far-reaching implications. Neither Picasso nor Braque theorized his discoveries. They were concerned with the technical innovation itself, exploiting it with ferocious prolixity before moving on to other methods. Picasso, who was personally uninterested in Duchamp, is regarded by some art critics as having unconsciously created a readymade himself in his 1943 piece *Bull's Head* (*Tete de Toro*), a sculpture composed of a narrow, springless bicycle saddle with handlebars soldered outward from the seat's rear end, so that the seat resembles a bull's head with handlebars for its horns.[10] By 1943, of course, Duchamp had fully realized the concept of the readymade and had more or less moved on to explore other ideas. Cubist collage first legitimized the presence of found materials in art; Duchamp, in turn, forced audiences to confront the idea that such objects can, in and of themselves, constitute art when placed in an art context. To look at a ready-made object as art we are forced to rethink our definition of what art is or can be — or even whether any definition of art is possible at all.

It was only a year after the Cubist invention of the term *collage* in 1912 that Duchamp mounted a bicycle wheel atop a kitchen stool, creating what was soon to be known as his first readymade. A year later, in 1914, he created his second and third readymades, one of which was his first true or "unassisted" readymade: a bottle-drying rack he picked up at a large housewares emporium in the center of Paris. "I have purchased this as a sculpture already made," he explained two years later in a letter to his sister.[11] The name *readymade* and the elaboration of the idea didn't come about until the winter of 1916, when Duchamp purchased an ordinary snow shovel at a hardware store in New York and inscribed on the reinforcement plate of its business end the title *In Advance of the Broken Arm*. Soon after he wrote his sister, asking her to secure two items in his Paris studio, the bottle rack and the first readymade, the bicycle wheel he mounted on a kitchen stool in 1913. "Here, in N.Y.," he wrote, "I have bought some objects in the same vein and I treat them as <u>readymade</u>."[12] This is Duchamp's first recorded use of the term, and it marks the launching point for his discovery of perhaps the single most important strategy in the "little game between 'I' and 'me'" he played, and in so doing, changed the future of the visual arts.[13]

As a concept collage has always involved the interruption of artistic media with outside elements. Duchamp's concept of the readymade disposes altogether with conventional artistic media and instead situates the interruption of outside elements within the institutional context of museums and the intellectual framework of artistic definition. His most famous enactment of such a gesture occurred in 1917, when he submitted a work to an exhibit hosted by the Society of Independent Artists, a group friendly to Dadaists and Surrealists. It was an ordinary urinal, turned on its side so that the phallic plumbing connection normally at its top pointed to the viewer; he signed the work with the pseudonym "R. Mutt." This piece, which Duchamp humorously titled *Fountain*, proved too much even for the avant-garde tastes of the Independent Artists, and the board rejected it, despite the fact that the exhibit was billed as unjuried, allowing anyone who paid a small submission fee to contribute. The board members found themselves in the uncomfortable position of echoing the critics from whom they were supposedly independent, declaring that R. Mutt's offering was "not art." This prompted no small embarrassment when Duchamp, himself a board member of the group, immediately resigned. A brilliant publicity stunt (among other things), this calculated little dustup has since evolved into one of the most famous incidents in twentieth-century art and has become a focal point for critical discussions seeking to define art's function and value. The Society of Independent Artists could not come to terms with the idea that an unaltered real-world object constitutes art. By forcing the Society to reject his work, Duchamp exposed important assumptions about the nature of art and created a megaphone for the ideas implicit in all of his readymades, ideas that profoundly shaped how subsequent artists have approached their own work.

Adequately summarizing the commentary on Duchamp's ready-mades would require a book in itself; of necessity I will simplify these ideas. Though I focus on those aspects of the readymades most relevant to Whitman, the concepts I stress — Duchamp's "critique of the retinal," his rejection of technical mastery as a definitive artistic value, and his dissolution of the boundaries of acceptable artistic materials — are core concepts of his legacy. Through his attack on what he called "retinal art," Duchamp redefined art as an interactive *process* negotiated between artist and audience, and thus explicitly dislocated the concept of art from the objects of aesthetic admiration generally thought to contain it. The critique of the retinal underlies what he and his successors have more flamboyantly called "the death of painting," a phrase stressing the perceived devolution of the relevance of art intended primarily for visual stimulation. Related to this, Duchamp rejected the notion that art is fundamentally an expression of the triumph of personal technique or style. Divorced from both its conventional objects of attention and the human mastery of paint or clay, art instead comes to reside wherever it is found, an attitude that has led to a radical expansion of viable outlets of expression. Filtered through his own predilections and fervor, Whitman anticipated these ideas with the innovations I have already explored in this study.

∽

Duchamp's "critique of the retinal" is now generally regarded as the most important of his ideas, an opinion he himself shared. Except for his early paintings, almost all of his work can be seen to varying degrees as being influenced by this concept; to a large extent its most extreme elaboration led to his supposed cessation of artistic production in favor of playing chess in 1923.[14] We see the seed of Duchamp's rejection of retinal art when, in the autumn of 1912, he visited the Salon de la Locomotion Aérienne and, pausing before a propeller with the painter Fernand Léger and the sculptor Constantin Brancusi, declared to the latter, "Painting is finished. Who can do better than that propeller? Tell me, can you do that?"[15] For Duchamp at least, painting was indeed almost finished, as his interest in the readymades and his related masterwork, *The Large Glass*, soon thereafter replaced his commitment to canvas and paint. A visual artist who frequently trafficked with poets, Duchamp was scornful of the popular idea of "the stupid painter" (an idea indirectly endorsed by Picasso and later, arguably, by what has been described as Pollock's "romantic primitivism") and sought an art that found its reception more in the mind than in the eye.[16]

Always cagey, Duchamp usually avoided straightforward summaries of his own ideas, but late in his life, in his dialogues with Pierre

Cabanne, he offered a candid account of what his readymades and other works critiqued:

> Since the time of Courbet, it's been believed that painting is addressed to the retina. That was everyone's error. The retinal shudder! Before, painting had other functions: it could be religious, philosophical, moral. If I had a chance to take an anti-retinal attitude, it unfortunately hasn't changed much; our whole century is completely retinal, except for the Surrealists, who tried to go outside it somewhat. And still, they didn't go so far! In spite of what Breton says he believes in judging from a Surrealist point of view, down deep he's still really interested in painting in the retinal sense. It's absolutely ridiculous. It has to change; it hasn't always been like this.[17]

What Duchamp shudders at is the idea of an art that "merely" pleases the eye. Like any artist, he is responding to the climate in which his early sensibilities were formed. This was the turn of the century and the era of Picasso and Braque, of Cézanne and Matisse, artists who, for all their innovations, still addressed their work to the eye, to ideas of beauty and ugliness, approaches to how things are seen, concepts of color and perspective and formal composition. Although their work was radical in a different way (the rejection of representational value was no small change in the visual arts), it is easy to see that Cubism and later Abstract Expressionism conserved traditional values, presenting art aimed primarily at conventional aesthetic experience: standing before a painted canvas, admiring and being moved by its formal qualities, its use of color, brushstroke, texture. The art of these movements advanced art's means but not necessarily its ends.

Duchamp and his readymades explicitly preclude the possibility of this kind of response, which is different from rejecting the delight one may take in the objects themselves. He conspicuously admitted the pleasure he found in his *Bicycle Wheel*, for example, comparing the experience of watching the blurred spokes of a spinning wheel with the simple pleasure of watching flames crackle in a fire. His analogy is instructive: both a bicycle wheel and a fireplace offer the readymade pleasure of things already around us, pleasures arising from human ingenuity perhaps, but not from artistic technique. Tilting a urinal and hanging it on a museum wall may perversely (and comically) emphasize the formal attraction of its porcelain shape, a quality the urinal was unlikely to enjoy in its former, more humble employment, but this is a pleasure the artist indicates rather than makes. Duchamp's only interventions as an artist were to choose the object, change the context in which it was presented, and give it a title. The artist leaves nothing to admire from the artistic perspective that even an adventurous audience from his milieu expected, and both his own creative relation to the art object and the relation he allows his audience to have with it are rendered almost completely conceptual.

In this respect his gesture is analogous to Whitman's in a poem such as "Song of the Broad-Axe." The poem's extensive unadorned list of words for things shaped from the axe also represents a rejection of conventional artistic value. Such a list is intentionally devoid of any aspect of formal ingenuity or craft, forcing us to attend to the words as things in and of themselves. If we admire or take pleasure in the list, it is for the words alone, not the poet's effort in structuring them, which is arbitrary or, at most, minimal in terms of intentional artistic agency. This of course is Whitman's strategically chosen method. By refusing the kind of control that a poet is conventionally expected to exert upon language, he subtracts himself from the poem during this key passage, forcing us to confront the words as autonomous entities, which is why he claims just prior to the list that "The axe speaks!" these words. As with Duchamp, who defended the works of his pseudonym R. Mutt by emphasizing that he *chose* the urinal, Whitman reduces his own artistic authority to a level of choice, since the most that can be said about his creative, technical relation to the list is that he selected these words to include. Even the order of the words seems intentionally arbitrary, since the items that Whitman's axe speaks can be easily rearranged without affecting the meaning of his poetic gesture. Whitman's casual aside toward the end of the list emphasizes its arbitrary nature: "Chair, tub, hoop, table, wicket, vane, sash, floor, / Work-box, chest, string'd instrument, boat, frame, and what not." Even for Whitman, who delighted in using colloquialisms in his poems, inserting a term like "what not" in a list seems intentionally prosaic and cavalier. As with the contemporary use of "etc.," the term suggests that if he wished, he could go on choosing examples at whim.

Whitman is even more confrontational in his dismissal of artistic control in the revised conclusion to the poem eventually titled "I Sing the Body Electric." In its original 1855 version the poem concludes with one of Whitman's typical authoritative proclamations:

> Have you seen the fool that corrupted his own live body? or the fool
> that corrupted her own live body?
> For they do not conceal themselves, and cannot conceal themselves.
>
> Who degrades or defiles the living human body is cursed,
> Who degrades or defiles the body of the dead is not more cursed.[18]

The poet asserts control over the poem and its message, summarizing this theme in the poem and providing a sense of authoritative finality. When the poem next appeared in the 1856 edition of *Leaves* Whitman had removed the final two declarative lines and replaced them with a remarkable catalog of human body parts, stretching for dozens of lines and presenting well over a hundred elements of the human form. There is an intentionally de-authorized feel to the list, similar to the effect in the list from "Song of the Broad-Axe"; here, however, he uses the intentional absence of poetic discrimination to offer a social and political critique. Most of Whitman's body parts are innocuous enough, and over the course of dozens of examples the passage assumes the feel of an anatomical catalog, such as one might encounter in medical literature (only here the body parts are presented in an aggressively colloquial diction). Toward the middle of the list Whitman names those parts of the male anatomy that conventionally went unmentioned, or were mentioned only in the sanitized vocabulary of clinical jargon:

> Wrist and wrist-joints, hand, palm, knuckles, thumb, forefinger, finger-joints, finger-nails,
> Broad breast-front, curling hair of the breast, breast-bone, breast-side,
> Ribs, belly, backbone, joints of the backbone,
> Hips, hip-sockets, hip-strength, inward and outward round, man-balls, man-root,
> Strong set of thighs, well carrying the trunk above,
> Leg-fibres, knee, knee-pan, upper-leg, under-leg
> (*LG* 100)

Harmless enough now, the poet's naming of the male sexual organs was regarded as almost pornographic in Whitman's day; this section of *Leaves* was one of the most frequently cited passages by those who criticized the sexual content of his writing. However, in the context of the poem, where the list moves from head to toe, his presentation of "man-balls" and "man-root" is logically dictated only by their physical placement in the body. As with the catalog in "Song of the Broad-Axe," this list is devoid of any aspect of poetic craft, shaped only by the author's choice of words, and here he uses this arbitrary, craftless quality to frame his inclusion of sexual organs as merely an indexical function of his anatomical catalog. It is as if Whitman were saying, I am not purposefully choosing to mention these "unmentionable" parts—this is simply where they are.

Both Whitman and Duchamp were sensitive to the implications of depending on personal choice as a definitive artistic value, and both exploited this aspect of their work. If the only qualification an object requires to be considered art is that an artist chose it, the question immediately arises: On what criteria was the artist's choice made? Duchamp was keenly aware of the temptation to assume that his choices were based on some new approach to aesthetic consideration. Was the artist attempting to present some new definition of beauty based on an industrial, mass-produced aesthetic? Such an assumption would be antithetical to his true intention, which was to deprecate aesthetic, or "retinal," value as the centerpiece of artistic experience. In later interviews Duchamp explicitly rejected the role of visual attraction in his choice of ready-made objects: "A point which I want very much to establish is that the choice of these 'readymades' was never dictated by aesthetic delectation." In another interview with Pierre Cabanne he elaborated on his criteria for selecting objects: "In general, I had to beware of its 'look.' It's very difficult to choose an object, because, at the end of fifteen days, you begin to like it or hate it. You have to approach something with indifference, as if you had no aesthetic emotion. The choice of readymades is always based on visual indifference and, at the same time, on the total absence of good or bad taste."[19]

Duchamp's emphasis on the visual indifference involved in his selection of readymades led him to some novel means to ensure that he was removing his own taste from the process of selection. In one note he instructs himself to "Look for a readymade / which weighs a weight / chosen in advance / first decide on a / weight for each year / and force all readymades / of the same year / to be the same weight."[20] He doesn't seem to have followed up on these instructions, but his speculations regarding such arbitrary criteria for the selection of ready-made objects reflect his aversion to the idea of subjective aesthetic preference. Whitman of course never envisioned such deliberate measures; however, he took pains to convey that his choices for what he would include were not based on aesthetic considerations. In *Democratic Vistas*, for example, he announces "a new founded literature, not merely to copy or reflect existing surfaces, or pander to what is called taste — not only to amuse, pass away time, celebrate the beautiful, the refined, the past, or exhibit technical, rhythmic, or grammatical dexterity" (*PW* 1:212). Like Duchamp, Whitman saw taste as a significant obstacle to vital artistic expression. For both, the idea of taste was corrupted by elite historical associations that implied an arbitrary, outdated set of values regarding the appropriate subject matter for art. Thus Whitman promised his readers an art form like nature itself, which "Makes no discriminations, has no conceivable failures, / Closes nothing, refuses nothing, shuts none out" (*LG* 221). Both artists theorized a form of artistic production that "makes no discriminations" about what can and cannot be art, but their strategies toward that goal differed wildly. Duchamp's minimalist approach severely constrained the process for selecting what could be art, presenting intentionally arbitrary criteria to reflect his belief that conventional values such as beauty were themselves arbitrary qualifiers, contingent upon historical inertia and imaginative complacency for their privileged status. Whitman, ever the maximalist, attempted to remove *all* criteria from his selection process, evoking an art without boundaries that would include everything in its embrace. Put more succinctly, where Duchamp says *Because art can include anything, I must not, myself, choose*, Whitman says *Because I, the artist, must choose, I must choose to include everything*. Both were responding to the same problem, even if their reactions were contradictory — or even, arguably, antithetical.

Although their strategies for artistic definition stood in opposition, in another sense they were parallel — not only in regard to their underlying goals, but in the objects their strategies ultimately tended to pursue. Like Duchamp, Whitman frequently presented ordinary objects of commercial production as objects worthy of our regard as art. Thus in "Song of the Broad-Axe" what "The axe speaks!" in the poem are the ready-made artifacts of industrial society. It is true, of course, that Duchamp and Whitman adopted very different relations to these objects. Where Whitman's catalogs and lists, especially in his early poems, usually affirm a celebratory relation to the things they present, Duchamp's engagement with the objects of his readymades is better described as a subversive critique. Readymades such as the formidably pronged *Bottle Drier (Bottlerack)* and his inscribed steel dog comb (*Comb*) exploit the sadistic visual appearance of the objects and suggest a dark underside to the consumer's relation to mundane commodities.[21] Others, such as *Fountain* and *Fresh Widow* (a French window whose panes are backed by black leather) bring out a perverse sexual character in the objects. All of these readymades play off the quality Marx described as "consumer fetishism": the tendency in capitalist society to sexualize and ascribe human qualities to ordinary commercial objects, seducing consumers with the promise of fantastic or erotic rewards. If Whitman's celebration of the objects of commercial production today strikes us as strange or naïve, it is worth keeping in mind that these objects were for the most part expressions of individual labor and were not generally imbued with the kind of false talismanic power Duchamp engaged. Whitman's broadaxe is the poet's symbol of the relation between humanity and the base materials of the earth, and so "Song of the Broad-Axe" naturally develops a different relation to domestic objects.[22] Nevertheless, though fundamentally different in their social context, both Whitman and Duchamp used these objects similarly in their relation to art. Neither mid-nineteenth-century poetry nor early twentieth-century visual art found much of a place for banal relics like a snow shovel or a wooden tub, and their unadorned interjection as art significantly interrupted aesthetic presumptions about suitable objects of artistic attention. Thus both artists used such objects to subvert and expand conventional artistic assumptions, Duchamp with visual media and Whitman with words.

As we have seen, a significant part of Whitman's project was to offer these words, transformed by their involvement in the poem, as the poetically realized materials of future artistic endeavor. He was frustrated by what he perceived as the disengagement of America's fledgling poets from their own native environment. He believed that his poetic contemporaries were crippled by nostalgia for outmoded European conventions. This presented a number of problems, not the least of which was a poetic vocabulary dislocated from the physical environment of its users. From a personal creative standpoint, Whitman's solution involved moving the act of writing beyond the shelter of one's desk and home and out into the light of day, actually composing in the presence of the people and objects his poems describe. This is what Whitman's friend and biographer Richard Maurice Bucke meant when he reiterated the poet's claim, "Certainly no book was ever more directly written from living impulses and impromptu sights, and less in the abstract."[23] But Whitman went beyond just writing in the presence of empirical reality and using the native words for what he found there. Like Duchamp, he sought a confrontational strategy to evoke the change he desired. It was not enough to say, These American words can be made into poetry, though this is one implication of his project. He asserted that the words already are poetry as they are used by people every day — not merely "poetic," as his contemporaries might say, but actually ready-made *poetry.*

This difference is crucial. Prior to Whitman, of course, poets had found aspects of "the poetic" in the "humble language" of ordinary speech. Selective (and often ironic) use of vernacular had long been a vital aspect of pastoral traditions, and Romantics often embraced the vocabulary of those not educated in poetry, as is perhaps most obviously emphasized in Wordsworth's *Lyrical Ballads.* Whitman's gesture in "Song of the Broad-Axe" is quite different. To allow that everyday language can be rendered poetic is ultimately to continue policing the borders of rarefied artistic discrimination. It is to say that I, the poet, can use these words poetically, transforming them into poetry through technical and imaginative proficiency. Where such poets had previously worked to lift such language into the stable artistic context of the poem, Whitman employed words as *ready-made* poetry to destabilize the artistic context itself, to redefine the essential idea of what a poem was and could do. To enact such a change, Whitman knew, it was necessary to interrupt the reception of his writing *as poetry* and force readers into new interpretive relations with the language before them. Readers educated to read poetry will naturally read it as poetry, situating even such strange poetic specimens as *Leaves of Grass* within received concepts of art, concepts that were anathema to Whitman's deeper ambitions, which involved nothing less than the acceleration of what he saw as a progressive evolution of human consciousness. Just as Duchamp sought to dislocate art from conventional art objects such as paintings and sculptures, Whitman dislocated poetry away from the poem, defining it instead as a perceptual and conceptual transformation negotiated between poet and reader. For both, art takes place not in the poem or painting, but between such objects and those who behold them. To awake their audiences to this understanding it was necessary to confront them with something that both was and was not "art."

It is for this reason, in part, that Dadaist work has often been described as "anti-art." There are valid reasons to associate Duchamp with Dada (Duchamp himself accepted the label when it served his purposes); however, in this respect the association is misleading. Where most Dadaist work was purely destructive, Duchamp is now recognized as having both negated previous artistic values and posited constructive alternatives. The destructive anti-art aspect of Duchamp's legacy is bluntly apparent in his readymades, which abandon all pretense of art as the term had been previously understood and which were initially rejected as such by all but a small coterie of the artist's friends and admirers.[24] The positive aspect of his work took longer to recognize. Although a few artists, such as Man Ray and Francis Picabia, were immediately affected by Duchamp's constructive ideas, the art world at large was preoccupied with the achievements of the Cubists and other prominent painters such as Matisse. In the 1940s and 1950s Robert Rauschenberg, Jasper Johns, and John Cage were among the first outside Duchamp's initial circle of friends to become intrigued by the conceptual and formal intricacies of his work.[25] In the 1960s the floodgates opened to such movements as Fluxus, Minimalism, Conceptualism, Performance, Land Art, and others, all of which have been informed, to varying degrees, by Duchamp's work. Although opinions vary about the value and importance of these movements, Duchamp's anticipation of them is seldom disputed.

The critic and theorist Thierry de Duve offers a succinct explanation of why Duchamp has proven so useful to recent artists when he describes him as "an artist who outstrips Picasso's importance, because of having transgressed the limits of painting and having submitted art in general to the linguistic turn that Conceptual art's task would be, precisely, to register."[26] As de Duve knows, Duchamp's influence extends beyond submitting art to the linguistic turn as articulated by French poststructuralism; he further predicted a "linguistic turn" in the sense of a visual art enacting (as opposed to conveying) a semantic content for its audience. In a broad sense, what Duchamp's idea and his readymades have led to is a radical pressure on the art object, so that for many, the products of art have become less important than, and in some cases even superfluous to, the conceptual or perceptual changes they are intended to produce. In more confrontational enactments the art object is completely forgone, just as Duchamp himself ostensibly stopped making art objects after 1923 to focus on playing chess.

One of the most extreme elaborations of the implications of Duchamp's critique comes from Joseph Kosuth, who declared in his seminal 1969 text "Art after Philosophy," "All art (after Duchamp) is conceptual (in nature) because art only exists conceptually." Kosuth asserts that objects are now "irrelevant" to art and that although artists may now elect to "employ" objects, art itself "is finally conceptual." Put another way, at a certain point the art object becomes nothing more than the "physical residue" of the acts of mind that truly constitute art and thus can be done away with. Explaining why he had finally stopped producing objects, Kosuth says that his friends, having lived through the recent New York art scene with him, had begun having such powerful sensory experiences of the ordinary world that "perhaps mankind was beginning to outgrow the need for art on that level."[27] Like Whitman, Kosuth sees art's function not "as aiming toward art or aestheticism," as Whitman put it, but as advancing the development of consciousness.[28] Also like Whitman, Kosuth's practices and those of others like him were profoundly alarming to many critics at the time. In a special issue of the College Art Association's *Art Journal* devoted to the subject of conceptual art, Irving Sandler insisted that such attitudes destroyed "every notion of what art should be."[29] Similarly Murray Krieger worried that conceptual art's "leap beyond Pop Art" would "complete the obliteration of the realm of art, its objects, its museums."[30] It is particularly interesting for my discussion that for artists like Kosuth and others, such as Claes Oldenburg — as well as for many of their critics — the terms of their statements often refer to the democratically accessible world of ordinary life in contrast to the "elite" world of art objects. If in the unlikely event these critics had been reading Whitman closely at the time, they might not have framed their discussions in such apocalyptic terms.

Decades before Duchamp and over a century before Kosuth and other conceptual artists, Whitman offered as radical an interpretation of art's function as did any of them. From his earliest published statements on poetic theory in the preface to the 1855 *Leaves* until his last major statement in "A Backward Glance O'er Travel'd Roads" Whitman instructs us again and again to regard his work not as poetry, but as something that can achieve the higher end of helping his audience "possess the origin of all poems" — that is, "possess the good of" the world all around us (LG 30). Duchamp seems not to have been a reader of Whitman, but if he had been, this artist who claimed without scorn that America's greatest art is its development of indoor plumbing would have surely been charmed by Whitman's descriptions of the material industry of man as works of art. In one of his most amusing lines Whitman, like Duchamp, even affirmed plumbing specifically as a source of artistic inspiration, claiming in "Song of the Exposition" (which he eventually placed directly after "Song of the Broad-Axe") that the muse will now be found "Bluff'd not a bit by drain-pipe, gasometers, artificial fertilizers, / . . . / She's here, install'd amid the kitchen ware!" Whitman's theoretical statements and the tropes he used to illustrate them were not approached with the same levity. They bear the stamp of his age in their lofty rhetoric and Romantic elevation of the natural world. For Duchamp such enthusiasms were, of course, passé. Art that celebrated the natural world had become a mainstay for many of the "retinal" artistic predecessors that he rejected, and he scorned and parodied the grandiose statements of "artistic genius," adopting a decidedly cooler and more whimsical rhetorical pose. But these are differences in temperament; scratch the surface, and we find striking parallels in their definitions of art and attitude toward the work that preceded them.

Before readers encountered a single poetic line of the first edition of *Leaves of Grass* Whitman worked to shape and guide their engagement with his work, confronting them with a challenging conceptual instruction manual in the form of his 1855 preface. This remarkable document, the first anti-art manifesto of America's nascent avant-garde, is peppered with claims that elevate agencies in the world over the agency of art. We are told that "the United States themselves are essentially the greatest poem" and also, in a long list that concludes the preface's third paragraph, that all manner of behavior in his country's citizens, from "their curiosity and welcome of novelty" to "their susceptibility to a slight," down to a simple physical gesture like "the President's taking off his hat to [the citizens] not they to him" is "unrhymed poetry" that "awaits the gigantic and generous treatment worthy of it." Here Whitman goes beyond more traditional Romantic descriptions of the poetic qualities of nature to include a democratic range of details of human behavior, from the mundane and petty to the noble as poetry more worthy than that of all lines of verse that already existed. In one of the preface's most famous statements, Whitman also surpassed his contemporaries' conceptions of art by explicitly rejecting it as a form of personal achievement, defining it instead in terms of its audience's response by claiming, "A great poem is no finish to a man or woman but rather a beginning" (LG 710, 727).

There are numerous statements in the preface that seem to anticipate conceptual art, perhaps the most precise and detailed of which is this attack on what Whitman perceived as the core elements of his contemporaries' approach to poetry:

> The poetic quality is not marshalled in rhyme or uniformity or abstract addresses to things nor in melancholy complaints or good precepts, but is the life of these and much else and is in the soul. The profit of rhyme is that it drops seeds of a sweeter and more luxuriant rhyme, and of uniformity that it conveys itself into its own roots in the ground out of sight. (LG 11)

Here we find an explicit, conceptual inversion of how the relation between art and artistic form is traditionally conceived. "Rhyme" and "uniformity" do not "marshall" the "poetic quality"; nor does emotion (as with Wordsworth) or poetic instruction ("good precepts").

238

Rather, as Kosuth would argue over a century later, art — for Whitman "the poetic quality" — exists independently of its embodiments and is the "life of" not only art objects, but of consciousness (of "the soul"). Furthermore the "profit of" artistic technique (here "rhyme" and "uniformity") is that it "conveys itself" into its abstract origins and disappears. The radical art movements of the 1960s produced few anti-aesthetic statements as radical as this one, nor did many conceptual artists make such bold claims as the following one for their own art: "Read these leaves in the open air every season of every year of your life [. . .] and your flesh shall be a great poem and have the richest fluency not only in its words but in the silent lines of its lips and face and between the lashes of your eyes and in every motion and joint of your body" (*LG*, 11). Such a clear expression is easily paraphrased: Read my poems and you shall not aesthetically *appreciate* but *become* art.

Whitman's most developed statement about aesthetics comes with his publication of *Democratic Vistas* in 1871. While aesthetic inquiry appears scattered all throughout this assemblage of previously written essays, the long, freshly written introduction to the *Vistas* and the final, previously unpublished section originally titled "Orphic Literature" contain some of his most acute theoretic propositions.[31] The discussion of art, aesthetics, and culture that he weaves into *Democratic Vistas* is complex and often contradictory, but out of the whole, often by a process of repeating his most important propositions and abandoning his detours, an extraordinary account of the state and future of art emerges. Neither Duchamp nor Kosuth nor any other radical artist of the past four decades has attacked the art and artists of their day as vehemently and decisively as Whitman does here. Perhaps Whitman's most spirited attack on his contemporaries comes when he extols, "Do you call those genteel little creatures

American poets? Do you term that perpetual, pistareen, paste-pot work, American art, American drama, taste, verse? I think I hear, echoed as from some mountain-top afar in the west, the scornful laugh of the Genius of these states." Yet at least the "genteel little creatures" who are American poets practice a viable, living art form. Painters, sculptors, and actors are not even worthy of Whitman's scorn. In the New World their art forms have perished: "Painting, sculpture, and the dramatic theatre, it would seem, no longer play an indispensable or even important part in the workings and mediumship of intellect, utility, or even high esthetics."[32] Whitman allows that "architecture remains, doubtless with capacities, and a real future," and music fares better, occupying still a "highest place," but he makes clear that "over all the arts, literature dominates, serves beyond all" (*PW* 2:207–8).[33] Whitman's use of the word "serves" in the previous sentence is especially telling, for it emphasizes again that art is not an end in itself. It is also important that, just as Duchamp did with such works as the *3 Standard Stoppages* and indirectly with his *Large Glass*, Whitman includes an art of science in his definition of literature: "Including the Literature of science, its scope is indeed unparallel'd" (*PW* 2:208). Both artists also exploited the terms and authority of pseudo-sciences, as is evidenced by Whitman's enthusiasm for phrenology and Duchamp's involvement with pataphysics.

Even though "literature dominates" the other arts, what Whitman allows for in *Democratic Vistas* is the *potential* of literature, not literature as he saw it at the time:

> I say a new founded literature, not merely to copy and reflect existing surfaces, or pander to what is called taste – not only to amuse, pass away time, celebrate the beautiful, the refined, the past, or exhibit technical, rhythmic, or grammatical dexterity – but a literature underlying life,

religious, consistent with science [. . .] teaching and training men [. . .] achieving the entire redemption of woman [. . .] is what is needed. (*PW* 2:372)

As with Duchamp, who rejected personal discrimination as a criterion for art, Whitman calls for a literature that will not "pander to what is called taste." Perhaps even more surprisingly for a poet praised for his descriptive facility, Whitman's dream literature also does not "celebrate the beautiful." It is a highly utilitarian (if extraordinarily ambitious) conception of art. It's hard not to hear the echo between Whitman's statement and Duchamp's call for an art that has other uses than the retinal, such as "religious, philosophical, and moral functions."[34] Indeed if we replace *literature* with *art* in Whitman's statement, Duchamp, who embraced a utilitarian role for the visual arts and who worked hard to make *The Large Glass* "consistent with science" (in its own perverse way), comes off as a likely candidate for one of the "poets to come" who would "hardly recognize" Whitman.

Whitman goes on to attack existing art throughout the *Vistas*, calling the "swarms of poems, literary magazines, dramatic plays, resultant so far from American intellect [. . .] useless and a mockery," declaring that they "suffice only the lowest level of vacant minds." Elsewhere he assails drama, declaring that it "deserves to be treated with the same gravity, and on a par with the questions of ornamental confectionery at public dinners, or the arrangement of curtains and hangings in the ballroom." He attacks poetry as "copious drivel" that "does not fulfill, in any respect, the needs and august occasions of this land."[35] One of his more amusing slanders of poetry is when he describes it as "causing tender spasms in the coteries, and warranted not to chafe the sensitive cuticle of the most exquisitely artificial gossamer delicacy." In a lengthy footnote to *Democratic Vistas* Whitman explicitly elevates work that is "esthetically defective" but spiritually capable over work that is successful on a mere aesthetic level, calling for us to "dismiss every pretensive production, however fine its esthetic or intellectual points, which violates or ignores, or even does not celebrate, the central divine idea of All."[36]

Beneath Whitman's gleeful scorn at the art of his contemporaries lies a cogent theory of art and a faith in what it *could* do. Whitman allows aesthetic consideration only a limited, preemptory role in the regard of art:

> It may be that all works of art are to be first tried by their art qualities, their image-forming talent, and their dramatic, pictorial, plot-constructing, euphonious and other talents. Then, whenever claiming to be first-class works, they are to be strictly and sternly tried by their foundation in, and radiation, in the highest sense, and always indirectly, of the ethic principles, and eligibility to free, arouse, dilate.[37]

So the traditional aesthetic qualities of literature — their "art qualities," as Whitman puts it (sounding like a late twentieth-century visual art critic) — *may* (he qualifies) have an initial function in setting forth the candidates for true art. The real measure of art, however, relates to its "foundation in, and radiation" of "ethic principles, and eligibility to free, arouse, dilate." A foundation in ethical principles is not a conceptual function of art; that is a traditional qualifier. But the final part of Whitman's standard is more radically suggestive. "Free," "arouse," and "dilate" have a number of connotations: liberatory, sexual, and, perhaps most conceptually suggestive, consciousness changing. As we've already seen, dilation is one of the most important organizing principles in Whitman's early poems, one that vitally informs his catalog technique.

A more subtle connotation emerges in a later passage:

> Books are to be call'd for, and supplied, on the assumption that the pro-
> cess of reading is not a half-sleep, but, in the highest sense, an exercise, a
> gymnast's struggle; that the reader is to do something for himself, must be
> on the alert, must him or herself construct indeed the poem, argument,
> history, metaphysical essay—the text furnishing the hints, the clue, the
> start or frame-work. Not the book needs so much to be the complete thing,
> but the reader of the book does. That were to make a nation of supple and
> athletic minds, well-train'd, intuitive, used to depend on themselves, and
> not on a few coteries of writers.[38]

This passage places Whitman firmly in line with Modernist poetic
theory emphasizing the necessity for poetry to be difficult, as well
as with Duchamp, all of whose important works, especially the
readymades, require viewers to "be on the alert" and "construct"
the art experience for themselves. As did the artist who provided
The Green Box to complicate *The Large Glass*, Whitman calls for
an art that furnishes "the hints, the clue, the start or frame-work."
Likewise Duchamp asserted, "The creative act is not performed by
the artist alone; the spectator brings the work in contact with the
external world by deciphering and interpreting its inner qualifications
and thus adds his contribution to the creative act."[39] Sounding like
a proto–reader response theorist, Whitman claims that the reader
completes the book, just as Duchamp suggests that the spectator
contributes to the creative act. Thus all true art for Whitman is, as
Duchamp put it describing *The Large Glass*, "definitively unfinished."
Likewise another connotation of "free" quoted in the earlier passage
emerges: true art, for Whitman, frees the audience *from art itself*. As
he puts it in "Song of Myself," "He honors my style most who learns
under it to destroy the teacher."

∾

As the previous chapters of this study have shown, long before Picasso pasted objects to his painted canvases or the Dadaists cut up newspapers and reassembled their language into strange new forms, Whitman cut up his own found and created text, arranging and rearranging the fragments until "the pieces fell properly into place." Duchamp's readymades are not collages; however, they and his theorization of them help us to pinpoint those aspects of collage that have been most important to the artists who followed. As Marjorie Perloff phrased it, "From Cubist collage, it is, after all, a short step to the Dada ready-made," and in this "short step," the implications of defining found material as art unfolded.[40] Whitman's relation to found art and readymades has been obscured by the fact that he composed most of the language in his poems, even if that language was extracted in fragments from his notebooks and collaged into new forms. Another factor complicating his reception is the fact that he was not nearly as confrontational as Duchamp in his use of this found material. Indeed, properly speaking, Whitman's implementation of found materials may be more closely related to montage than collage. Montage, a technique usually associated with photography or film, is generally regarded as a less disjunct, smoothed-over use of found materials. The critic Gregory Ulmer differentiates the techniques by describing collage as "a transfer of materials from one context to another" and montage as "the 'dissemination' of these borrowings through the new settings."[41] He suggests that in montage there is a greater tendency to subsume the collaged materials in the context of a larger whole, a proposition that has been recently echoed by the poet and critic Charles Bernstein, who defines collage as "the use of different textual elements without recourse to an overall unifying idea." In contrast montage is "the use of contrasting images toward the goal of one unifying theme."[42]

Aspects of Whitman's writing resemble both descriptions, and there are even occasional instances when he produced what today would be called a "found poem," a form more directly analogous to Duchamp's readymades. Late in his life Whitman seems to have become more interested in the form, or at least in explicitly disclosing his use of "found poetry" to his readers. In a late poem titled "Mirages," created about a year before he died, he included a subheading directly beneath the title: "(Noted verbatim after a supper-talk outdoors in Nevada with two old miners)." The poem that follows reads as one of Whitman's typical catalogs, this one describing mirage images purportedly seen by a miner and his companion. Whitman himself does not comment on these images, and his voice is, at least ostensibly, left out of the poem, the point of which seems to be to evoke the sense of mystery experienced by the men who witnessed these images in their desert travels. Framed as a found poem "Noted verbatim" after overhearing it, the poem's true nature is more complex. Whitman never traveled as far west as Nevada, so if the poem was indeed overheard he is lying about its origins. Interestingly, however, he still insists that he had no hand in the poem, presenting what at least appears to be uncrafted language, a ready-made poem that the aged and bedridden poet would have had to discover in his previously written notes.[43] This faux found poem, then, is likely a hoax, yet the implications of explicitly presenting it as found remain. It embodies Whitman's attitude toward language, his belief that the immediate language of perceived reality is already poetry, regardless of whether or not it is crafted by a poet. The poem also discloses, at least by implication, his very real compositional process of collaging text from his notebooks. Whereas today we have become used to the idea of a poet offering ready-made found poetry in the midst of other self-composed work, in Whitman's day the practice was anything but familiar. If there is a previous known example of something this close to found poetry, I am not aware of it.

Another related later work originally published in *November Boughs* (1888) also resembles a found poem in that it is mostly composed of titles of Whitman's previously published works. "Now precedent songs. Farewell." opens with a brief salute from the poet, followed by this list:

> "In Cabin'd Ships," or "Thee Old Cause" or "Poets to Come"
> Or "Paumanok," "Song of Myself," "Calamus," or "Adam,"
> Or "Beat! Beat! Drums!" or "To the Leaven'd Soil they Trod,"
> Or "Captain! My Captain!" "Kosmos," "Quicksand Years," or
>   "Thoughts,"
> "Thou Mother with Thy Equal Brood," and many, many more
>   unspecified
>   (*LG* 534)

Following this list Whitman defines his understanding of the true nature of his created works, explaining that his poems' true essences are distinct from their embodiment on the page: "The personal urge and form for me — not merely paper, automatic type and ink." As usual he insists that the most valuable aspect of art is not the art product but the personal and conceptual exchange between artist and audience. Echoing an assertion expressed throughout his work, he also stresses his belief that his poems are part of an ongoing process, culminating from the art and language that preceded him: "Each song of mine — each utterance in the past — having its long, long history." He seems to have been disposed toward reaffirming this evolutionary scope before he died, and he returns to the theme in other late works, such as "Old Chants," a poem composed almost entirely of a list of great writers and their works, which are defined as the "chiefest debt" of the "New World" and, by implication, himself (LG 547).

In his 1881 poem "Reversals" Whitman simply salvages some thematically linked lines from a longer poem, "Respondez!" written a quarter of a century earlier, demonstrating that some of his found poems were discovered in his previously published work. In yet another late poem he presents work framed not as a found poem but as the inverse of one, in language that mirrors something overheard by presenting its opposite. Like "Mirages," "The Rounded Catalogue Divine Complete" includes a subheading defining the poem's origins:

> [Sunday, <u>Went this forenoon to church. A college professor, Rev. Dr.,</u> gave us a fine sermon, during which I caught the above words; but the minister included in his "rounded catalogue" letter and spirit, only the esthetic things, and entirely ignored what I name in the following:] (LG 554)

Like "Mirages," "The Rounded Catalogue Divine Complete" is entirely a catalog, with no framing device but the poem's title and subheading. In this case his catalog is of aspects of reality omitted in the sermon he claims to have heard at church, of "The devilish and the dark, the dying and diseas'd," of "Venom and filth, serpents, the ravenous sharks, liars." As with "Mirages," however, Whitman appears to be contriving a false context to frame his poem for his readers. Drafts of the poem suggest that it did not originate with a sermon, as Whitman experimented with alternative introductory material before deciding to include the aforementioned subheading.[44] Although likely biographically irrelevant, the subheading is notable for its stating what I have argued is implicit throughout the poet's use of the catalog technique: that such lists represent Whitman's primary device in countering his audience's limiting appetite for "the esthetic things," as he phrases it. As with his extensive list from "Song of the Broad-Axe," he explicitly presents his catalog technique as a riposte to those who would assimilate his work into limiting preconceptions of art's function in the world.

These brief late poems may lack the scope and conceptual efficacy of the major poems he composed as a younger and healthier man, but they reveal a new form of self-reflection in Whitman, as, bedridden and dying, he looked back on his life's work. Shortly before he passed on, in one of the most remarkable statements he made about his own writing, Whitman sought one last time to explain his work to his friends. He had been brought down from his room by his disciple Horace Traubel to speak with about thirty people assembled to celebrate his seventy-second birthday in 1891. Aware of his impending death and of the urgency of last words, he described the origins and effects of *Leaves of Grass*, his "experimentation in strange ways, not such as usually go to make poetry and books and grand things." Whitman elaborates:

> I still think — I have always thought — that it escapes me myself, its own author, as to what it means, and what it is after, and what it drifts at. . . . I accept and consider the book as a study. But behind all that . . . remains a subtle and baffling, a mysterious, <u>personality</u>. My attempt at "Leaves of Grass" — my attempt at my own expression — is after all this: to thoroughly equip, absorb, acquire, from all quarters, despising nothing, nothing being too small — no science, no observation, no detail — west, east, cities, ruins, the army, the war (through which I was) — and after all that consigning everything to the personal critter.

It is to reveal this, "the fellow, man, individuality, person, American," for what it most deeply is: "something curious, indescribably divine . . . the compound individuality that is in everyone."[45]

Whitman's project is to awaken people to their compound inner makeup, to the atomistic, all-encompassing diversity that he sees at the heart of identity, and his book, as he saw it, was a separate "personality" altogether — its own being, related to but not really him. He defines this independent subjectivity as a kind of absorbing device, a conduit, through which flow all the fragmentary details, all the pieces and parts of a world, and that consigns them "to the personal critter" that is each individual reader. As we have seen in this study, his method is to set in motion the fragments of a world by way of words — catalogs, lists, pieces of language both taken and made — through his readers, to render the reader, like his book, a conduit, active and open, to a passage of details that reflect the reader's own inner diversity, "the compound diversity that is in everyone." This for Whitman is the process of dilation, the enlarging of the self so that, containing all, it can identify with all, united in the "kelson of creation." Pursuing this goal, consciously or unconsciously, the poet stumbled upon the method we now call collage.

The story of *Leaves of Grass* is both personal to each individual who reads it and historical to all of us. However we respond to it, whatever the force it exerts upon its audiences, we must also recognize Whitman's achievement as an artist. The conventional, transatlantic conception concerning the roots of modernism is complicated and enriched by our recognition of Whitman's originality. Signature modernist techniques such as collage are routinely assumed to have originated in Europe, often in Paris, and usually beginning with visual arts media; however, closer looks at the history of these practices continue to reveal the model's inadequacies. Art historians, for example, have increasingly emphasized the role that tribal African masks and ancient Iberian sculpture played in establishing key aspects of Cubism, and literary scholars have begun to recognize the importance of modernist writing outside the frame of Franco-American confluence. Recognizing Whitman's role in pioneering the use of found art and collage composition further undermines conventional assumptions about some of the most important and exciting aspects of art in the twentieth century. Although the word itself did not yet exist, the history of collage as a Western art practice does not begin with Picasso or Braque, or even with the visual arts. The defining features of collage, so far as we can tell, received their first major expression in mid-nineteenth-century Brooklyn. They were discovered by an imaginative young newspaperman named Walter Whitman, who was living a nomadic lifestyle at the time, moving from house to house out of economic and practical necessity, bringing along with him trunks containing all of his life's possessions, the most precious of which were his fated collection of notebooks, paper scraps, and various journalistic, historical, and scientific (as well as pseudo-scientific) ephemera. Poring over this material, energized by dreams of literary greatness and metaphysical grandeur, Whitman at some point landed on an effective formal vehicle for his maverick instincts in style and structure. This capacious and flexible poetic line proved the perfect complement to the habits he had developed in the newspaper business, using scissors and glue to manually cut and paste both borrowed and original material into new forms. Thus collage was born, emerging from its long prehistory in commercial media and grassroots creations such as scrapbooks and quilts, to find its landmark expression in Western art in the form of *Leaves of Grass.*

Notes

INTRODUCTION

1. When possible, I have endeavored to include images of the most critical of Whitman's manuscripts where they are discussed in this study. All of the images described in this book can be found in digital form at the online Walt Whitman Archive (www.whitmanarchive.org). In most cases the best way to access them is though the link "Finding Aids for Manuscripts at Individual Repositories," found in the "Manuscripts" section. In some cases the images reproduced in this book have been resized or colorized slightly to enhance legibility.

1. HOW WHITMAN USED HIS EARLY NOTEBOOKS

1. Previous scholars have also called it the "albot Wilson" notebook because of their dependence on a poor quality microfilm copy.

2. See Gail Fineberg, "LC's Missing Whitman Notes Found in N.Y.," *Library of Congress Gazette*, February 24, 1995, http://memory.loc.gov/ammem/wwhtml/gazette1.html; Birney, "Missing Whitman Notebooks."

3. The scans are available at the Library of Congress's American Memory site, http://memory.loc.gov/ammem/collections/whitman/index.html.

4. *The Uncollected Poetry and Prose of Walt Whitman*, hereafter UPP.

5. Shephard, "Possible Sources," 67n.

6. To my knowledge the only other scholar who accurately dated the notebook, at least in writing, was Floyd Stovall in "Dating Whitman's Early Notebooks."

7. Grier, "Walt Whitman's Earliest Known Notebook."

8. Higgins, "Wage Slavery."

9. Erkkila, *Whitman the Political Poet*, 50.

10. Allen, *The Solitary Singer*, 134.

11. Loving, *Walt Whitman: The Song of Himself*, 147–49, 502–3.

12. Krieg, *A Walt Whitman Chronology*, 18.

13. Bucke, *Cosmic Consciousness*; *Walt Whitman's Leaves of Grass: The First (1855) Edition*, ed. Malcolm Cowley; Chari, *Whitman in the Light of Vedantic Mysticism*.

14. See Binns, *A Life of Walt Whitman*, 51; Holloway, *Whitman: An Interpretation*; Pollak, *The Erotic Whitman*. For a debunking of the story of Whitman's New Orleans sexual encounter, see Loving, *Walt Whitman: The Song of Himself*, 122–23.

15. Many of the notebooks and manuscript images not reproduced here are or will soon be available for viewing at the online Walt Whitman Archive (http://www.whitmanarchive.org). Except in special instances (which I note in the text), all manuscript transcriptions contained herein are my own and are based on images from the Walt Whitman Archive or the Library of Congress's American Memory Web site, http://memory.loc.gov.

16. These notebooks include "Talbot Wilson," "Memorials," and the "Perceptions and Senses;" see Whitman, *Notebooks and Unpublished Prose Manuscripts*, 1:60–61, 125, 139–140; hereafter *NUPM*.

17. Walt Whitman, *Leaves of Grass: Comprehensive Reader's Edition*, 718, hereafter *LG*; [Walt Whitman], "Walt Whitman and His Poems."

18. Davis, *The Principles of Nature*.

19. See Reynolds, *Walt Whitman's America*, 262.

20. In a letter to Sarah Tyndale in 1857 Whitman wrote, "Andrew Jackson Davis puts *matter* as the subject of his homilies, and the primary source of all results—I suppose the soul among the rest. Both [Davis and Cora L. V. Hatch, another spiritualist] are quite determined in their theories. Perhaps when they know much more, both of them will be much less determined." Walt Whitman, *The Correspondence*, 1:43, hereafter *Corr*, qtd. in Kuebrich, *Minor Prophecy*, 206. Despite the dismissive tone of the letter, Whitman seems to have at least been somewhat influenced by spiritualism. Kuebrich, who perhaps overstates the case, draws numerous analogies (38–40), as do Reynolds, *Walt Whitman's America*, 262–64, and Stovall, *The Foreground of Leaves of Grass*, 154–55.

21. On this portion of the leaf Whitman defines unfamiliar terms, as he does

in many of the notebooks composed from this period in his life, especially his homemade dictionary or "Words" notebook. See Whitman, *Daybooks and Notebooks*, 3:664–727, hereafter DBN.

22. For this and other images in this document, I have enhanced the color contrast to render the text more legible.

23. Stovall, "Dating Whitman's Early Notebooks," 198–201.

24. Bucke, *Walt Whitman*, 137.

25. Bradley, "Whitman's Fundamental Metrical Principle."

26. Allen, *The New Walt Whitman Handbook,* 215–24.

27. Conversely one of the rare, late Tupperians used Whitman's heightened reputation in an attempt to rescue Tupper's, an ironic reversal of fortunes given the authors' acclaim in their time. Derek Hudson opined, "There is little doubt that Walt Whitman (whom Tupper incidentally abominated) was influenced by Tupper's innovation—and that free-versifiers in general, down to T. S. Eliot, who have so thoroughly familiarized us with this form, or lack of form, have all been moving (horrified though they may be to hear the news) under the original impetus of Martin Tupper." Hudson, *Martin Tupper*, 43.

28. Hollis, *Language and Style*, 30.

29. See Coulombe, "'To Destroy the Teacher'"; Cohen, "Martin Tupper," 25; Zweig, *Walt Whitman: The Making of the Poet,* 149–50.

30. See also DBN 3:770–71.

31. This notebook, often called the "Perceptions or Senses" notebook, is filed as Notebook LC #86 at the Library of Congress. The entire notebook is available for viewing at the American Memory Web site, http://memory.loc.gov; see also NUPM 1:126–27.

32. See also DBN 3:766–70.

33. See also NUPM 1:62.

34. See also NUPM 1:1349

35. See also NUPM 1:287.

36. *Facsimile of Two Rivulets: Author's Edition* (Camden NJ, 1876), Special Collections Department, University of Iowa Libraries, 29.

37. Emerson, *Essays*, 17–18.

38. See for example Chari, *Whitman in the Light of Vedantic Mysticism,* 65–69, 107, 139.

39. Ed Folsom gathers together the various statements Whitman made about composing the first edition in "'Many MS. Doings and Undoings.'"

40. Burroughs, *Walt Whitman as Poet and Person*, 83.

41. Qtd. in Myerson, *Whitman in His Own Time*, 173–74.

42. Bucke, *Walt Whitman*, 135.

43. Ibid., 137.

44. Folsom, "'Many MS. Doings and Undoings,'" 169.

45. Bucke, *Walt Whitman*, 25, 135.

46. Symonds, *Walt Whitman: A Study*, xxii.

47. Traubel, *With Walt Whitman in Camden*, 8:351.

48. Traubel, *Camden's Compliment*, 4; interview in Myerson, *Whitman in His Own Time*, 20.

49. See also DBN 3:775, 776.

50. These paragraphs are pasted together from three separate scraps of paper of the same type. The first paragraph is on one scrap; the next three paragraphs are the second; and the last is on the third; see also NUPM 1:101.

51. This notebook is filed in the Library of Congress as Feinberg #697. It is sometimes referred to as the "Crossing Brooklyn Ferry Notebook" or "George Walker" (the first two words on one of its inside covers); see also NUPM 1:233.

52. Allen, *The New Walt Whitman Handbook*, 209.

2. PACKING AND UNPACKING THE FIRST *LEAVES OF GRASS*

1. See Allen, *The Solitary Singer*, 106–7; Krieg, *A Walt Whitman Chronology*, 23.

2. For more details on the current state of the house on Ryerson, see Berman, "Walt Whitman's Ghost." On a personal note, I myself live in Clinton Hill, about six blocks south of Whitman's former residence on Ryerson. For decades Clinton Hill was a predominantly black, working-class neighborhood. In recent years it has emerged as more of a mixed-ethnicity, middle-class neighborhood, one that has experienced a good deal of gentrification as a result of the Pratt Institute, subway access, and relatively close proximity to Manhattan. Some local initiatives to commemorate the last surviving Whitman house have been proposed, but nothing has come of it at the time of this writing.

3. Whitman mentioned his family's "trunks" several times in his letters. In May 1863, for example, he inquired, "Mother, is George's trunk home & of no use, there? I wish I had it here, as I must have a trunk," and a month later he wrote, "If I should succeed in getting a transportation ticket that would take me to New York & back, I should be tempted to come home for two or three days, as I want some MSS & books, & the trunk, &c." He also mentioned his and his family's trunks in letters of 1864, 1872, and, in separate requests to Charles Eldridge and Peter Doyle, three times in 1873 (*Corr* 1:105, 107, 200; 2:178, 247, 250–51).

4. For an account of Whitman's room in Camden, see Broderick, "The Greatest Whitman Collector."

5. Keller, *Walt Whitman in Mickle Street*, 32.

6. Traubel, *With Walt Whitman in Camden*, 1:155.

7. The question of whether the poems of the first edition were titled or untitled is unclear. On the one hand, Whitman inserted the identical phrase "Leaves of Grass" before each of the first six poems in the first edition. He may have intended each of these poems (and perhaps the remaining ones) to have assumed this identical title. On the other hand, the phrase may have been used simply as a form of division between poems, similar to a running head at the top of the page. Alternately he may have thought of these repeated phrases as something in between a title and a placeholder, intentionally suggesting an ambiguity as to the nominal status of his works. That at least is the effect he seems to have achieved. Regardless, I need to refer to these poems in another manner here, as it would be impossible to distinguish between them if we called them all by the title "Leaves of Grass."

8. Whitman himself tended not to differentiate the poems of the first edition at all, sometimes referring to the entire first edition as if it were one long poem called "Leaves of Grass" or referring to them en masse as "his leaves." However, in an important manuscript preserved at the University of Texas at Austin's Harry Ransom Humanities Research Center, he clearly refers to the first poem of the 1855 *Leaves of Grass* by its first-line title, "I celebrate myself."

9. Whitman, *Leaves of Grass: 100th Anniversary Edition*.

10. In what follows, then, when I refer to "Song of Myself" I mean to

indicate the deathbed edition of the poem, and by "I celebrate myself" I mean the first poem of the 1855 edition of *Leaves*. I use the same form of distinction with regard to the other poems of the first edition, except when it is necessary to explain which version I am discussing because the first-line title remained the final title.

11. See Folsom and Price, *Re-Scripting Walt Whitman*, 23–25; and Folsom's original essay from his Web site, *Whitman's Manuscript Drafts of "Song of Myself" Leaves of Grass, 1855*, http://bailiwick.lib.uiowa.edu.

12. A *kelson* or *keelson* is a nautical term for the wood that runs along the centerline of a ship that strengthens the ship's keel.

13. Whitman later came to use the word "clusters" to describe the various sections of *Leaves of Grass*.

14. Schmidgall, "1855: A Stop-Press Revision."

15. Genoways, "'One goodshaped and wellhung man.'"

16. Traubel, *With Walt Whitman in Camden*, 8:351.

17. Line 941 of the final edition of the poem.

18. Line 243 of the final edition as a "jay" instead of a "mocking bird."

19. Line 98 of the final edition of the poem.

20. Line 668 of the final edition of the poem.

21. Folsom, "'Many MS. Doings and Undoings,'" reprinted with revisions in Folsom and Price, *Re-Scripting Walt Whitman*.

22. Bucke, *Walt Whitman*, 172.

23. Cowley, introduction to *Leaves of Grass*, x; Martin, *The Homosexual Tradition in American Poetry*, 9.

24. E. H. Miller, *Walt Whitman's Poetry*, 73.

25. These lines, which occur on only two leaves, do not show that Whitman had yet developed his first-person voice; they seem rather crude in comparison to lines in the "Talbot Wilson" notebook. A reference to Whitman's "brother . . . practicing at the piano" shows that the writing came after 1852, when Whitman bought his brother Jeff a piano.

26. R. S. Mishra and James Perrin Warren have discussed this notebook previously. Mishra works accurately from William White's transcription of this passage in *Daybooks and Notebooks* and describes, among other things, how the "basic problem that haunts Whitman in the notes is how to establish

a link between his homosexuality and his power and identity as a poet." See "'The Sleepers' and Some Whitman Notes," *Walt Whitman Quarterly Review* 1 (June 1983): 30. Although White's transcription makes clear that the object of the poet's attention here was a man, Warren, who cites White as his manuscript source, ignores this fact and presents Whitman in a suspiciously heterosexual light. Warren also blatantly overstates the relationship of the notebook to the published poem, referring to it as the "'Sleepers' Notebook" even though a very small portion of the poem is drafted here and claiming that Whitman "worked on several versions" of the six clear lines of "I wander all night" that originally appeared in this notebook, when in fact he worked on only two versions. If there was indeed a "Sleepers" notebook in which Whitman worked broadly on the poem, it would seem to have been either lost or destroyed. See Warren, "'Catching the Sign,'" 18; DBN 3:764.

27. The natural extension of this observation is that Whitman—at least the Whitman of the early to mid-1850s—was more comfortable with his sexuality than most previous scholars have acknowledged.

28. Warren, "'Catching the Sign,'" 22.

29. Whitman was most familiar with the 1847 edition of Webster's dictionary. For this study, I have used an 1891 reprinting: Noah Webster, *An American Dictionary of the English Language* (Springfield MA: G. & C. Merriam, 1847); Noah Webster, *An American Dictionary of the English Language*, revised by Chauncey A. Goodrich (Chicago: Donohue & Henneberry, 1891). For more information on Whitman and dictionaries, see Folsom, *Walt Whitman's Native Representations*, chapter 1.

30. Martin, *The Homosexual Tradition in American Poetry*, 11.

31. Webster, *An American Dictionary*, (1847, 1891).

32. Ibid.

33. The transcription is originally from Bucke's *Notes and Fragments* (CPW 10:33), where the list begins with these phrases: "Airscud. / Airdrift." Regarding the incongruity of these two items, Grier notes, "Since Bucke frequently conflated distinct MS, there is no reason to assume that the first two entries have any connection with the others," suggesting that in the original the first two items were from a separate MS (NUPM 1:196).

34. The phrases I refer to are from section 9 of "I Sing the Body Electric" and

section 24, l.530 from "Song of Myself." "I celebrate myself" also contains the phrases, but they do not appear until the 1856 version of the poem eventually called "I Sing the Body Electric" ("Poem of The Body" in the 1856 version).

35. Line 130 of the poem, where Whitman uses a metaphor of a whale whose "tap is death" as he speaks from the point of view of a slave, was originally part of a longer prose passage in a notebook at the Library of Congress Harned Collection (DBN 3:763). Another phrase in the poem, "emerging from gates" from line 10, is anticipated by the first page of the "efflux of the soul" notebook by the phrase "comes through beautiful gates," though the same passage in the notebook was used directly for line 95 of "Song of the Open Road"; see DBN 3:764.

36. This is the overall thesis of *Walt Whitman's Pose*.

37. Reprinted as Kennedy, "Walt Whitman's Indebtedness to Emerson."

38. Stovall, *The Foreground of Leaves of Grass*, 296–305.

39. For Shephard's description of Whitman's derivations for "O Hymen! O Hymenee!" see *Walt Whitman's Pose*, 150, 179–80; for "Dilation" see 178; Stovall, *The Foreground of Leaves of Grass*, 220–21. Whitman seems to have copied (with some amendments) the passage from Sand's novel onto a separate manuscript leaf before using the idea and some of its language for "Dilation." See NUPM 1:83.

40. See Allen, "Walt Whitman and Jules Michelet"; Allen, *The New Walt Whitman Handbook*, 268–70.

41. See Hedge, "*Prose Writers of Germany* as a Source"; Stovall, *The Foreground of Leaves of Grass*, 195.

42. See Goodrich, *The World As It Is*.

43. See Genoways, "Civil War Poems."

44. See also NUPM 1:304. As I discussed in the previous chapter, Whitman exploited local expertise similarly (or at least exhorted himself to) with his self-instruction to "get from Mr. Arkhurst the names of all insects" for his unwritten "Poem of Insects."

45. Shephard, *Walt Whitman's Pose*, 141.

46. This passage, which I have been unable to find in its actual manuscript form, was described by Bucke as "written as note to following sentence in magazine article, dated Oct., '51, on Keats' 'Hyperion'; 'It is perhaps safe to

affirm that originality cannot be attained by seeking for it, but only eccentricity — oddity and eccentricity, which the great artist avoids as he values his immortality.'" See *CPW* 6:37.

47. OED.

48. This manuscript is part of a larger collection of notes Whitman made on essays in the *Edinburgh Review*. As we can tell from his notes elsewhere, he was reading old essays. At the bottom of one page, he pastes a clipping and adds the date "May '57." The page from which I have been citing these notes is from a different essay, so we can't be sure when he wrote these notes, but the confidence of his tone in defining what great artists do and his interest in defending "light reading" in preparation for art suggest a date considerably later than 1845.

49. David S. Reynolds develops a similar idea in *Beneath the American Renaissance* (and, less directly, in *Walt Whitman's America*).

50. French, "Reading 'Song of Myself,'" 76–77.

51. OED.

52. Pierre Joris, from a paper delivered at the 1997 Eric Mottram Conference in London.

53. See Singer, "Connoisseurs of Chaos"; Larson, "'Scraps, Orts and Fragments,'" chapter 1.

54. Killingsworth, *The Growth of "Leaves of Grass."* Killingsworth's book discusses much more than "organic form" in Whitman studies, though that is a substantial topic of the book.

55. Triggs, "The Growth of 'Leaves of Grass,'" 102.

56. Allen, *The New Walt Whitman Handbook,* 67–68.

57. J. E. Miller, *Walt Whitman,* 38.

58. The fragmentary quality in Whitman's work has been noted by Gilles Deleuze, who finds in Whitman a sense of "spontaneity or the innate feeling for the fragmentary." See *Essays,* 56–60.

59. Olson, *Human Universe,* 52.

60. Wilson, *Romantic Turbulence,* 119.

3. KOSMOS POETS AND SPINAL IDEAS

1. See Whitman's "Starting Newspapers" from *Specimen Days* (*PW* 286–87), and Brasher, *Whitman as Editor,* 17–21.

2. For an excellent summary of Whitman's work during this period, see Greenspan, *Walt Whitman and the American Reader*, 39–87; for in-depth discussions of the *Daily Eagle* period, see Brasher, *Whitman as Editor*.

3. *NUPM* 1:211. Grier says the notebook from which this list is extracted is missing from the Library of Congress, and indeed I have not been able to locate it. The transcription is based on photostats and on previous transcription from *UPP* and Furness.

4. Parker, "Unrhymed Modernity."

5. Readers interested in an examination of actual newspaper pages that Whitman wrote that present the news in this manner are referred to the *Brooklyn Daily Eagle* online Web site, where users can access fully searchable scans of the newspaper's entire run, including the issues that Whitman edited between 1846 and 1848. http://www.brooklynpubliclibrary.org.

6. Parker, "Unrhymed Modernity," 165.

7. Brasher, *Whitman as Editor*, 25.

8. For a direct visual comparison of this manuscript leaf to a typical front page of a newspaper that Whitman edited, see the online *Brooklyn Daily Eagle* (http://eagle.brooklynpubliclibrary.org/), produced by the Brooklyn Public Library.

9. "Virginia Elections," *Brooklyn Daily Eagle and King Country Democrat*, April 29, 1847, 2.

10. Greenspan, *Walt Whitman and the American Reader*, 108.

11. *LG* 115; *Brooklyn Evening Star*, October 10, 1845, reprinted in Greenspan, *Walt Whitman and the American Reader*, 54. In a telling exercise in prosody, Greenspan breaks up into poetic lines the column from which this quote is excerpted, resulting in a passage that resembles lines from *Leaves of Grass*:

Boy, or young man, whose eyes hover over these lines!

How much of your leisure time do you give to loafing?

What vulgar habits of smoking cigars, chewing tobacco, of making
frequent use of blasphemous or obscene language have you begun
to form?

What associations and appetites are you idly falling into, that future
years will ripen in wickedness or shame?

> Consider these questions as addressed, not to everybody in general, but
> to *you* in particular – and answer them honestly to your own heart.
> The one who speaks to you through this printed page, never has spo-
> ken, and probably ever will speak to you in any other way;
> But it would be a deep and abiding joy for him to know that he had
> awakened wholesome reflection in your mind, even if it lasts for
> only a passing five minutes. (107)

Although Whitman as poet was never so prudish as to chastise his audience for smoking or cursing, Greenspan's point is well taken.

12. From the notes of Harrison S. Morris's 1887 conversation with the poet, qtd. in Blodgett, "Walt Whitman's Poetic Manuscripts," 35–36.

13. From *Democratic Vistas* (PW 2:367, 396); "Origin of Attempted Seces-sion" (PW 2:433); "Poetry To-Day – Shakspere – The Future" (PW 2:486); "A Word about Tennyson" (PW 2:570); and "The Bible as Poetry" (PW 2:546), respectively.

14. Whitman's spinal idea for "Passage to India" was to demonstrate "That the divine efforts of heroes, & their ideas, faithfully lived up to, will finally prevail, and be accomplished however long deferred" (NUPM 2:928). His spinal idea for "Song of the Redwood Tree" is among his most elaborately worked out: "I (the tree) have fill'd my time and fill'd it grandly All is prepared for you – my termination comes prophecy a great race – great as the mountains and the trees / Intersperse with *italic* (first person speaking) the same as in 'Out of the Cradle endlessly rocking'" (qtd. in LG 206).

15. For a good introduction to the Oulipo and their creative practices, see Jacques Roubaud's introduction to *The Oulipo and Combinatorial Art*, reprinted in Brotchie and Matthews, *Oulipo Compendium*, 37–44.

16. Even such a conceptual artist as Marcel Duchamp admitted that his ready-mades – which set out to abolish the idea of subjective creativ-ity – nevertheless involve some sense of spontaneous individualism, even if the immediate creativity involved amounted to nothing more than the act of selecting his art objects for presentation.

17. Queneau's *100,000,000,000,000 Poems*, for example, offers readers a series of ten fourteen-line sonnets, in which each line is interchangeable and can

replace a corresponding line in another sonnet. The result: 100,000,000,000,000 potential sonnets, which readers are invited to create at will with cut-up lines. William S. Burroughs, along with his friend Brion Gysin, created texts made solely from cut-up writing by both themselves and others and, echoing Whitman in his notebooks, theorized that practice as a kind of "language experiment." Much of Ashbery's *The Tennis Court Oath* is collaged from French newspapers, and later poems such as his cento "The Dong with the Luminous Nose" are created entirely from others' lines. See Brotchie and Matthews, *Oulipo Compendium*, for a reprinting of Queneau and John Ashbery, *The Tennis Court Oath*.

18. Garrison, "Walt Whitman," reprinted in Myerson, *Whitman in His Own Time*, 70–75.

19. For a more detailed discussion of this manuscript, see Sill, "'You Tides with Ceaseless Swell.'" Sill's discussion is illuminating, though I take issue with many of his assumptions about the chronology behind Whitman's drafts of specific lines.

20. From the preface to the 1855 edition of *Leaves* (LG 715).

21. The phrase "earliest and most important notebook" was coined by the twentieth-century biographer and critic Emory Holloway in a note glued to its cover.

22. Traubel, *With Walt Whitman in Camden*, vol. 2.

23. Both definitions from the online OED.

24. In the only complete, published version of this notebook, the editor William White refers to this as Whitman's "home-made word book, *Words,*" and describes it as Whitman's incomplete "dictionary project" (DBN 3:664). I refer to this notebook hereafter as simply the "Words" notebook, based on paper labels affixed to the cover and spine, on which is written in Whitman's hand, "Words."

25. The relevant online OED definitions are:

> 4. *trans.* To relate, describe, or set forth at length; to enlarge or expatiate upon.
>   *Obs.*
> 5. *intr.* To discourse or write at large; to enlarge, expatiate. Const. *of* (obs.), *on, upon.*

The reference to Dickens is from his early novel *Nicholas Nickleby* (1838).

26. Shephard, *Walt Whitman's Pose*, 177–78. The passage from Sand reads, "The unknown refused to explain himself. 'What could I say to you that I have not said in another (my own) language? Is it my fault that you have not understood me? You think I wished to speak to your senses, and it was my soul spoke to you. What do I say! It was the soul of the whole of humanity that spoke to you through mine.'"

27. *NUPM* 1:145. This notebook, which has been referred to as the "Memorials" notebook, appears to have been lost. It was originally filed in the Harned Collection of the Library of Congress as LC #84.

28. The line maintained this form in the first three editions of *Leaves*. The word "kosmos" was briefly omitted in the 1867 edition, then restored in the line "Walt Whitman am I, a Kosmos, of mighty Manhattan the son." His final 1881 version of the line reads, "Walt Whitman, a kosmos, of Manhattan the son."

29. Qtd. in Price, *Walt Whitman: The Contemporary Reviews*, 18. Norton's review is also available online at the Walt Whitman Archive.

30. Digital images of this notebook are not yet available at the Walt Whitman Archive.

31. The OED lists a third spelling of the word as "cosmus" and a derivative secondary definition of the word as "order, harmony: the opposite of *chaos*."

32. Another possibility is that Whitman was playing on the commonly used noun *cosmopolitan*, which indicated (according to the 1848 Webster's) "a person who has no fixed residence; one who is nowhere a stranger, or who is at home in every place; a citizen of the world," and combining and intensifying that denotation with the expansive "Kosmos." *Cosmopolitan* comes from roots *cosmos* and *polis*, meaning citizen of the world.

33. Mouth-to-mouth resuscitation was not accepted as a medical practice until the late 1950s, though other techniques had been tried, such as expelling air with bellows and attempting to stimulate the lungs by strapping patients to a trotting horse.

34. See, for example, Folsom and Price's description in *Re-Scripting Walt Whitman*, 18–19.

35. The phrase is from Whitman's famous statement that he "sometimes think[s] the *Leaves* is only a language experiment—that it is an attempt to give the spirit, the body, the man, new words, new potentialities of speech." Whitman, *An American Primer*, viii–ix.

36. Rosenthal, "'Dilation' in Whitman's Early Writing," 15.

37. "Come closer to me" received its final title, "A Song for Occupations," in 1881. The complete line in its original form reads, "The light and shade—the curious sense of body and identity—the greed that with perfect complaisance devours all things—the endless pride and outstretching of man—unspeakable joys and sorrows."

38. "The bodies of men and women engirth me" received its final title, "I Sing the Body Electric," in 1867. The complete, original line reads, "The fullspread pride of man is calming and excellent to the soul."

39. As a loose single-leaf manuscript fragment, this draft was not included in either Grier's *Notebooks and Unpublished Prose Manuscripts* or White's *Daybooks and Notebooks*, and so it has received scant attention from Whitman scholars.

4. POEMS OF MATERIALS

1. On July 6 an ad for the first edition of *Leaves of Grass* appeared in the *New York Tribune*. Critics have speculated that *Leaves* first went on sale on the Fourth of July; however, as Allen points out, bookstores were unlikely to have been open on that date (*Solitary Singer*, 149). Around this time Whitman also mailed out complimentary copies to reviewers and prominent New England literary figures including Emerson.

2. The first poem of the 1855 *Leaves* ("I celebrate myself") was titled "Poem of Walt Whitman, an American" in the 1856 edition and "Walt Whitman" in subsequent editions until 1881, when it received its familiar title, "Song of Myself."

3. The remaining spinal ideas found in the "Dick Hunt" notebook have the following titles: "Poem of the Library," "Poem of Precepts," "Poem of Joys and Works," "Poem of Legacies," "Poem of Large Personality," "Poem of (my brothers and sisters) artists, singers, musicians," "Poem of Tears," "poem of (American) Materials," "Poem of Criminals," and "Poem of the Past"; see *NUPM* 1:246–80.

4. See Harris, "Whitman's Leaves of Grass," 172.

5. The 1856 edition of *Leaves* contained 32 poems; the 1860 edition contained 146 new poems, for a total of 178. If his note about a "New American Bible" refers to *Leaves of Grass*, he overestimated his output by 187 poems.

6. In what may be a related note, Whitman appears to contemplate a cluster for *Leaves of Grass* comprised of what he calls "*Religious Canticles*." In these notes, Whitman divides his output into "Poems" and "Lessons" and defines the characteristics that distinguish them. The note implies that they are to be separate projects.

7. Whitman makes numerous remarks in the 1855 Preface that depict his book in biblical terms. Another note describes "Founding a new American Religion." Whitman also compared the number of words in the 1860 *Leaves* to the number in the Bible, with the apparent intention of exceeding the biblical count.

8. Pasted to the bottom of this note in paper of the same type is another note that reads, "Put in my poems American things, idioms, materials, persons, groups, minerals, vegetables, animals, &c." See *NUPM* 1:351.

9. Grier comments in a footnote that the remark may have originated with "Fitz James O'Brien, who was called 'M. Le Baron' by his friends at Pfaff's" (*NUPM* 1:351).

10. See *NUPM* 1:335. The salient lines are in *LG* 18, 481: "I will make the poems of materials, for I think they are to be the most spiritual poems" ("Starting from Paumanok," l.70) and "Strong and sweet shall their tongues be, poems and materials of poems shall come from their lives, they shall be makers and finders" ("Mediums," l.8).

11. This leaf's relation to the preface is indicated by a small comment in its top margin: "for Preface." Whitman makes other remarks on this leaf that I discuss later in the chapter. See also *NUPM* 1:95.

12. All quotations in this paragraph are from the original 1856 poem.

13. *NUPM*: 1:246–80, 270. See also Hollis, "Whitman's Word-Game."

14. Bucke, *Walt Whitman*, 25.

15. Whitman's poetic output dwindled about the same time he became bedridden. Although we cannot say so conclusively, the events seem related, suggesting the possibility that his much discussed flagging of creative powers was due to his lack of access to sensory perceptions outside his home.

16. As Genoways has noted, for example, a significant amount of the Civil War material used in *Drum-Taps* was derived almost entirely from newspaper accounts; see Genoways, "Civil War Poems." See also Barrett, "'Cavalry Crossing a Ford.'"

17. Qtd. in Shephard, *Walt Whitman's Pose*, 197.

18. Esther Shephard is perhaps the most insistent of such critics; see *Walt Whitman's Pose*.

19. Howard J. Waskow has described a similar concept from a more formalist perspective. See *Whitman: Explorations in Form*.

20. Myerson, *Walt Whitman: A Descriptive Bibliography*, 27.

21. Diana Horton, botanist, University of Iowa, personal interview, October 25, 2005.

22. John Downer, font historian and designer, Iowa City, telephone interview, October 26, 2005. Confirmed by comparison with examples of the Scotch Roman face from Lawson, *Anatomy of a Typeface*.

23. The City of Williamsburgh was an independent town until it was annexed into the City of Brooklyn as the so-called Eastern District in 1855. Over the years the *h* was gradually dropped from common public spellings. See Eugene L. Armbruster, *Brooklyn's Eastern District* (Brooklyn NY: Author, 1942).

24. For more on Whitman's last-minute inclusion of the 1855 Preface, see Folsom, "Walt Whitman's Working Notes." See also Folsom and Price, *Re-Scripting Walt Whitman*, 30.

25. Though it seems less likely, it is also possible that Whitman based his cover lettering on the type itself; however, in this scenario as well the cover design would have come late in the overall process of creating the book.

26. Folsom, *Whitman Making Books*, 19.

27. See Genoways, "'One goodshaped and wellhung man.'"

28. The following lines from the second poem of the first edition of *Leaves of Grass,* eventually titled "A Song for Occupations," were excised from the poem in 1881:

Come closer to me,
Push closer to me and take the best that I possess,
Yield closer and closer and give me the best you possess.

This is unfinished business with me . . . . how is it with you?
I was chilled with the cold types and cylinder and wet paper between
us.

29. For example, Whitman refers to *Leaves* as "This printed and bound book" and, perhaps referring to one of those truths described in "Song of the Rolling Earth" "that print cannot touch," in the poem eventually titled "A Song for Occupations," he writes:

There is something that comes to one now and perpetually,
It is not what is printed, preach'd, discussed, it eludes discussion and
    print,
It is not what is printed in a book, it is not in this book (*LG* 77, 213)

30. *Leaves of Grass: 1855 Facsimile Edition*, 57.

31. The text on this leaf is composed in pencil, but the overstruck lines are in ink, suggesting that Whitman wrote and crossed over the note at different times.

32. *Leaves of Grass: 1856 Facsimile Edition*, 146.

33. Reynolds, *Walt Whitman's America*, 353.

34. This manuscript, the location of which was unknown to both Allen and Traubel, was for decades believed lost. It has quite recently been found in the collection of the New York Public Library's Henry W. and Albert A. Berg Collection. It contains much material that is not described in the transcription appearing in *Complete Writings* 3:161, which has been the sole known source for this manuscript for many decades. See the Walt Whitman Archive, http://www.whitmanarchive.org/manuscripts/figures/nyp.00122.001.jpg.

35. *Complete Writings*, 3:161. As described in the previous note, this is not an accurate transcription. In the actual manuscript the title "Broadaxe" appears above the rhymed sestet, and the material concerning the "irregular tapping of rain" appears in a separate area at the top of the leaf. To the left and below the rhymed sestet later used in "Broad-Axe Poem" are a series of brief descriptions of what appear to be erotic metaphors, including reference to "loveblows / loveblossoms / loveleaves / loveclimbers / loveverdure / lovebranches loveroot." These references, as well as some development of

what is meant by "loveroot" at the bottom of the leaf, suggest that the opening sestet for "Broad-Axe Poem" was associated with sexuality when Whitman was composing the lines.

36. Allen, *The New Walt Whitman Handbook*, 239–40.

37. *Leaves of Grass: 1856 Facsimile Edition*, 141.

38. See note 35.

39. For the Brooklyn notebook in which Whitman drafted lines toward "Broad-Axe Poem" and kept notes of his games of Twenty Questions, see "Dick Hunt" in *NUPM* 1:246–80. For a Civil War notebook with similar notes, see "Hospital Book 12," *NUPM* 2:723–30. See also Hollis, "Whitman's Word-Game."

40. Consider similar subject matter in the opening stanza of the original version of "A Song for Occupations," where Whitman is "chilled" by the "cold types and wet paper" between him and his readers. See also Whitman's late poem "A Font of Type."

41. Hewitt's pamphlet, *On the Statistics and Geography of the Production of Iron*, which details the production of iron in the United States, seems to have been used by Whitman to inform his descriptions of the mining, smelting, and tempering of iron in "Broad-Axe Poem." Whitman refers to Hewitt's pamphlet on the inside cover of the so-called "Crossing Brooklyn Ferry" notebook ("George Walker"), a notebook in which he drafts many of the lines used in "Broad-Axe Poem."

42. See Whitman's "Crossing Brooklyn Ferry Notebook" ("George Walker"); *NUPM* 1:233.

43. *Leaves of Grass: 1856 Facsimile Edition*, 211.

44. Whitman lived to see the Brooklyn Bridge render ferries between Brooklyn and Manhattan obsolete. See Geffen, "Silence and Denial"; Haw, "American History."

45. Qtd. in Price, *Walt Whitman: The Contemporary Reviews*, 32.

46. "And that a kelson of the creation is love" is a crucial image in the poem eventually titled "Song of Myself." Whitman also used an important ship image in "Poem of The Sayers of The Words of The Earth" ("A Song of the Rolling Earth"), and he toyed with the idea of using the image of a ship on the cover of his first edition.

47. "Walt Whitman, a Brooklyn Boy," *Brooklyn Daily Times*, September 29, 1855, 2.

48. The appendix, which Whitman wittily titled "Leaves-Droppings" (echoing the phrase "eavesdropping"), gathers a variety of reviews, both positive and negative. The appendix was dropped after the second edition. For the direct parallel described here, see *Leaves of Grass: 1856 Facsimile Edition*, 361.

49. "Crossing Brooklyn Ferry," LG 165.

5. WHITMAN AFTER COLLAGE / COLLAGE AFTER WHITMAN

1. The situation is similar to the method Whitman used in relation to gay identity, mining (in the years before the word *homosexual* entered the lexicon) the diction of phrenology (*adhesiveness*) and inventing words like "camerado."

2. Just as a rifacimento reinterprets and recasts a previously existing art work, so Whitman was recasting his own poems into new and evolving forms.

3. Picasso's first artwork in this mode is generally thought to be *Still Life with Chair Caning*, a work in which he pasted oil cloth, scraps of newspaper, and a piece of rope to his painting; Braque's first experiment in this mode was *Fruit Dish and Glass*, a composition involving pieces of wallpaper and newspaper glued to his canvas.

4. In a more general sense art involving pasted fragments of paper finds much earlier origins and can perhaps be traced all the way back to around 200 BC and the invention of paper in China (tenth-century Japanese calligraphers later developed the technique significantly). Collage-like practices in the Western world have long existed outside the context of art, including scrapbooks and examples of what we would today call photo montages.

5. Berlin Dada, in particular, often continued to be explicitly political, and Zurich Dada can be seen as such as well. For more on the political subtext of collage, see the work of the art historian Patricia Leighton.

6. It should be noted that in a broader sense the composer Charles Ives experimented with proto–collage sampling even earlier than Perry. Colin Rowe and Fred Koetter, *Collage City* (Cambridge MA: MIT Press, 1978). Lee "Scratch" Perry's song that introduced sampling to the world was his 1968 hit

single "People Funny Boy" from the album *Upsetter*. Perry would go on to become instrumental in the creation of the collage-inflected reggae subgenre now know as dub. For more on the history of collage-like practices in music, see Mcleod, *Freedom of Expression* ®.

7. *The American Heritage Dictionary of the English Language, Fourth Edition* (New York: Houghton Mifflin, 2004).

8. By no means do I intend to limit collage to the dictionary definitions just described; however, I do hope they offer a useful starting point to explore what the term has come to mean in actual practice.

9. Marika Mihalyi Visvesvara has written a dissertation on just this aspect of Whitman's published writing, "Collage Technique and Epic Traits," comparing the autonomous end-stopped lines of his catalogs to certain collage-related techniques in modernist poetry, focusing mostly on Guillaume Apollinaire. The study, unfortunately, is superficial and flawed. Visvesvara somehow managed to write an entire dissertation on collage in Whitman's writing while remaining unaware that his poems actually used snippets of borrowed text. His notebooks and manuscripts go completely unnoted, and there is no reference whatsoever to Whitman scholarship, such as Floyd Stovall's *The Foreground of Leaves of Grass*, that documents the collage-like appropriations in the very lines she describes.

10. Later the assemblage was cast in bronze. Picasso made many pieced-together sculptures from the junk in his studios, most of which were lost or destroyed. Many of these pieces were not regarded as artwork at all by Picasso, such as the many toys he created for his daughter Maia. Considerably earlier, in 1914, he included a real spoon in a sculpture titled *Glass of Absinth*. Like his already extant collages on canvas, *Glass of Absinth* challenged conventional notions of artistic media; however, the work is more sculptural collage than readymade, since it is primarily composed of hand-crafted materials (in this case, painted bronze).

11. Marcel Duchamp to Suzanne Duchamp, January 1916, Archives of American Art, Smithsonian, Washington DC.

12. Marcel Duchamp to Suzanne Duchamp, around January 15, 1916, Archives of American Art, Smithsonian, Washington DC.

13. Qtd. in Kuh, *Artist's Voice*, 82.

14. Although Duchamp claimed to have quit producing art, it has since been revealed that he continued to produce neo-readymade molded objects, as well as his final masterwork, *Étan Donnés*.

15. Qtd. in Ades, Cox, and Hopkins, *Marcel Duchamp*, 69.

16. Rosalind Krauss, among others, has argued that Pollock's work has more to do with Duchamp than might superficially appear. Indeed Pollock can be seen as an interesting analogue to Whitman. Pollock's technique has been described as "all-over," and the rhetoric of inclusiveness (everything thrown together) is part of his ambition and his reception; notably he uses industrial house paint and throws the detritus of everyday life (coins, cigarette butts, etc.) onto his canvases. See Krauss, *The Optical Unconscious*.

17. Cabanne and Duchamp, *Dialogues with Marcel Duchamp*, 43.

18. *Leaves of Grass: 1855 Facsimile Edition*, 82.

19. Cabanne and Duchamp, *Dialogues with Marcel Duchamp*, 48.

20. Qtd. in Ades, Cox, and Hopkins, *Marcel Duchamp*, 154, 156.

21. *Comb* is inscribed with the ominous if puzzling sentence "3 OU 4 GOUT-TES DE HATEUR N'ONT RIEN A FAIRE AVEC LA SAUVAGERIE," which is conventionally translated as "3 or 4 drops of height have nothing to do with savagery." Although I have not encountered the suggestion in Duchamp criticism, I would suggest that Duchamp also meant to indicate the literal if improper translation "3 or 4 drops of height have nothing to do with *the savage* [italics mine]," humorously reflecting back both on the consumer and the combed dog.

22. Though, as we have seen, Whitman's "Broad-Axe Poem" too is portrayed in a sexual light and seems to have been associated with sexuality in the author's mind while creating the poem. See chapter 4, note 35.

23. Bucke, *Walt Whitman*, 25–26.

24. Conventional wisdom has long held that the same could be said for Whitman and the first edition of *Leaves of Grass*. As convenient as this would be for my argument here, a growing body of evidence suggests that the early editions of *Leaves of Grass* were better received by the public than has been previously recognized. See, for example, the recently discovered early photograph of an unknown young woman proudly displaying her copy of the 1856 *Leaves* in an ordinary portrait, as well as my own discovery

that the well-known philanthropist and ironmaster Abram S. Hewitt quoted Whitman in an 1856 speech. That year Hewitt was at the center of important social circles in New York, and he later went on to become the city's mayor, as well as a U.S. congressman. It seems unlikely that he would have known Whitman's work well enough to quote it if *Leaves'* reception was as limited as previously believed. See Folsom, "The Sesquicentennial"; Hewitt, *On the Statistics and Geography*.

25. Cage and Duchamp did eventually become friends and enjoyed playing chess together.

26. de Duve, "Echoes of the Readymade."

27. Kosuth, "Art after Philosophy," 94, 87, 23.

28. Walt Whitman, "A Backward Glance O'er Travel'd Roads," in *Walt Whitman: Poetry and Prose*, 671.

29. Sandler, "Modernism, Revisionism."

30. Krieger, *Arts on the Level*, 56.

31. "Democracy" was first published in *Galaxy* in December 1867; "Personalism" was published (also in *Galaxy*) in May 1868. "Orphic Literature," from which I extract many of the quotations here, was not published prior to the appearance of *Democratic Vistas* in 1871. The *Vistas* are composed of these three essays and a lengthy twenty-two-paragraph introduction that was added for the occasion.

32. Whitman, *Democratic Vistas*, 979, 958.

33. Interestingly architecture is the only artistic enterprise that evaded the scorn of all the major modernist avant-garde movements of the early twentieth century. Part of the reason for this, I would argue, is that architecture possesses an inherently utilitarian component. Whitman and later avant-garde artists were in agreement that art should evince results other than emotional or aesthetic stimulation, a view that architects, by nature of their medium, had always embraced.

34. Cabanne and Duchamp, *Dialogues with Marcel Duchamp*, 43.

35. Whitman, *Democratic Vistas*, 412.

36. Ibid., 418.

37. Ibid., 1011.

38. Ibid., 424–25.

39. Marcel Duchamp, from "Session on the Creative Act" at the Convention of the American Federation of Arts, Houston, April 1957.

40. Perloff, *The Futurist Moment*, 52.

41. Ulmer, "The Object of Post Criticism," 84.

42. Charles Bernstein, "Pound and the Poetry of Today," in *My Way*.

43. It is also possible that this is a late example of what Genoways and others have been discovering about some of the poems in *Drum-Taps*, that it is lifted from a newspaper or magazine piece, another way Whitman collages and plagiarizes to create poetry. If it is a newspaper piece, this may in fact have been a reported actual conversation, even if Whitman himself never overheard it.

44. These manuscripts, from the Charles E. Feinberg Collection at the Library of Congress, include discarded lines such as this aborted introduction: "Buried and hid beneath the mountains of soil . . . A lustrous sapphire blue, eternal, vital, slumbers ready (what is the part the wicked and the loathsome bear within the latent scheme?)" (*LG* 554).

45. Traubel, *With Walt Whitman in Camden*, 8:598; see also Shephard, *Walt Whitman's Pose*, 197–98.

Bibliography

Ades, Dawn, Neil Cox, and David Hopkins. *Marcel Duchamp*. New York: Thames and Hudson, 1999.

Allen, Gay Wilson. *The New Walt Whitman Handbook*. New York: New York University Press, 1975.

———. *The Solitary Singer: A Critical Biography of Walt Whitman*. New York: Macmillan, 1955.

———. "Walt Whitman and Jules Michelet." *Etudes Anglaises* 1 (May 1937): 230–37.

Ashbery, John. *The Tennis Court Oath*. 1962. Hanover NH: University Press of New England, 1997.

Barrett, Betty. "'Cavalry Crossing a Ford': Walt Whitman's Alabama Connection." *Alabama Heritage* 54 (Fall 1999): 6–17.

Berman, Paul. "Walt Whitman's Ghost." *New Yorker*, June 12, 1995: 98–104.

Bernstein, Charles. *My Way: Speeches and Poems*. Chicago: University of Chicago Press, 1999.

Binns, Henry Brian. *A Life of Walt Whitman*. London: Methuen, 1905.

Birney, Alice. "Missing Whitman Notebooks Returned to the Library of Congress." *Walt Whitman Quarterly Review* 12 (Spring 1995): 217–29.

Blodgett, Harold W. "Walt Whitman's Poetic Manuscripts." *West Hills Review: A Walt Whitman Journal* 2 (Fall 1980): 35–36.

Brasher, Thomas L. *Whitman as Editor of the Brooklyn Daily Eagle*. Detroit MI: Wayne State University Press, 1970.

Broderick, John C. "The Greatest Whitman Collector and the Greatest Whitman Collection." *Quarterly Journal of the Library of Congress* 27 (1970): 109–11.

Brotchie, Alastair, and Harry Matthews, eds. *Oulipo Compendium*. London: Atlas Press, 1998.

Bucke, Richard Maurice. *Cosmic Consciousness: A Study in the Evolution of the Human Mind*. New York: E. P. Dutton, 1923.

———. *Walt Whitman*. Philadelphia: David McKay, 1883.

Burroughs, John. *Walt Whitman as Poet and Person*. New York: J. S. Redfield, 1867.

Bradley, Sculley. "Whitman's Fundamental Metrical Principle." In *On Whitman*, edited by Edwin H. Cady and Louis J. Budd, 49–72. Durham NC: Duke University Press, 1987.

Cabanne, Pierre, and Marcel Duchamp. *Dialogues with Marcel Duchamp*. New York: Viking, 1971.

Chari, V. K. *Whitman in the Light of Vedantic Mysticism*. Lincoln: University of Nebraska Press, 1964.

Cohen, Matt. "Martin Tupper, Walt Whitman, and the Early Reviews of *Leaves of Grass*." *Walt Whitman Quarterly Review* 16 (Summer 1998): 22–31.

Coulombe, Joseph L. "'To Destroy the Teacher': Whitman and Martin Farquhar Tupper's 1851 Trip to America." *Walt Whitman Quarterly Review* 13 (Spring 1996): 199–209.

Cowley, Malcolm. Introduction to *Leaves of Grass: The First (1855) Edition*, by Walt Whitman, vii–xxx. New York: Penguin, 1959.

Davis, Andrew Jackson. *The Principles of Nature, the Divine Revelations, and a Voice to Mankind*. New York: S. S. Lyon and Wm. Fishbough, 1847.

De Duve, Thierry. "Echoes of the Readymade: Critique of Pure Modernism." *October* 70 (Fall 1994): 93–129.

Deleuze, Gilles. *Essays: Critical and Clinical*. Minneapolis: University of Minnesota Press, 1997.

Emerson, Ralph Waldo. *Essays: Second Series*. In *The Complete Works of Ralph Waldo Emerson*. New York: Houghton Mifflin, 1968.

Erkkila, Betsy. *Whitman the Political Poet*. New York: Oxford University Press, 1989.

Folsom, Ed. "Many MS. Doings and Undoings: Walt Whitman's Writing of the 1855 *Leaves of Grass*." In *From Wordsworth to Stevens: Essays in Honour of Robert Rehder*, edited by Anthony Mortimer, 167–89. Oxford: Peter Lang, 2005.

———. "The Sesquicentennial of the 1856 *Leaves of Grass*: A Daguerreotype of a Woman Reader." *Walt Whitman Quarterly Review* 24 (Summer 2006): 33–34.

———. *Walt Whitman's Native Representations*. New York: Cambridge University Press, 1994.

———. "Walt Whitman's Working Notes for the First Edition of *Leaves of Grass*." *Walt Whitman Quarterly Review* 16 (Fall 1998): 90–95.

———. *Whitman Making Books / Books Making Whitman: A Catalog and Commentary*. Iowa City IA: Obermann Center for Advanced Studies, 2005.

Folsom, Ed, and Kenneth M. Price. *Re-Scripting Walt Whitman: An Introduction to His Life and Work*. Oxford: Blackwell, 2005.

———, eds. *Walt Whitman Archive*. 2006. http://www.whitmanarchive.org.

French, R. W. "Reading 'Song of Myself.'" *San Jose Studies* 12, no. 2 (1986): 75–83.

Furness, Clifton J., ed. *Walt Whitman's Workshop: A Collection of Unpublished Manuscripts*. Cambridge: Harvard University Press, 1928.

Geffen, Arthur. "Silence and Denial: Walt Whitman and the Brooklyn Bridge." *Walt Whitman Quarterly Review* 1 (March 1984): 1–11.

Genoways, Ted. "Civil War Poems in 'Drum-Taps' and 'Memories of President Lincoln.'" In *A Companion to Walt Whitman*, edited by Donald D. Kummings, 522–38. Malden MA: Blackwell, 2006.

———. "'One goodshaped and wellhung Man'": Accentuated Sexuality and the Uncertain Authorship of the Frontispiece to the 1855 Edition of *Leaves of Grass*." In *Leaves of Grass: The Sesquicentennial Essays*, edited by Susan Belasco, Ed Folsom, and Kenneth M. Price, 87–123. Lincoln: University of Nebraska Press, 2008.

Goodrich, S. G. *The World as It Is and How It Has Been; or a Comprehensive Geography and History, Ancient and Modern*. New York: J. H. Colton, 1855.

Greenspan, Ezra. *Walt Whitman and the American Reader*. New York: Cambridge University Press, 1990.

Grier, Edward. "Walt Whitman's Earliest Known Notebook." *PMLA* 83 (October 1968): 1,453–56.

Harris, W. C. "Whitman's Leaves of Grass and the Writing of a New American Bible." *Walt Whitman Quarterly Review* 16 (Winter-Spring 1999): 172–90.

Haw, Richard. "American History/American Memory: Reevaluating Walt Whitman's Relationship with the Brooklyn Bridge." *Journal of American Studies* 38 (April 2004): 1–22.

Hedge, Eleanor. "*Prose Writers of Germany* as a Source for Whitman's Knowledge of German Philosophy." *Modern Language Notes* 51 (June 1946): 381–88.

Hewitt, Abram S. *On the Statistics and Geography of the Production of Iron.* New York: W. C. Bryant, 1856.

Higgins, Andrew C. "Wage Slavery and the Composition of *Leaves of Grass*: The 'Talbot Wilson' Notebook." *Walt Whitman Quarterly Review* 20 (Fall 2002): 53–77.

Hollis, C. Carroll. *Language and Style in* Leaves of Grass. Baton Rouge: Louisiana State University Press, 1983.

———. "Whitman's Word-Game." *Walt Whitman Newsletter* 4 (1958): 74–76.

Holloway, Emory. *Whitman: An Interpretation in the Narrative.* New York: Knopf, 1926.

Hudson, Derek. *Martin Tupper: His Rise and Fall.* London: Constable, 1949.

Keller, Elizabeth. *Walt Whitman in Mickle Street.* New York: M. Kennerley, 1921.

Kennedy, William Sloane. "Walt Whitman's Indebtedness to Emerson." In *An Autolycos Pack of What You Will,* edited by William Sloane Kennedy. 1897. West Yarmouth MA: Stonecraft, 1927.

Killingsworth, M. Jimmie. *The Growth of "Leaves of Grass": The Organic Tradition in Whitman Studies.* Columbia SC: Camden House, 1993.

Koetter, Fred, and Colin Rowe. *Collage City.* Cambridge MA: MIT Press, 1978.

Kosuth, Joseph. "Art after Philosophy, I, II." In *Idea Art,* edited by Gregory Battcock, 22–97. New York: Dutton, 1973.

Krauss, Rosalind. *The Optical Unconscious.* Cambridge MA: MIT Press, 1993.

Krieg, Joann P. *A Walt Whitman Chronology.* Iowa City: University of Iowa Press, 1998.

Krieger, Murray. *Arts on the Level: The Fall of the Elite Object.* Knoxville: University of Tennessee Press, 1981.

Kuebrich, David. *Minor Prophecy: Walt Whitman's New American Religion.* Bloomington: Indiana University Press, 1989.

Kuh, Katharine, ed. *Artist's Voice: Talks with Seventeen Artists.* New York: Harper & Row, 1962.

Larson, Lesli Anne. "'Scraps, orts and fragments': Polyscopia in Cinematic and Literary Modernism." PhD diss., University of Oregon, 2000.

Lawson, Alexander S. *Anatomy of a Typeface.* Boston: Godine, 1990.

Loving, Jerome. *Walt Whitman: The Song of Himself.* Berkeley: University of California Press, 1999.

Martin, Robert K. *The Homosexual Tradition in American Poetry: An Expanded Edition.* Iowa City: University of Iowa Press, 1998.

Mcleod, Kembrew. *Freedom of Expression®: Overzealous Copyright Bozos and Other Enemies of Creativity.* New York: Doubleday, 2005.

Miller, Edwin H. *Walt Whitman's Poetry.* New York: New York University Press, 1961.

Miller, James E., Jr. *Walt Whitman.* New York: Twayne, 1962.

Myerson, Joel. *Walt Whitman: A Descriptive Bibliography.* Pittsburgh: University of Pittsburgh Press, 1993.

———, ed. *Whitman in His Own Time.* Expanded Edition. Iowa City: University of Iowa Press, 2000.

Olson, Charles. *Human Universe.* Edited by Donald Allen. New York: Grove, 1967.

Parker, Simon. "Unrhymed Modernity: New York City, the Popular Newspaper Page, and the Forms of Whitman's Poetry." *Walt Whitman Quarterly Review* 16 (Winter/Spring 1999): 163–64.

Perloff, Marjorie. *The Futurist Moment: Avant-Garde, Avant Guerre, and the Language of Rupture.* Chicago: University of Chicago Press, 1986.

"Poet at Work: Walt Whitman Notebooks 1850s–1860s." *American Memory.* Library of Congress. http://memory.loc.gov, accessed June 26, 2007.

Pollak, Vivian R. *The Erotic Whitman.* Berkeley: University of California Press, 2000.

Price, Kenneth M., ed. *Walt Whitman: The Contemporary Reviews.* Cambridge, England: Cambridge University Press, 1996.

Reynolds, David S. *Beneath the American Renaissance: The Subversive Imagination in the Age of Emerson and Melville.* New York: Knopf, 1988.

———. *Walt Whitman's America*. New York: Knopf, 1995.

Rosenthal, P. Z. "'Dilation' in Whitman's Early Writing." *Walt Whitman Review* 20, no. 1 (1974): 3–15.

Sandler, Irving. "Modernism, Revisionism, Pluralism, and Post-Modernism." *Art Journal* 40 (1980): 345–47.

Schmidgall, Gary. "1855: A Stop-Press Revision." *Walt Whitman Quarterly Review* 18 (Summer-Fall 2000): 74–76.

Shephard, Esther. "Possible Sources of Some of Whitman's Ideas in *Hermes Mercurius Trismegistus* and Other Works." *Modern Language Quarterly* 14 (March 1953): 60–81.

———. *Walt Whitman's Pose*. New York: Harcourt, Brace, 1938.

Sill, Geoffrey M. "'You Tides with Ceaseless Swell': A Reading of the Manuscript." *Walt Whitman Quarterly Review* 6 (Spring 1989): 189–97.

Singer, Ben. "Connoisseurs of Chaos: Whitman, Vertov, and the Poetic-Survey." *Literature/Film Quarterly* 15 (1987): 247–58.

Stovall, Floyd. "Dating Whitman's Early Notebooks." In *Studies in Bibliography: Papers of the Bibliographical Society of the University of Virginia* 24 (1971): 197–204.

———. *The Foreground of Leaves of Grass*. Charlottesville: University Press of Virginia, 1974.

Symonds, John Addington. *Walt Whitman: A Study*. London: John C. Nimmo, 1893.

Traubel, Horace L., ed. *Camden's Compliment to Walt Whitman*. Philadelphia: David McKay, 1889.

———. *With Walt Whitman in Camden*. Vol. 1. Edited by Sculley Bradley. Boston: Small, Maynard, 1906.

———. *With Walt Whitman in Camden*. Vol. 2. New York: Rowman and Littlefield, 1962.

———. *With Walt Whitman in Camden*. Vol. 8. Edited by Jeanne Chapman and Robert Macisaac. Carbondale: Southern Illinois University Press, 1992.

Triggs, Oscar Lovell. "The Growth of 'Leaves of Grass.'" In *The Complete Writings of Walt Whitman*. Edited by Richard Maurice Bucke, Thomas Biggs Harned, Horace L. Traubel, and Oscar Lovell Triggs. New York: G. P. Putnam's Sons, 1902.

Ulmer, Gregory. "The Object of Post Criticism." In *The Anti-Aesthetic: Essays on Postmodern Culture*, edited by Hal Foster. Port Townsend WA: Bay Press, 1983.

Visvesvara, Marika Mihalyi. "Collage Technique and Epic Traits in Modernist Poetry: A Stylistic and Thematic Study of Poems by Walt Whitman, Guillaume Apollinaire, and T. S. Eliot." PhD diss., University of California, Berkeley, 1982.

Warren, James Perrin. "'Catching the Sign': Catalogue Rhetoric in 'The Sleepers.'" *Walt Whitman Quarterly Review* 5 (Fall 1987): 16–34.

Waskow, Howard J. *Whitman: Explorations in Form*. Chicago: University of Chicago Press, 1966.

Whitman, Walt. *An American Primer*. Edited by Horace Traubel. Boston: Small, Maynard, 1904.

———. *The Complete Prose Works of Walt Whitman (CPW)*. 6 vols. Edited by Richard Maurice Bucke. New York: G. P. Putnam's Sons, 1902.

———. *The Complete Writings of Walt Whitman*. Edited by Richard Maurice Bucke, Thomas Biggs Harned, Horace Traubel, and Oscar Lovell Triggs. New York: G. P. Putnam's Sons, 1902.

———. *The Correspondence (Corr)*. 6 Vols. Edited by Edwin Haviland Miller. New York: New York University Press, 1961–77. Volume 1: *1842–1867* (1961); Volume 2: *1868–1875* (1961); Volume 3: *1876–1885* (1964); Volume 4: *1886–1889* (1969); Volume 5: *1890–1892* (1969); Volume 6: *A Supplement with a Composite Index* (1977).

———. *Daybooks and Notebooks (DBN)*. 3 vols. Edited by William White. New York: New York University Press, 1978. Volume 1: *Daybooks, 1876–November 1881*; Volume 2: *Daybooks, December 1881–1891*; Volume 3: *Diary in Canada, Notebooks, Index*.

———. *Leaves of Grass: 1855 Facsimile Edition*. San Francisco: Chandler, 1968.

———. *Leaves of Grass: 1856 Facsimile Edition*. Woodbridge CT: Research Publications, 1982.

———. *Leaves of Grass: Comprehensive Reader's Edition (LG)*. Edited by Harold W. Blodgett and Scully Bradley. New York: New York University Press, 1965.

——. *Leaves of Grass: 100th Anniversary Edition*. Edited by David S. Reynolds. New York: Oxford University Press, 2005.

——. *Notebooks and Unpublished Prose Manuscripts (NUPM)*. 3 vols. Edited by Edward F. Grier. New York: New York University Press, 1984. Volume 1: *Family Notes and Autobiography, Brooklyn and New York*; Volume 2: *Washington*; Volume 3: *Camden*; Volumes 4, 5, and 6: *Notes*.

——. *Prose Works, 1892 (PW)*. 2 vols. Edited by Floyd Stovall. New York: New York University Press, 1963–64. Volume 1: *Specimen Days* (1963); Volume 2: *Collect and Other Prose* (1964).

——. *The Uncollected Poetry and Prose of Walt Whitman (UPP)*. Edited by Emory Holloway. Gloucester MA: Peter Smith, 1972.

——. "Walt Whitman and His Poems." *United States Review* 5 (September 1855): 205–12.

——. *Walt Whitman: Poetry and Prose*. New York: Penguin Books, 1996.

——. *Walt Whitman's Leaves of Grass: The First (1855) Edition*. Edited by Malcolm Cowley. New York: Penguin, 1959.

Wilson, Eric. *Romantic Turbulence*. New York: St. Martin's, 2000.

Zweig, Paul. *Walt Whitman: The Making of the Poet*. New York: Basic, 1984.

Index